Leisure Studies

A2

William Collins' dream of knowledge for all began with the publication of his first book in 1819. A self-educated mill worker, he not only enriched millions of lives, but also founded a flourishing publishing house. Today, staying true to this spirit, Collins books are packed with inspiration, innovation and practical expertise. They place you at the centre of a world of possibility and give you exactly what you need to explore it.

Collins. Do more.

Published by Collins

An imprint of HarperCollins*Publishers*

77 – 85 Fulham Palace Road
Hammersmith
London
W6 8JB

Browse the complete Collins catalogue at www.collinseducation.com

10 9 8 7 6 5 4 3 2 1

ISBN-13 978 0 00 720039 9

ISBN-10 0 00 720039 0

British Library Cataloguing in Publication Data
A Catalogue record for this publication is available from the British Library

Commissioned by Graham Bradbury
Cover design by Blue Pig Design Limited
Cover picture courtesy of Powerstock
Series design by Patricia Briggs
Book design by Ken Vail Graphic Design
Indexed by Patricia Baker
Picture research by Thelma Gilbert
Production by Sarah Robinson

Printed and bound by Butler and Tanner, Frome

This high quality material is endorsed by Edexcel and has been through a rigorous quality assurance programme to ensure that it is a suitable companion to the specification for both learners and teachers.

This does not mean that its contents will be used verbatim when setting examinations nor is it to be read as being the official specification – a copy of which is available at www.edexcel.org.uk

Acknowledgements

I would like to give thanks to the fellow professionals who helped me put this together and to Jane and Joseph for the many hours they gave me to write the book.

Ray Barker

The author and publishers would also like to thank the following for their help: Mike McCarthy; Tanya Wright; Chris Jones; Graham Saffery; Sebastian Clayton; Julie Gibson; Helena Page, Publisher Relations Manager at Edexcel.

The publishers would like to thank the following for permission to reproduce pictures on these pages (t) = top, (b) = bottom, (l) = left, (r) = right:

p.11 (tl) Empics, (bl) Rex Features; (r) Alamy/Danita Delmont; p.12 (t) Empics; (b) Alamy/Photo Library Wales; p.14 Rex Features; p.18 Empics; p.24 Rex Features; p.30 Rex Features; p.36 Photos.com; p.41 (t) Alamy/Visions of America; (b) Alamy/INSADOC Photography; p.42 Photos.com; p.44 Alamy/Gari Wyn Williams; p.48 Alamy/Imagestate; p.50 Alamy/Jeff Greenberg; p.52 Alamy/Nigel Hicks; p.54 Alamy/Chris Laurens; p.55 Alamy/AllOver Photography; p.57 Empics; p.58 Rex Features; p.62 Mike McCarthy; p.67 Empics; p.68 Courtesy of BUNAC Travel Services; p.73 Alamy/Nick Hanna; p.74 Empics; p.75 Alamy/Justin Kase; p.76 Rex Features; p.84 Corbis; p.86 Photos.com; p.88 Alamy/Adrian Sharrett; p.93 Science Photo Library/CC Studio; p.98 Empics; p.101 Empics; p.102 Alamy/Steve Nichols; p.104 Empics; p.106 Alamy/Directphoto.org; p.107 Empics; p.108 (t) Alamy/Steve Steley; (b) Alamy/Eddie Gerald; p.109 Alamy/David Hancock; p.110 Rex Features; p.114 Wendy Gray; p.118 Corbis; p.119 (t) Empics; (b) Empics; p.120 Rex Features; p.121 (t) Science Photo Library/BSIP Laurent; (b) Advertising Archives; p.124 Empics; p.125 Empics; p.126 Corbis; p.127 Photofusion; p.130 Empics; p.131 Empics; p.132 Empics; p.134 Empics; p.135 Empics; p.136 Rex Features; p.139(t) Alamy/Neil Setchfield; (b) Photofusion; p.140 Empics; p.142 Alamy/Paul Doyle; p.143 Courtesy Sports & Activity Development Reading County Council; p.146 Rex Features; p.147 Michael Upchurch & Kate Wigley; p.148 Rex Features; p.149 Empics; p.151 Empics; p.152 Photos.com; p.156 Empics; p.161 Graham Saffery.

The publishers gratefully acknowledge the following for permission to reproduce copyright material. Every effort has been made to contact the holders of copyright material, but if any have been inadvertently overlooked, the Publishers will be pleased to make the necessary arrangements at the first opportunity. The publishers would be happy to hear from any copyright holder that has not been acknowledged.

Thanks to:

p.17 HF Holidays for the case study material; p.23 Leisure Opportunities magazine for the David Lloyd case study; p.70 The John Lyon School Sports Centre for the job advert; p.71 West of England Sports Partnership and Sports West for the job advert; p.72 PGL Travel Ltd for their recruitment brochure; p.77 Anywork Anywhere for a screenshot of their website; p.85(t) PGL Travel Ltd for their application form; (b) LA Fitness for a screenshot of their website; p.129 The National Railway Museum for their leaflet; p.130 The Guardian and Marcus Christenson for the article on Sepp Blatter; p.134 Kick it Out for the interview with Harpal Singh; p.137 Eurogamer Network Ltd for the article on EM Media; p.153 Pleasure Island Family Theme Park for their leaflet.

Contents

About this book 6 Table of organisations used as examples 8

Unit 4 Leisure in Action 10–65

4.1 Choice of event

Topic 1 Choosing your event 12

4.2 Feasibility of event

Topic 2 Investigating the feasibility 18

Topic 3 Aims, objectives and customers 24

Topic 4 Marketing your event 30

Topic 5 Resources, finance and staffing 36

Topic 6 Administration, timescales, targets and evaluation 42

4.3 Teamwork

Topic 7 Effective teamwork skills 48

4.4 Carrying out the event

Topic 8 Carrying out your event 54

4.5 Evaluating the event

Topic 9 Evaluating your event 58

Industry focus and useful links 62

How Unit 4 is assessed 64

Unit 5 Employment in Leisure 66–117

5.1 Employment practices in leisure

Topic 1 Different types of employment in leisure: Part one 68

Topic 2 Different types of employment in leisure: Part two 74

5.2 Recruitment and selection in leisure

Topic 3 Effective recruitment processes 80

Topic 4 Effective selection processes 84

5.3 Employment issues in leisure

Topic 5 Orientation and working practices 88

Topic 6 Organisational working practices 94

5.4 Motivating staff in leisure

Topic 7 Motivating staff 98

5.5 Employment law

Topic 8 The law and discrimination 104

Topic 9 The law and working conditions 108

Industry focus 114

How Unit 5 is assessed 116

Unit 6 Current Issues in Leisure 118–183

6.1 Issues in leisure

Topic 1 Lifestyle and health 120

Topic 2 Equality, diversity and inclusion 126

Topic 3 Sex, gender and race 130

Topic 4 Events, festivals and traditions 136

Topic 5 Government and policy in leisure 140

Topic 6 The media and commercial issues 146

6.2 Leisure research project

Topic 7 Selecting and planning a research project 152

Topic 8 Final planning and writing of your research proposal 158

Industry focus 161

How Unit 6 is assessed 163

Useful websites 164 Glossary 167 Index 173

About this book

Welcome to A2 Leisure Studies. This textbook is written specifically for students taking the Edexcel Leisure Studies award and provides you with the underpinning knowledge to be successful in both the coursework set by your school or college (internal assessment) and the one-and-a-half hour test set by Edexcel (external assessment).

Collins *Leisure Studies A2 for Edexcel* is divided into three units. Each unit in this book corresponds to a unit of the Edexcel A2-level leisure studies specification.

Unit	Title	How is this unit assessed?
4	Leisure in Action	Internal assessment
5	Employment in Leisure	External test
6	Current Issues in Leisure	Internal assessment

The units in this book have been divided into topics and each topic provides a manageable chunk of learning covering the subject content of an Edexcel unit. The contents list at the beginning of this book and at the start of each unit will show you how the topics correspond to the Edexcel Leisure Studies A2-level specification.

Activities provide you with an opportunity to develop your understanding about specific aspects of a topic and practise your skills. Most activities are designed for you to work on your own, with a partner or in a small group.

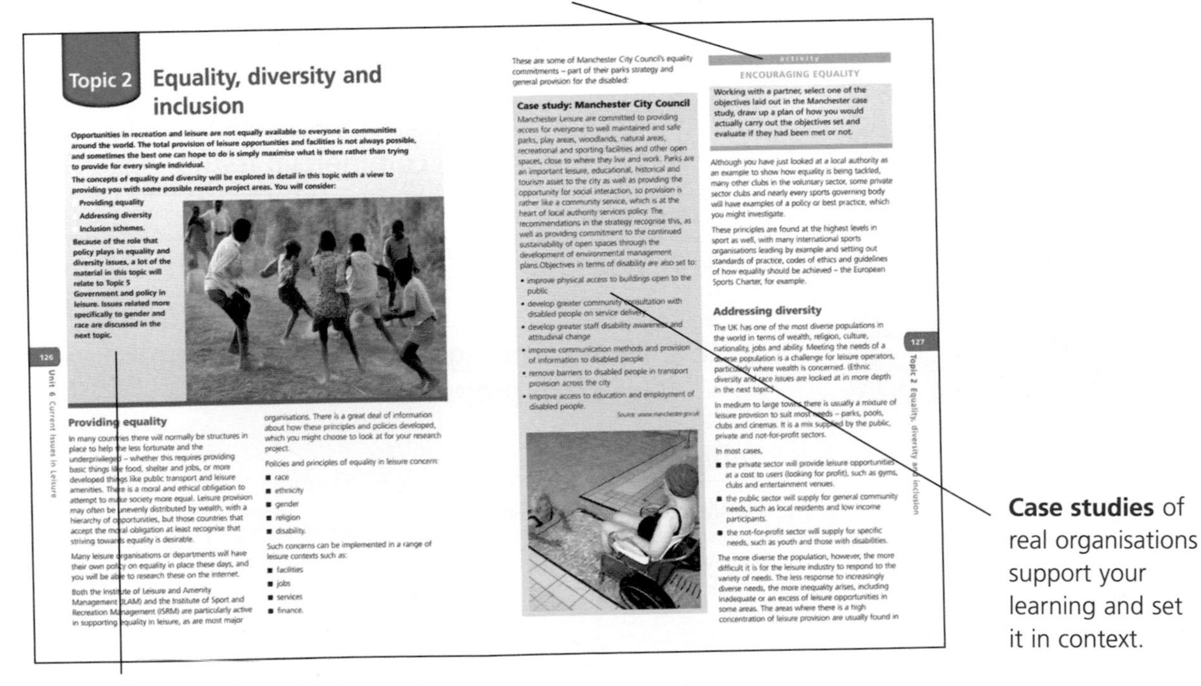

126

Unit 6 Current Issues in Leisure

Topic 2 Equality, diversity and inclusion

Opportunities in recreation and leisure are not equally available to everyone in communities around the world. The total provision of leisure opportunities and facilities is not always possible, and sometimes the best one can hope to do is simply maximise what is there rather than trying to provide for every single individual.

The concepts of equality and diversity will be explored in detail in this topic with a view to providing you with some possible research project areas. You will consider:

- **Providing equality**
- **Addressing diversity**
- **Inclusion schemes.**

Because of the role that policy plays in equality and diversity issues, a lot of the material in this topic will relate to Topic 5 Government and policy in leisure. Issues related more specifically to gender and race are discussed in the next topic.

Providing equality

In many countries there will normally be structures in place to help the less fortunate and the underprivileged – whether this requires providing basic things like food, shelter and jobs, or more developed things like public transport and leisure amenities. There is a moral and ethical obligation to attempt to make society more equal. Leisure provision may often be unevenly distributed by wealth, with a hierarchy of opportunities, but those countries that accept the moral obligation at least recognise that striving towards equality is desirable.

Many leisure organisations or departments will have their own policy on equality in place these days, and you will be able to research these on the internet.

Both the Institute of Leisure and Amenity Management (ILAM) and the Institute of Sport and Recreation Management (ISRM) are particularly active in supporting equality in leisure, as are most major organisations. There is a great deal of information about how these principles and policies developed, which you might choose to look at for your research project.

Policies and principles of equality in leisure concern:

- race
- ethnicity
- gender
- religion
- disability.

Such concerns can be implemented in a range of leisure contexts such as:

- facilities
- jobs
- services
- finance.

These are some of Manchester City Council's equality commitments – part of their parks strategy and general provision for the disabled:

Case study: Manchester City Council

Manchester Leisure are committed to providing access for everyone to well maintained and safe parks, play areas, woodlands, natural areas, recreational and sporting facilities and other open spaces, close to where they live and work. Parks are an important leisure, educational, historical and tourism asset to the city as well as providing the opportunity for social interaction, so provision is rather like a community service, which is at the heart of local authority services policy. The recommendations in the strategy recognise this, as well as providing commitment to the continued sustainability of open spaces through the development of environmental management plans. Objectives in terms of disability are also set to:

- improve physical access to buildings open to the public
- develop greater community consultation with disabled people on service delivery
- develop greater staff disability awareness and attitudinal change
- improve communication methods and provision of information to disabled people
- remove barriers to disabled people in transport provision across the city
- improve access to education and employment of disabled people.

Source: www.manchester.gov.uk

activity

ENCOURAGING EQUALITY

Working with a partner, select one of the objectives laid out in the Manchester case study, draw up a plan of how you would actually carry out the objectives set and evaluate if they had been met or not.

Although you have just looked at a local authority as an example to show how equality is being tackled, many other clubs in the voluntary sector, some private sector clubs and nearly every sports governing body will have examples of a policy or best practice, which you might investigate.

These principles are found at the highest levels in sport as well, with many international sports organisations leading by example and setting out standards of practice, codes of ethics and guidelines of how equality should be achieved – the European Sports Charter, for example.

Addressing diversity

The UK has one of the most diverse populations in the world in terms of wealth, religion, culture, nationality, jobs and ability. Meeting the needs of a diverse population is a challenge for leisure operators, particularly where wealth is concerned. (Ethnic diversity and race issues are looked at in more depth in the next topic.)

In medium to large towns there is usually a mixture of leisure provision to suit most needs – parks, pools, clubs and cinemas. It is a mix supplied by the public, private and not-for-profit sectors.

In most cases,

- the private sector will provide leisure opportunities at a cost to users (looking for profit), such as gyms, clubs and entertainment venues.
- the public sector will supply for general community needs, such as local residents and low income participants.
- the not-for-profit sector will supply for specific needs, such as youth and those with disabilities.

The more diverse the population, however, the more difficult it is for the leisure industry to respond to the variety of needs. The less response to increasingly diverse needs, the more inequality arises, including inadequate or an excess of leisure opportunities in some areas. The areas where there is a high concentration of leisure provision are usually found in

127

Topic 2 Equality, diversity and inclusion

Case studies of real organisations support your learning and set it in context.

Explanatory introduction to the topic explains what you will need to learn about each topic.

Diagrams and examples support and clarify all the explanations in the text.

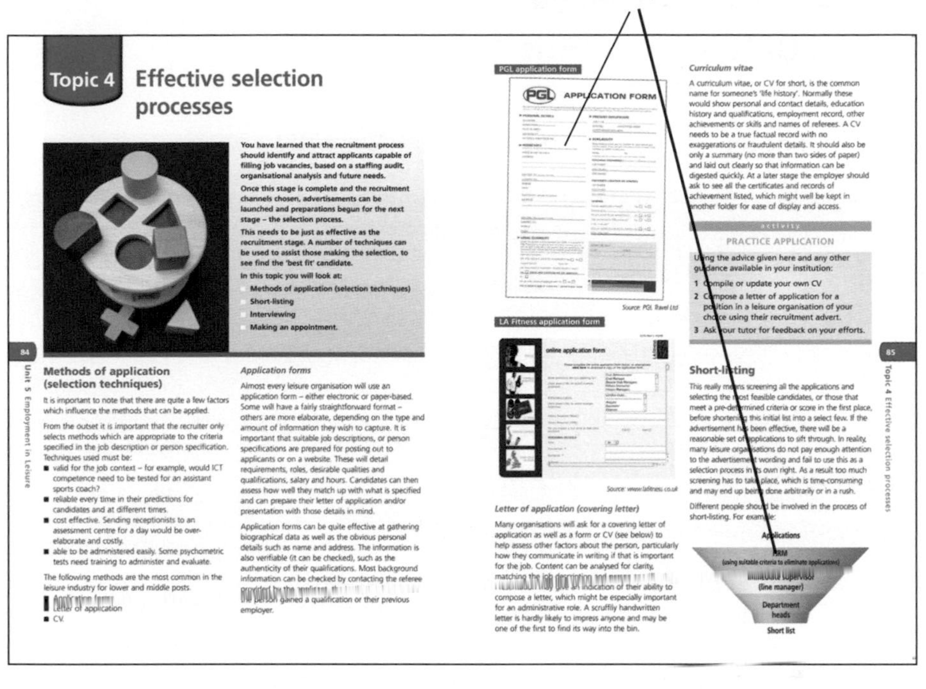

Topic 4 Effective selection processes

You have learned that the recruitment process should identify and attract applicants capable of filling job vacancies, based on a staffing audit, organisational analysis and future needs.

Once this stage is complete and the recruitment channels chosen, advertisements can be launched and preparations begun for the next stage – the selection process.

This needs to be just as effective as the recruitment stage. A number of techniques can be used to assist those making the selection, to see find the 'best fit' candidate.

In this topic you will look at:

- **Methods of application (selection techniques)**
- **Short-listing**
- **Interviewing**
- **Making an appointment.**

84

Unit 5 Employment in Leisure

Methods of application (selection techniques)

It is important to note that there are quite a few factors which influence the methods that can be applied.

From the outset it is important that the recruiter only selects methods which are appropriate to the criteria specified in the job description or person specification. Techniques used must be:

- valid for the job context – for example, would ICT competence need to be tested for an assistant sports coach?
- reliable every time in their predictions for candidates and at different times.
- cost effective. Sending receptionists to an assessment centre for a day would be over-elaborate and costly.
- able to be administered easily. Some psychometric tests need training to administer and evaluate.

The following methods are the most common in the leisure industry for lower and middle posts.

- [illegible]
- Letter of application
- CV.

Application forms

Almost every leisure organisation will use an application form – either electronic or paper-based. Some will have a fairly straightforward format – others are more elaborate, depending on the type and amount of information they wish to capture. It is important that suitable job descriptions, or person specifications are prepared for posting out to applicants or on a website. These will detail requirements, roles, desirable qualities and qualifications, salary and hours. Candidates can then assess how well they match up with what is specified and can prepare their letter of application and/or presentation with those details in mind.

Application forms can be quite effective at gathering biographical data as well as the obvious personal details such as name and address. The information is also verifiable (it can be checked), such as the authenticity of their qualifications. Most background information can be checked by contacting the referee [illegible] the person gained a qualification or their previous employer.

PGL application form

PGL APPLICATION FORM

Source: PGL Travel Ltd

LA Fitness application form

online application form

Source: www.lafitness.co.uk

Letter of application (covering letter)

Many organisations will ask for a covering letter of application as well as a form or CV (see below) to help assess other factors about the person, particularly how they communicate in writing if that is important for the job. Content can be analysed for clarity, [illegible] an indication of their ability to compose a letter, which might be especially important for an administrative role. A scruffily handwritten letter is hardly likely to impress anyone and may be one of the first to find its way into the bin.

Curriculum vitae

A curriculum vitae, or CV for short, is the common name for someone's 'life history'. Normally these would show personal and contact details, education history and qualifications, employment record, other achievements or skills and names of referees. A CV needs to be a true factual record with no exaggerations or fraudulent details. It should also be only a summary (no more than two sides of paper) and laid out clearly so that information can be digested quickly. At a later stage the employer should ask to see all the certificates and records of achievement listed, which might well be kept in another folder for ease of display and access.

activity

PRACTICE APPLICATION

Using the advice given here and any other guidance available in your institution:

1. Compile or update your own CV
2. Compose a letter of application for a position in a leisure organisation of your choice using their recruitment advert.
3. Ask your tutor for feedback on your efforts.

Short-listing

This really means screening all the applications and selecting the most feasible candidates, or those that meet a pre-determined criteria or score in the first place, before shortening this initial list into a select few. If the advertisement has been effective, there will be a reasonable set of applications to sift through. In reality, many leisure organisations do not pay enough attention to the advertisement wording and fail to use this as a selection process in its own right. As a result too much screening has to take place, which is time-consuming and may end up being done arbitrarily or in a rush.

Different people should be involved in the process of short-listing. For example:

Applications

HRM (using suitable criteria to eliminate applications)

[illegible] supervisor (line manager)

Department heads

Short list

85

Topic 4 Effective selection processes

This book has been produced with considerable input from current practitioners in the leisure industry. Each unit contains an **Industry Focus** interview:

Unit 4 Leisure in Action features Mike McCarthy, Events Manager, The Spa Complex, Scarborough.

Unit 5 Employment in Leisure features Tanya Wright, Receptionist, Brentford Fountain Leisure Centre, Hounslow Borough.

Unit 6 Current Issues in Leisure features Graham Saffery, a teacher at Blackpool Sixth Form College.

industry focus

The industry focus for this unit is a young leisure centre worker called Tanya who has first-hand experience of many of the employment practices in a leisure centre in London. She was recently made a permanent member of staff having had casual status before.

The centre is Brentford Fountain in Hounslow Borough, which offers a fairly typical picture of a local authority leisure centre, with activities and classes for all ages:

- Pool sessions
- A play/party centre for small children
- Trampolines
- Summer sports camps and courses
- Rackets sports
- Health suite and gym.

The local authority runs several centres, and a leisure card is available for all centres. Prices are affordable and opening times are 7am to 10pm weekdays and 9am to 6pm weekends.

We interviewed Tanya in the summer of 2005 when she had just been made a permanent member of staff.

Her job title is 'Receptionist'. Her duties are quite diverse as you can see from the following list:

- Controlling admissions and ticket sales
- Dealing with bookings and enquiries
- Arranging hire and sale of equipment and merchandise
- Accounting for monies taken
- Operating cash tills and other sales equipment
- Controlling lost property and valuables left for safe-keeping
- Undertaking clerical and other duties instructed by the manager
- Keeping the reception area tidy
- Promoting the Centre's image
- Helping to host functions, if required.

Her working pattern before her new permanent status was:

- Casual: she had to book shifts for every two weeks, with a limit of 48 hours per week maximum (regularly, but not guaranteed).

Now she works:

- Full-time, permanent: Working a four-week rota, averaging 36 hours per week.

Tanya, Leisure Centre Worker
Brentford Fountain, Hounslow Borough, London

114

Unit 5 Employment in Leisure

A wide range of leisure organisations has been included and the table on pages 8–9 will help you to locate them in this book. When you are building your understanding of the industry and completing assessments you will find the internet an invaluable source of information. To help you in your research, details of useful websites are given on pages 164–165.

Good luck with your GCE A2-level studies. This book provides you with interesting, supportive and motivating learning materials that we hope will help you to succeed in your leisure studies course.

Table of organisations used as examples

Unit 4 Unit 5 Unit 6

Organisation	Focus	Page
Accolade Corporate Events UK	aims of event companies (activity) technological changes and advantages	25 32
Acorn Adventure	seasonal work	72
Advertising Standards Authority	recruitment advertising	83
Advisory Conciliation and Arbitration Services	staffing plan selection processes disciplinary and grievance procedures	82 87 96
Anywork Anywhere	casual work abroad (activity)	77
BBC	healthy living campaigns	125
Blackpool Sixth Form College	Unit 6 industry focus	161
Bourne Leisure	staff development and training (case study)	100
Bristol City Council	flexible working annual leave entitlements	90 92
British Heart Foundation	heart disease	122
British Olympic Association	influencing policy decisions	141
British Paralympics Association	special population leisure needs	125
Business Link	maternity, paternity and adoption leave	95
Camp Beaumont	seasonal work	72
Capital Sport	aims of event companies (activity)	25
Carmarthen Council	inclusion schemes	129
Chartered Institute for Personnel Development	staffing plan selection processes	82 87
Charter Mark	industry quality awards staff development and training	28 100
Chichester District Council	leisure policy and crime (case study)	142
Childline	child protection	113
Commission for Racial Equality	the law and discrimination campaigns for leisure equality	107 135
Concerto Group	aims of event companies (activity)	25
Connexions	apprenticeships	78
David Lloyd Leisure	assessing feasibility – great mile runs (activity)	23
Department for Culture, Media and Sport	leisure policy issues	141
Department for Education and Skills (DfES)	leisure policy issues	141
Department for Environment, Food and Rural Affairs	leisure policy issues	141
Department for Work and Pensions	leisure policy issues	141
Department of Health	healthy living campaigns leisure policy issues	125 141
Department of Trade and Industry (DTI)	working time regulations annual leave entitlements notice periods redundancy, redeployment and dismissal working time regulations	91 92 95 96 110
Disability Rights Commission	the law and discrimination	107
Disney	corporate culture (activity)	102
Drugs in Sport	negative use of drugs	123
DTB International – Hospitality and Events Management	aims of event companies (activity)	25
EM Media	the aims and purpose of events	137
English Federation of Disability Sport	special population leisure needs	124
Equal Opportunities Commission	the law and discrimination	107
FIFA (Fédération Internationale de Football Association)	hallmark events	10
Flamingo Land	seasonal work	72
Football Association (FA)	influencing policy decisions	141
Greenwich Leisure Limited	casual staff (case study)	76
Haven Holidays	seasonal work	72
Health and Safety Executive (HSE)	sickness and absence employment of children health and safety regulation	93 111 112
Henley Royal Regatta	casual staff	76
HF Walking Holidays	roles within a team (case study)	17
Highland Council	inclusion schemes	129
Hit Racism for Six	campaigns for leisure equality	135
Hounslow Borough Council	Unit 5 industry focus	114
Institute of Leisure and Amenity Management (ILAM)	aims of event companies (activity) providing equality influencing policy decisions	25 126 141

Organisation	Topic	Page
Institute of Sport and Recreation Management (ISRM)	providing equality	126
	female participation	132
	influencing policy decisions	141
International Association of Athletics Federations (IAAF)	negative use of drugs	123
International Convention Centre, Birmingham	the economic value of events	139
International Olympic Committee (IOC)	assessing feasibility	10
International Organisation of Standardization (ISO)	industry quality awards	28
Investors in People	industry quality awards	28
	flexible working	90
	staff development and training	100
LA Fitness	application forms	85
Leisure Opportunities magazine	annual leave entitlements (activity)	92
Leisurejobs	employment in leisure	68
Let's Kick Racism Out of Football	under-representation (case study)	134
	campaigns for leisure equality	135
London 2012	financial planning	38
	event timescales	43
	voluntary work	78
	motivation	98
	organisational culture (activity)	102
	environmental value of events	139
Long Way Round (Ewan McGregor and Charlie Boorman)	supporting team members (case study)	56
Manchester City Council	providing equality	127
	race and ethnicity	133
	homosexuality	133
Maximillion Events Ltd	aims of event companies (activity)	25
McDonald's	diet (activity)	123
Mencap leisure needs	special population	124
National Railway Museum	inclusion schemes	129
National Society for the Prevention of Cruelty to Children (NSPCC)	child protection	113
National Statistics	sources of leisure data	159
People 1st	seasonal work (case study)	73
PGL	seasonal work	72
	application forms	85
Quest	industry quality awards	28
	staff development and training	100
Raleigh International	voluntary work	77
Reading Borough Council	leisure policy and crime (case study)	143
Royal Ascot	casual staff	76
Royal National Institute for the Blind	special population leisure needs	124
Scarborough Borough Council	leisure policy issues (case study)	142
Scarborough Spa	unit 4 industry focus	62
Sense (UK deafblind charity)	special population leisure needs	124
Silverstone (home of British Grand Prix)	health and safety	45
SkillsActive	apprenticeships	78
Social Exclusion Unit	inclusion schemes	128
Sport England	advice for planning	18
	voluntary work	77
	leisure policy and regeneration (activity)	144
Sporting Equals	racial equality	133
Team Ellen (Ellen MacArthur)	teamwork (case study)	52
TimeBank	voluntary work	77
Trade Unions Council (TUC)	working time regulations (activity)	92
UK Sport	negative use of drugs	123
Weight Watchers	healthy living campaigns	125
Welcome Host	customer service training scheme	27
Westminster Council	inclusion schemes	129
Wimbledon (All England Lawn Tennis Club)	security procedures	47
	casual staff	76
Women's Sports Foundation	female participation	132
World Anti-Doping Agency	negative use of drugs	123

Attending leisure events such as concerts, sports matches or exhibitions are significant and often memorable ways in which people use their leisure time. The leisure industry accounts for over 25% of total consumer expenditure in the UK.

Events occur in many sectors of the leisure industry. For example:

- Voluntary sector events, such as a battle re-enactment given by enthusiasts.
- Public sector events in sport, such as Scarborough's Annual Triathlon.
- Private sector events, such as the opening launch of a new gym.
- Partnership events also occur, with participants coming from clubs (in the voluntary sector) to facilities run by a local authority (public sector) and with sponsorship provided by the private sector.

Events can occur regularly, occasionally, or just be a 'one-off'. Some large-scale, prestigious events, called 'Hallmark events' – such as the FIFA World Cup and the Olympic Games – move around, and tickets are highly sought after. Recall how much money and effort went into London's successful bid for the 2012 Olympics.

Event companies exist which offer a huge range of corporate, sports and bespoke events – cocktail receptions, for instance, Christmas parties, exhibitions, team-building days, the Henley Royal Regatta (rowing) or Cowes Week (sailing).

Whatever its size, frequency or scale, in order for an event to happen a number of key things need to occur – a suitable and feasible event needs to be selected; a plan has to be made and a team of people have to stage the event.

These are the themes which will be developed in this unit:

- Choosing an event
- Assessing its feasibility
- Teamwork for the event
- Planning the event
- Carrying out the event
- Evaluating the event

The three key areas of this unit are:

Planning the event

Carrying out the event

Evaluating the event

Think about the bidding process that the International Olympic Committee (IOC) goes through to award the Olympic Games. They receive proposals and plans from countries trying to win the Games and have to decide which venue's plan is the most feasible, the best planned and the most likely to satisfy participants, spectators and the media.

You, as event professionals, will have to keep records of your inputs and involvement in some sort of diary, file or logbook, so that you can use the information for your portfolio and evaluation later. Event managers usually keep a manual so that they can refer to it the next time a similar event comes round, so your log will be the equivalent of this.

In tackling your event you will be able to draw on the knowledge, information and skills from other units, such as health and safety (Unit 2), budgeting (Unit 2) and customer service (Unit 3). Staging an event will bring together many broad and specific aspects of this course. You should also try to study some local events – or even national ones – to assess what aspects go into the planning, staging and evaluation so that you might pick up some good ideas.

Much of what goes on in the leisure industry is event-based, and learning how to plan and stage an event will give you valuable insights into the skills needed to work in the industry. Organising a trip on a river cruise for a group, visiting a theme park or staging a small performance or show are some examples of small-scale efforts you might be able to achieve. You might be able to run your event to benefit others, such as a charity, and not just plan and carry it out to meet the assessment needs. Don't forget that even if your effort does not go totally smoothly you will still be able to identify what you could do better next time.

Unit 4

Leisure in Action

4.1 Choice of event

Topic 1	Choosing your event	12

4.2 Feasibility of event

Topic 2	Investigating the feasibility	18
Topic 3	Aims, objectives and customers	24
Topic 4	Marketing your event	30
Topic 5	Resources, finance and staffing	36
Topic 6	Administration, timescales, targets and evaluation	42

4.3 Teamwork

Topic 7	Effective teamwork skills	48

4.4 Carrying out the event

Topic 8	Carrying out your event	54

4.5 Evaluating the event

Topic 9	Evaluating your event	58
	Industry focus and useful links	62
	How Unit 4 is assessed	64

Topic 1 Choosing your event

You are going to be working in a team to stage your leisure-related event. The event itself must meet the needs of the assessment, so it's essential that you choose your event wisely. Your tutor may be able to guide you at this stage.

To make the best choice you need to consider what type of leisure-related event you and your team-mates could run. It has to generate enough interest to keep everyone motivated, have enough roles and responsibilities to make sure everyone can contribute meaningfully and give you the opportunity to achieve the assessment criteria for the unit.

This topic will take you through the initial stages of Leisure in Action, with guidance about:

- **Thinking about a suitable leisure-related event**
- **Assessing the complexity of the event**
- **Choosing your event**
- **Selecting your team and its structure**
- **Allocating roles for all in the team**
- **Meeting assessment needs**
- **Recording your involvement.**

Thinking about a suitable leisure-related event

The diversity of the leisure industry, as covered in Unit 1, should help you in your search for a suitable event. You might choose something which is 'active' in nature – for example, a sporting or activity theme. You might choose a more 'passive' event such as a group visit to a leisure location. The majority of your participants might be involved competitively or they might be spectators. It might be a new kind of event or it might copy a well-known event but be on a smaller scale, such as a fashion show.

The type of participants might be an important factor in helping you decide on a suitable event. Will it be an event for your class, for people in your neighbourhood, or perhaps for a particular age group?

The scale of the event will need to be determined too, and its effects on planning time, logistics and objectives. The location for your event will also be a consideration. Will it need to be held indoors or can it be run outside? Will it need specific leisure resources, such as rackets and balls? It is necessary to think about these aspects too.

Indoor sports events are easier to run year round.

Below are some leisure-related events that have been run in the past which might give you ideas. Look at these different examples of events and consider how the following factors were important:

	Day trip to Alton Towers	A visit to the Masters Tennis Tournament at the Royal Albert Hall	Local treasure hunt	Firework display
Are the participants active/passive?	Usually active (although they may choose not to).	The spectators are passive.	Active.	Mostly passive.
Does the event require spectators?	No.	Yes.	No.	Yes.
Is the event participant-specific? How?	No, although it may suit younger people more.	Fans of the game.	No.	No.
Is scale important?	No, the group can be any size.	Yes, there are limits on the number of spectators.	No.	No.
Is the event innovative?	No.	Yes.	It depends how it is run.	No.
Is the event static or transportable?	Static.	Static.	Transportable.	Transportable.
Is the event reliant on specific resources?	No	No.	It depends on scale.	Yes – fireworks.
Is the event seasonal?	It may be better to go when good weather is more likely.	Annual tournament but not dependent on weather.	It may be better to go when good weather is more likely.	Usually around 5th November or New Year.

Some leisure events are seasonal in nature. If the event is carried out in your summer term then an outdoor event is more likely. You might be able to theme an event by checking a calendar of festivities, holidays and other notable dates. A Valentine's theme, for example, could work for certain events in February.

Your local area might have a tradition that you could incorporate, such as walking in the Lake District or a themed visit to historic parts of London.

Whatever you choose eventually, keep in mind that it must be leisure-related.

Assessing the complexity of the event

As well as being leisure-related, your chosen event needs to be complex enough to be a real challenge, giving you the opportunity to stretch yourself and gain a real sense of achievement at the end. If it is not complex enough and too simple, you run the risk of not being able to:

- involve and motivate everyone in the team
- maintain interest from participants
- meet the assessment criteria well.

In order to decide how best to proceed, you should consider the following suggestions about what should be kept simple and what might need to be more complex:

1. The aims and objectives of your event should not be too complex. Use the KISS principle – 'keep it suitably simple'!
2. The people you will involve as customers or participants need to be realistically manageable. Use the KISS principle here as well.
3. Think how complex the marketing of the event might be. You may use various promotional techniques and several people.
4. The management and application of physical resources will nearly always be complex. Small teams can be allocated here to cover aspects such as location and travel.
5. If finance is involved then you may have to take responsibility for collecting and recording cash taken, or banking cheques. You should try to keep the processes and responsibilities simple.
6. Individual roles should be simple and clear, but all come together to represent a complete set of roles, working towards a team effort.
7. Administrative responsibilities will be complex and need to be shared – don't expect one person to carry out this role alone.

8. Responsibility for health, safety, security and legal aspects are also too complex to be carried by one person. This is a difficult area, with legal implications if you get it wrong, so seek professional help.
9. Targets and deadlines (timescales) will be varied, but the team needs to have a shared responsibility for them as the staging of the event approaches.

From these outlines you should be able to see whether the event will be complex enough to keep everyone busy and where the greatest difficulties lie. This will help you to know where you need to allocate the most people and time, and where it is advisable to stick to the KISS principle. As a cautionary note, be careful not to make your event over-complicated so that it runs beyond your control.

Choosing your event

Would a music event make your shortlist?

By now you should have an idea of how complex your leisure event needs to be, to give you the best chance of achieving a good grade.

Coming up with a workable idea and finding some appropriate team-mates might be quite difficult. The following methods will help you with the selection process:

- Brainstorming ideas.
- Creating a short list.
- Selecting your team and its structure.
- Deciding the parameters of your event.

Once you have chosen, you will investigate the feasibility of your chosen event in the next topic. If your choices do not work at that stage, you can always return to this section and restart the process of choosing your event.

Brainstorming ideas

You are probably quite familiar with this technique for coming up with suggestions. You can tackle this aspect as a whole class with your teacher, monitoring and noting ideas. Everyone is allowed to contribute a few ideas for event headings at this stage. One person's idea might spark someone else's, or two simple ideas might be combined to produce a more complex one. It is an evolutionary process. Be polite and don't ridicule suggestions you might think are unsuitable or silly; instead consider those suggestions that could be changed into more workable ideas.

Stop occasionally to agree which ideas are favoured and could be carried forward for further discussion – and which should be discarded.

activity

YOUR BRAINSTORMING SESSION

1 **Arrange a brief meeting with your teacher and classmates to brainstorm ideas for possible events. Keep a record of ideas, preferences and your inputs. You might want to do an internet search first to gather some ideas from the professional event companies.**

2 **By the end of the session, through the processes of discussion (and perhaps voting) try to select a short list of possible events which would suit the number of teams formed. Keep a record of decisions and your inputs.**

Creating a short list

Your teacher should be present during the drawing up of a short list as they will have to approve and advise. You might arrange more than one meeting to allow people time to investigate ideas or develop questions about ideas. Also, carry forward one or two spare ideas as back-up event ideas.

At the selection meeting, each short-listed suggestion should be given a fixed time for discussion, and notes made about what issues arise. At the end of the discussion, vote for the events that you think your class could do well, or, if your teams are already formed, bid for the event you like best.

Selecting your team and its structure

Even if your teams have been pre-selected, there are a number of factors to be taken into account which might determine the effectiveness of the teams, such as:

- The number of people in your team.
  Five to six people would generally be enough for an event team, unless a really complex event was planned for the whole class. Your teachers will be able to advise you about this, and any constraints that might apply to your institution, or to the delivery of the unit. A small event might be run with around five, but team members might have to take on more roles and responsibilities (and may not have all the skills needed). A more complex event, with more logistics, may require eight or nine people, but you may find all the skills you need amongst the team.
- Team structure.
  You can use the diagram below as a starting point for how you might set up your team's structure.
- Skills and abilities.
  It is best to assess everyone's skills and abilities to see if you have a good range. Remember the phrase 'too many cooks spoil the broth', so try to have diverse skills and abilities in your team.
  The structure helps with spreading skills out across your team, but you are likely to need most of the following:
  - good verbal communicators
  - good organisers and leaders
  - someone with computer competence
  - someone with the ability to notice weaknesses in your plans.

Working out your roles (see below) should be easier now. Clearer responsibilities will come later when the actual details of the event are known, but if you can match up people to roles at this stage it will help when you are investigating the feasibility of your event in Topic 2.

The minimum roles you will probably need.

- A co-ordinator
- Someone in charge of finances
- Organisers of resources
- A promotions co-ordinator
- Two to three team workers who take on various roles
- An expert who can be called upon for technical advice.

Deciding the parameters of your event

With your idea agreed in broad terms, there are some other key factors that will determine the parameters (limits) you need to work within. These parameters need to be identified before you assess feasibility. Factors that need to be examined include: Can you obtain a specific venue to stage your event? What is the actual date of the event? Who will be your customers? Most of these factors will be within your control, but some might not.

To some extent this will guide your eventual event format and team structure, so knowing these at an early stage is valuable.

Structure diagram for an event team

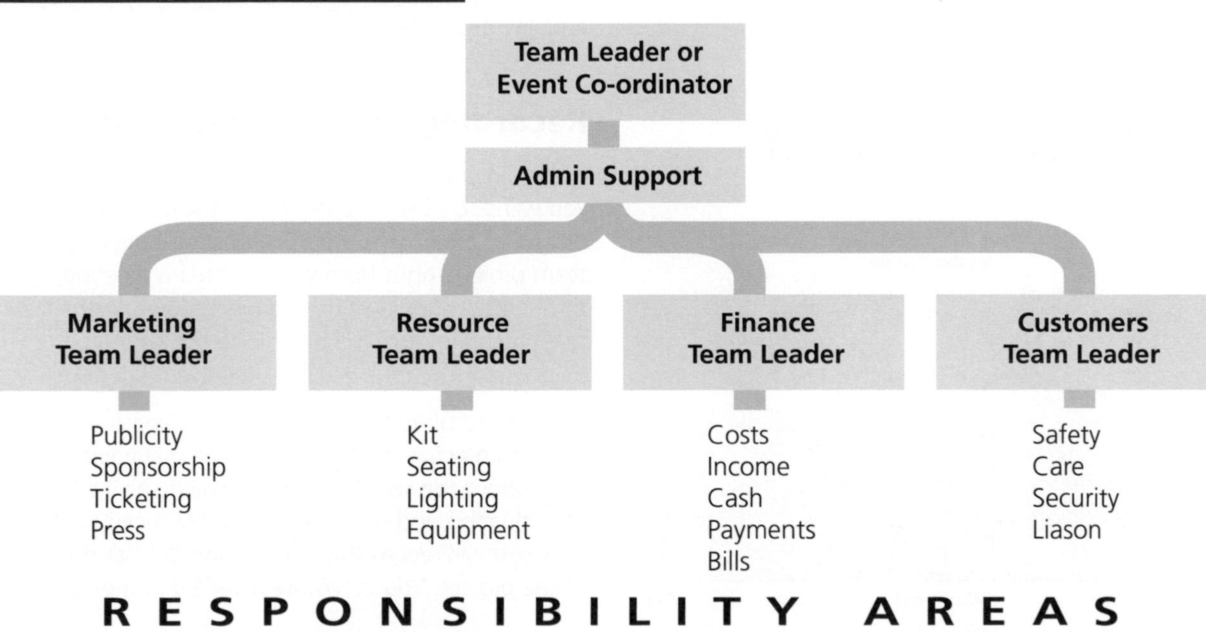

activity

DRAWING YOUR PARAMETERS

Start to create a spider diagram or flow chart, which captures early information graphically (date, location, timescale). This can be added to as ideas progress.

Allocating roles for all in the team

Once you have explored your event's complexity and it is clear that everyone should be able to play a sufficient role from start to finish, your team needs to begin to flesh out the detail of roles and tasks to assess what the actual workload will be for everyone. The case study opposite provides an example of the range of tasks within one organisation. The distribution of workload will have to be done fairly to ensure that work is equally shared, that everyone has a substantial role, sticks to their tasks and stays engaged with the project throughout.

Someone with an insubstantial role might not feel they have a full part to play. As a result, they might disengage from the project. Regular team meetings should highlight anyone not doing their share or their allotted tasks, and quick action should be taken to remedy any current or potential problems.

At the same time, be aware of the risks of overburdening someone or allowing them to take on too much. This is a recipe for frequent errors or delays in task completion. The diagram below gives you a visual image of how best to work together.

Here are some ideas to help you evolve a balanced set of roles for different stages of the planning and running of the event:

Swingometer chart of performance

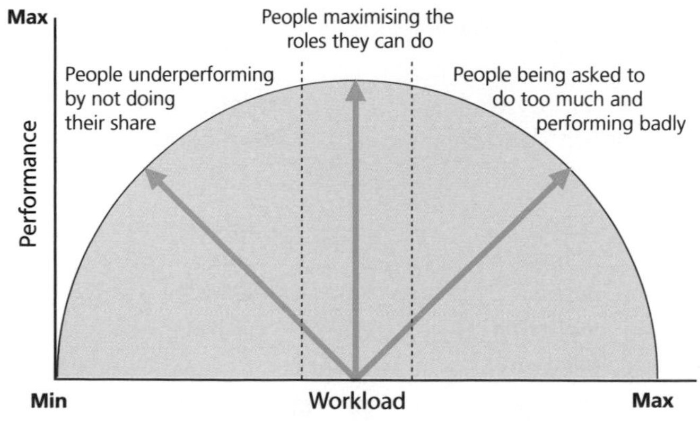

- Stage One – Researching
  Everyone is involved in finding out information, exploring costs, and discussing what resources might be needed and the interest levels of likely customers.
- Stage Two – Reporting findings and selecting the final event scenario.
  Everyone should feed back here and take part in the decision-making process, which might involve a vote, if you wish.
- Stage Three – planning tasks and allocating roles.
  This must involve everyone in as equal a way as possible. Tasks and roles will correspond to aspects like finance, marketing, resource management, customer care, health, safety and security. If there is not enough work to go around, your team may have to set some new aims and objectives or include new logistics.
- Stage Four – Carrying out pre-event roles.
  It may be important for someone (such as a co-ordinator) to oversee how everyone is coping and reallocate roles if someone is struggling.
  Refer again to the diagram of event team roles on page 15.
- Stage Five – running the actual event.
  This is where new roles (which have been planned and agreed) may be taken on, according to the needs of the day – parking co-ordinator, first aider, announcer or transport manager, for example.
- Stage Six – Completion and feedback.

You can use the above stages as a guide to when roles need to be allocated, monitored, evaluated and changed.

There may be peaks and troughs of activity for some people as each phase unfolds, but over the course of the event period, there should be an underlying equality of inputs.

Recording your involvement

Although you will run the project as part of a team, you will also need to produce a personal logbook or diary that records your particular contribution to the team project, right from your first team meeting, through the running of the project, down to the last team meeting. You will be able to use your records to help when you are evaluating the event later on.

Your record of your own contribution and that of your team is an active process: it must be maintained throughout the whole project. It will be a vital source of evaluation and review material. You need to decide how you will record this information right at the start of the project. You could use a variety of methods

Case study: HF Walking Holidays

This case study features a walking holiday company offering leisure treks all over Britain, the rest of Europe, and beyond. HF Walking Holidays have been organising walks for over 90 years. Each trip is a unique event for the participants, but a well practised formula for the teams of staff who try to ensure a quality experience every time. The teams have to:

- Devise guided and self-guided walks – at various levels
- Plan the routes – over varying terrain
- Select leaders – with good communication, first aid and navigations skills
- Arrange logistics – to cover transport, luggage and accommodation each night
- Compile info packs for guests – to include 'what items to bring'
- Arrange menus and eating stops
- Offer advice on fitness and diet
- Accommodate group bookings
- Schedule – dates, levels of walk, accommodation, and routes to fit together into a cohesive package and event
- Cover conditions of booking
- Ensure that insurance covers all eventualities
- Maintain a website
- Deal with customers' and providers' payments.

This is another list of extensive practical matters, some of which you might take note of if needed for your event.

What key factors have not been listed in this case study that are found in most events?

and should prepare these during the planning stage, so that you become familiar with them and can fill them in efficiently. Formats might include:

- ring binder divided into sections
- diary with pages for notes
- electronic
- wall planner or flow chart
- video recording
- photographs or tapes
- observer comments
- participant statements
- tutor observations.

Whichever format you select, it has to cover two main areas: process and content. Process means all the actions or procedures gone through by the team, such as planning, tasks allocated, customer care, deadlines, and any revisions made, along with notes on advice sought. Content means the topics covered. This must include records of:

- personal and team contributions
- how roles (briefings) were maintained
- how disruptions were handled
- how health, safety and security aspects were maintained
- how well the team co-operated and whether it adhered to the plan.

The format of the logbook should be discussed with your teacher to establish what is acceptable.

Your logbook should also contain copies of all relevant materials, such as:

- minutes from team meetings
- schedules of tasks
- checklists and briefings
- diary of activities
- reports on research
- costs of resources
- contacts for providers
- contingency plans
- emergency procedures.

activity

CREATING A PERSONAL LOG BOOK

Create a logbook suitable for recording your own contribution to the running of your project and those of your fellow team members. The logbook should have enough space and section divisions to cover the processes and contents already discussed.

Topic 2 Investigating the feasibility

Investigating the feasibility of your event forms an important part of the planning stage. A feasibility study is a study designed to determine the practicability of a system or proposal – in your case, a leisure event. Your findings for this type of study will take shape in the form of a plan that will explain various important aspects of your event. Investigating its feasibility should be the first *real* piece of research into your event. This topic will introduce each of the elements of your required plan with a focus on gathering data in order to make decisions on feasibility or help you to re-plan. Those elements are:

- **Aims and objectives**
- **Assessing customer or participant needs**
- **Marketing the event**
- **Physical resource needs**
- **Financial feasibility**
- **Staffing of the event**
- **Administration**
- **Timescales and targets**
- **Investigating legal aspects**
- **Reviewing and evaluating the event.**

As you plan, you are beginning to realise the vision you had in Topic 1. Sport England's advice at this stage of planning a project is to 'think long term and think quality'.

Testing feasibility

There are many benefits derived from assessing feasibility and the planning that follows:

- It helps to reduce risk and uncertainty.
- It eases people into their roles.
- The team thinks through their event logistics and resource needs in a logical sequence.
- It uncovers unrealistic assumptions which may have been made, such as cost of materials.
- It establishes whether the preparation period (timescale) is sufficient.
- Finally, it establishes whether the event could actually happen – or where changes need to be considered to realise the project.

Planning an event is a lot like the process people go through when setting up their first business. And when small businesses fail, it is usually due to not testing feasibility enough and a lack of planning.

Sources of help for testing feasibility

1. You can pick up a leaflet from most banks on 'starting a new business' which is a similar process.
2. Local business guidance organisations should be able to answer some of your questions on how to assess feasibility.
3. Project management textbooks will have some feasibility testing suggestions (your event is a project of sorts).
4. Go online and contact a professional event company for advice.
5. Use local contacts who regularly organise events, such as sports development officers.

activity

LOOKING AT HOW PROFESSIONALS ASSESS FEASIBILITY

Using at least three of the sources given previously, gather some examples of what is done by professionals to assess feasibility. Compare these with findings from other groups.

Aims and objectives

The aim of the event needs to be clear to everyone and agreed by them. Don't have too many aims and don't confuse aims and objectives. Aims are overviews of what you want to achieve and are more qualitative in nature, such as, 'to stage a successful netball event for under-18 girls' or 'to provide a safe and fun day at the beach for under-9s'. Objectives are more quantifiable, such as, 'selling 200 tickets for the disco event' or 'attracting 125 charity runners for a fun run'. Aims and objectives have to be agreed as a team and should be noted down and added to your development chart or diagram.

Assessing customer or participant needs

A range of methods might be used to assess customer or participant needs:

- Carrying out a small survey, using simple questionnaires.
- Writing to any organisations you hope to involve, to ask if they are interested – and what their needs might be.
- Sampling opinions or interviewing likely participants.
- Making initial approaches to potential sponsors to assess their preferences or criteria for sponsorship.
- Advertising – asking for email, text or phone responses to the idea.

If responses are good, you can go ahead. If feedback is negative, discuss what changes you could make to meet the needs expressed. At worst you might have to change the events parameters (aims and objectives, location and date).

Marketing the event

The marketing of the event is the next aspect to be assessed. Guidelines for this can be constructed around the four main P's of marketing (and probably incorporated into your customer survey investigation).

- Product – If you have clear aims and objectives then it should be easy to describe your product such as 'a fashion show for beach wear' or 'a visit to TV studios to watch a soap being filmed'.
- Place (the location) – This should be a well known or popular place that your customers are familiar with. You need to check its availability and also any costs to hire. Always have a back-up location. If it is an outdoor venue, keep an indoor 'wet weather' alternative in your plans too.
- Price – This is the most crucial and complex aspect to assess for it will have many component parts. The price has to be worked out to cover all costs in most cases, unless you are able to find a subsidy through sponsorship. Your final pricing strategy will be governed by your event aims and objectives. For instance, if you aim to stage a 'free event' you are likely to need sponsorship. If one of your objectives is to 'break even' through ticket sales, you will have to work out how many tickets you need to sell. (See break-even diagram on page 33, Topic 4). If your objective is to make a profit to donate to charity, you need to decide what this profit might be. In addition, you will have to assess what customers are willing to pay for your proposed event. Weigh this up against the costs you will incur and decide if the price is viable. You may decide you have to change some plans to reduce costs and bring the price down.
- Promotion – Until you have clarified Product, Place and Price your team cannot really begin any promotional activities because information about the event's main features needs to be clear. You will want to avoid any misinformation – that could be a recipe for a 'non-event'. It is likely you will choose a range of methods to promote your event so the information needs to be correct before these are launched.

Promotional techniques could include advertising, direct marketing, public relations, sales promotion and sponsorship. For an event, this might involve posters, website information, flyers (see overleaf) or giving talks. This gives you a marketing mix of opportunities to suit the product, customers, budget, locations, image and timing.

Promotional flyers

Physical resource needs

Physical resource needs can cover a huge range of specific and general needs and are likely to be different for every type of event. However, it is useful to classify things to help allocate roles for researching how feasible they are:

- Raw materials – pens, paper, blank videos, T-shirts, caps, tickets, receipts, consumables.
- Equipment – chairs, tables, clocks, cash box, computers, balls, streamers.
- Venue-specific resources – parking cones, lighting, signs, tents.
- Premises-specific resources – storage, fire extinguishers, first aid boxes.
- Facilities – toilets, pay kiosk, stalls serving food, changing areas.

Techniques which might be useful in researching physical resource needs are:

- The relevant team members sit down and 'visualise' what they think will be needed, and make notes to be submitted at a team meeting.
- Putting yourself in the customer's place and envisaging what you would like to find.
- Brainstorming all the needs in a group and discussing the priorities.

activity

PHYSICAL RESOURCES IN PRACTICE

Imagine you have been given responsibility for identifying the resources needed for one aspect of a team event – either marketing or sports equipment. The event will be a day-long, six-team volleyball tournament based in a school sports hall. Refreshments are to be provided. What would be needed?

Financial feasibility

You are going to have to assess this very carefully, covering income and expenditure for a range of event needs:

- What are the start-up costs? Initial purchases need to be investigated promptly, such as licences, permits, hall hire or raw materials.
- What overall budget does the event need? This will be derived from each cost centre and will cover marketing, staffing, resource needs and contingencies.
- What income can you expect and where will it come from? If you have set targets you will have to set prices to cover costs and meet those targets (perhaps through ticket sales), donations, secondary spending or sponsorship.
- How will you handle all of these cash flows – ensuring safety, security and correct record keeping?
- Will there be any insurance costs for cancellation, accident or damage?
- Will you need to budget for unseen costs, such as repairs, refunds, damage, loss, surcharges or VAT?

It is clear that this should not all be entrusted to one person. A team of two would be best, covering income and expenditure – with records and receipts being kept and constant reporting and monitoring of progress.

Staffing of the event

There are three sources of staffing which you might need to plan for – yourselves, tutors, and external assistance. These are your most important resources – the glue that will hold your event together and see it succeed. Many will have to take on dual roles or multi-task over the period of the event planning and running, so choose well. *Your* time of course, will be provided free, as no doubt will that of tutors, but any external help – expert advice or speakers, for example – may need some of their costs covering. If your event needs additional staff some volunteers could be sought amongst family and friends. Evaluate how many staff you will need, doing which tasks and for how long. Always keep someone spare for contingencies or for absences on the day. Be sure you identify roles for each person and can describe clearly the task you will wish them to carry out. Use your team structure diagram to expand and illustrate these.

Administration

The level of administrative (admin) support will depend on how complex your event is. Dividing the process into three stages might help your feasibility assessments:

1. Before the event

What will you need at the research and planning stage? Admin is likely to consist of a computer and someone keeping a hard copy of meeting notes. Some word processing of letters of enquiry and access to the internet and telephone system may be needed too. All individuals will need to keep their own log or record system. A good team will identify early what systems they are likely to need for recording routine tasks and reports – and the non-routine or exceptional pieces of work. At the planning stage you are more likely to need to record regular enquiries, transactions and bookings. While you may not have any emergencies or accidents, a method of recording these non-routine events must be in place. Don't get caught out – you will need them for legal purposes. Think also of how much your systems might cost, how fast and accurate they will be and what information needs to be stored and retrieved in what format. Will information be secure, yet easily accessible? How will graphics be created?

2. During the event

There will be less admin going on during the event, but you could be gathering customer feedback and may need access to your database for quick reference. The system will need to be able to administer bookings and ticket sales if that is a key feature. Other broader issues might include preparation of press releases, capture of digital photos, refunds, new notices, participants' details, results and emergency contacts.

3. After the event

Much data about the event will be needed after the event for the team's use, so your admin system needs to accommodate this, as it may affect your assessment needs. 'Thank you' letters will need to go out, data will need to be analysed, customer surveys carried out and reports prepared. Will your system allow this – with access for all? Costs will need to be considered too, whether you are using an electronic system or not.

Timescales and targets

By now, your team will have set a date for the event (or have been given one). When your feasibility investigation is completed the team needs to reassess whether the timescale is still adequate for the complexity planned. If you have doubts, simplify the event logistics so that they will fit more comfortably within the timescale and *always* leave extra time for planning and preparation. Similarly, your targets may have been too ambitious (or too modest) at the outset compared to what you know after the feasibility phase, so be prepared to adjust these too.

Investigating legal aspects

This feasibility test must be done thoroughly so that you stay within the law. At this stage you need to set someone the task of assessing what legislation may apply to your event and gathering advice as to what you need to do to comply with the regulations or guidelines. It is likely that they will have to consult experts on health and safety over issues of hazards, first aid, fire, security, and evacuation plans. When the planning truly begins, risk assessments will be needed for all these considerations. Your resource investigator will need to ensure that lack of compliance will not lead to problems later with cancellation or delay, and will not incur high insurance costs and liability for damage or injury.

Reviewing and evaluating the event

This aspect – assessing the satisfaction of customers, the team performance and the overall event success – is primarily for your team's benefit. As a team, you must agree how best you can do this, so that it is simple and effective. Evaluation should really be ongoing – through personal evaluation of inputs and reflection on performance so far. Your team might choose to see how it is doing against its targets at certain key stages. There are various ways of reviewing and evaluating:

- peer feedback
- comparison with targets
- performance charts
- satisfaction surveys
- scoring and rating systems.

Some charts and other criteria will be discussed in the next topic.

Finally, do not forget to discuss what might go wrong – and devise some contingency plans.

At the end of the feasibility stage you need to have a full team meeting to reassess all the matters and issues that your feasibility study has thrown up.

You must have complete agreement and confidence that the event fits within the parameters and can

Model of teamwork – Task and individual needs

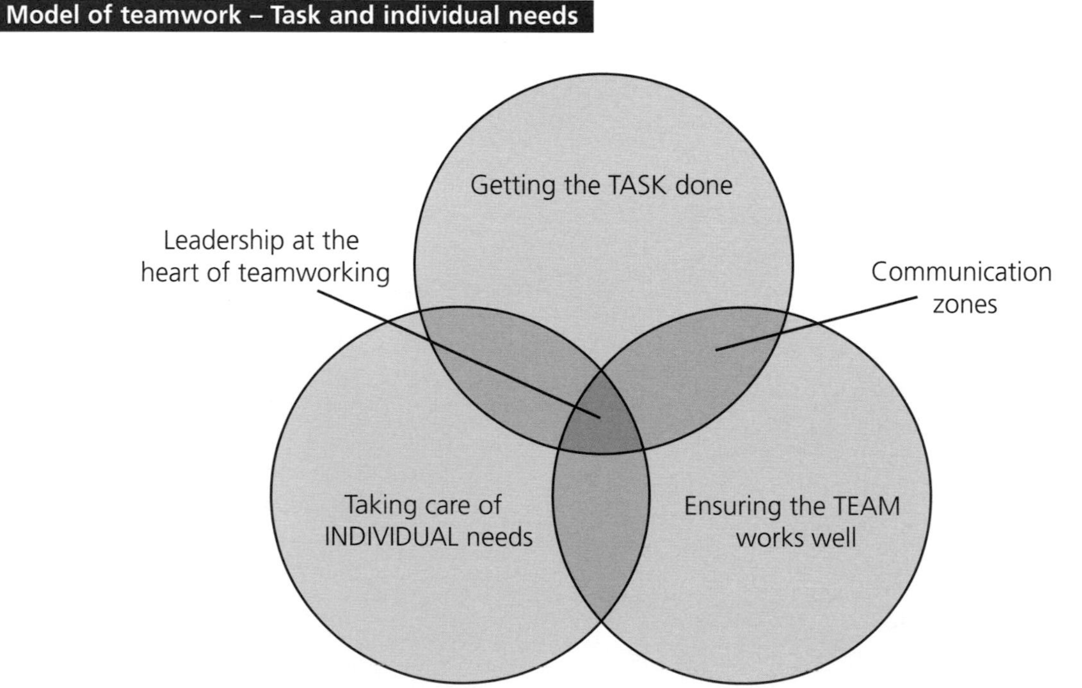

Source: Adapted from 'John Adair's Model of Teamwork'

work, and can meet the team, task and individual assessment requirements.

activity

ASSESSING FEASIBILITY

Assess the feasibility of the following event. Use the headings from this topic to help you. Hopefully you will come across new ideas which will help you when assessing your event.

Case study: David Lloyd Great Mile Runs

This case study features a type of event within the scope of your assessment requirements – a 'charity run'. Each May in various large UK cities 'David Lloyd Great Mile Runs' are staged. Organised by David Lloyd Leisure and Nova International, their aim is to 'get a million people to run a million miles' in total for charity. The objective is to build on the £25,000 raised to date. Celebrities from the world of sports attend and take part. The leisure company also staged a virtual gym and mini tennis courts exhibition alongside the run. The mile is felt to be a manageable distance for the young and moderately fit people (the target group).

Source: Leisure Opportunities, May 2005

Topic 3 Aims, objectives and customers

In the last topic we emphasised the need for your team to *fully* check your initial plans in order to assess the feasibility of the event's logistics before you commit to your planning process. With this done, you can begin the planning proper.

Your plan, although it will give much detail, still needs to have elements of flexibility in it to accommodate any changes which occur leading up to your event. It is also worth reminding you to keep your logbook records up to date, because once details are worked out for each role, task or function you will need to have a written record to refer to.

It is always useful to begin the planning process with a summary of the event, just to keep everyone clear about its nature and its aims. This summary is what professionals call the 'project overview'. Elements of the plan will correspond to those that you tested for feasibility, and in the next two topics we shall work through some guidelines for you to follow. A model of an event plan is shown on the right.

The guidelines will of course only be general in nature, but hopefully you can adapt them to suit your event, team and location. In this topic we will cover:

- Aims and objectives
- Customer needs.

Event planning diagram

Aims and objectives

In the feasibility section, you were encouraged to keep your aims simple and clear. This allows the vision or message about your event to come across clearly, so that it is readily understood by potential customers, by team members and by members of staff. You may wish to amend your aims and objectives in the light of information which has emerged from the feasibility investigation.

Aims

Aims provide an overview. Some you might consider are shown below:

- Complete the event on time and to budget.
- Provide a memorable experience.
- Ensure participants have a safe and successful day.
- Ensure the event team work well together and use all their capabilities and resources fully.

activity

DIFFERENT COMPANIES: SAME AIMS?

Carry out some online research on some of the event companies listed below to assess what their various aims are. Do they have any common themes?

DTB International (hospitality and events management) www.dtbsportsandevents.com

Accolade Corporate Events UK www.accolade-corporate-events.com/

The Concerto Group (integrated event solutions) www.concertogroup.co.uk/

Capital Sport www.capital-sport.co.uk

ILAM (Institute of Leisure and Amenity Management) www.ilam.co.uk/

Maximillion Events Ltd www.maximillion.co.uk/events

Objectives

Objectives are quantifiable in nature, and will largely determine success. You will also be able to use them for the evaluation process – which is needed for the assessment.

One of the most common ways of remembering the nature of objectives is using the acronym **SMART**:

Objectives should be:

Specific – applied to one area only – budget, for example.

Measurable – set in quantities – tickets sold, for example.

Agreed – by all the team.

Realistic – within the capabilities of the team and the plan.

Timed – given a set period in which to be achieved.

Objectives can be applied to many areas of the event such as finance, marketing or resources. It is up to each person or group responsible for one particular area to set their own objectives, in line with the overall event targets. Remember you will be judged on how well you meet these targets.

Objectives can be set for various stages of the event planning and implementation process so that progress can be checked for adherence to deadlines, advance bookings, use of resources or budget (see flowchart). This way the team can spot and manage any problems that occur before they become unmanageable.

Objectives flowchart

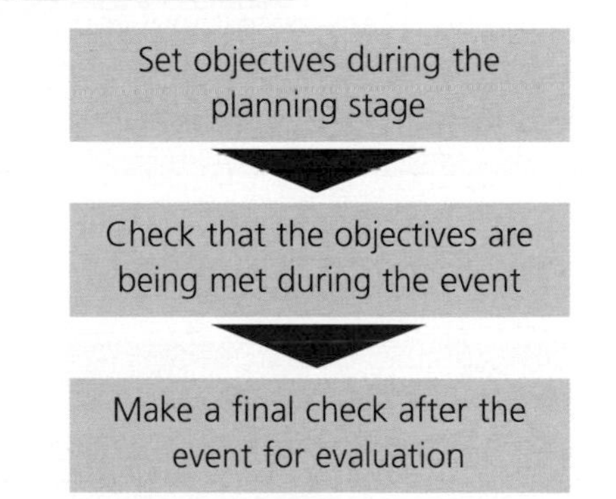

This style of running an event is called a goal-setting technique. In the leisure industry, failure to meet such goals might have certain consequences for an organisation staging events:

- Their image may be damaged.
- The costs may run over budget and cause them to make a loss.
- They may run out of planning time and have to make some hasty – and possibly poor – decisions.
- Customers might come away with an unfavourable experience and never use that organisation or venue again (loss of repeat business).

activity

WHO GOT IT WRONG?

Can you think of an actual project that *failed* to reach its goals recently? Why was this? Could it happen to your project?

Here are some other types of objectives you might set:

- Increase interest in a particular sport – for instance, raise the numbers of people taking part in roller hockey by five per cent. Sport development schemes often have this as a core objective.
- Increase customer awareness and sales of leisure goods – an objective that a leisure retailer might set.
- Create a more favourable image in a potentially hostile environment.
- Provide community benefits, such as putting on an event which is enjoyed by the under-privileged or which channels income into benefiting others.
- Make a profit. This is an objective that all commercial leisure operators will have.

activity

DISCUSSING OBJECTIVES

Discuss with your team-mates how you might tackle each of these objectives and identify any problems that you might encounter.

Customer needs

There are two types of customers involved with events: external customers – the participants and spectators, and internal customers – the team, the staff and suppliers you are dealing with.

External customers

For external customers you can identify your target group either demographically or geographically: A demographic analysis might give you:

- specified age ranges as target groups
- lifestyle preference, target groups, based for example on entertainment, sport or active/passive attitudes.

Geographic groups would probably be those 'in your neighbourhood' or 'on your campus' who have easy access to the event location.

The advantage of classifying your customers this way is that you can be more specific with your event content and marketing materials. This is called 'product positioning'. You can then select the promotional techniques (see table below) that you feel are likely to be most effective in attracting your customers.

Some customer needs may be less obvious for your event, so you must identify these and try to plan for them. Some examples might be:

- people who arrive as a group and want to be together
- VIPs at your event might need reserved seats
- disabled visitors will definitely need consideration
- babies and toddlers or mums/dads with young children

Promoting your event to the customer

Promotional techniques	*Use for an event*
Advertising	Publicity, display or broadcast of the event in a positive way, via newspapers, displays, radio, TV, posters and leaflets.
Personal selling	Direct contact with customers – face to face or over the telephone, selling to suit their needs.
Public relations	A planned attempt to create a favourable image of the event and its activities, via stories for the newspapers and celebrity endorsements.
Sales promotion	Short-term activities designed to encourage people to come to the event – special offers, demonstrations, competitions, all linked to the event.
Direct marketing	Sending the promotional material directly to the customer – mailshot or leaflet drop.
Publicity brochures	Circulation of leaflets and brochures at likely outlets.
Sponsorship	Display of the sponsor's name or products at an event can be very valuable and attract spectators. This needs to be done carefully to meet the sponsor's needs.

- older visitors/spectators or participants
- people with different cultural needs
- there may even be some gender issues – make sure that there are no barriers to access or participation for females/males.

Internal customers

Your internal customer strategy is very different, but just as important.

As a team, you need to build good relationships with tutors and other staff you may use on campus and with the outside organisations and individuals you deal with for your event. Here are some good principles to follow in all these cases:

- Establish good communication channels
- Always be polite
- Listen carefully to any instructions given
- Give clear information
- Deliver what you promise.

These are part of your marketing mix, and you need satisfied internal customers for a successful event.

activity

DIFFERENT CUSTOMERS: DIFFERENT NEEDS

A local college has, after nearly six years, raised enough money and found enough sponsors to have a new sports hall built. Imagine you are the team appointed to stage the official opening, with a celebrity and a few local dignitaries attending. You decide to put on a student display to entertain the crowd and give the press something to photograph. Can you identify the different types of customers you will have to liaise with and what their differing needs may be?

Meeting customer needs

When staging an event you will have a complex set of customer needs. It is very important to identify what might apply to your customers' needs and plan how your team will meet them.

Good internal and external customer relations are of great value to event organisers because they:

- create a good working environment
- produce positive and responsive relationships
- ensure that appreciation and recognition are more readily given
- Create a 'happy team image', which is more likely to attract sponsorship, increase sales or donations and be seen by customers.

Attitude and behaviour are the key to good customer service – putting yourself in the place of the customer helps you to envisage how you would like to be treated. No one likes rudeness, delays or ambiguous information.

Many organisations will have a 'customer charter' to help guide staff.

Probably the most-used customer service training scheme in the leisure and tourism industry is 'Welcome Host' promoted by the English Tourism Council. Their course includes aspects such as:

- communication skills
- complaint handling
- making positive first impressions
- providing customer information.

Research shows that training clearly provides benefits, so it is something that you might work into your plans, including perhaps, some role play for those who are less confident, but might need to deal with the public over the phone (or face-to-face).

There are some simple guidelines you can follow:

- Make sure that you at least satisfy expectations – but better still exceed them
- Don't pressure people into buying or participating
- Make staff and customers feel valued
- Ensure that any information you pass on is accurate
- Respond to complaints, problems and queries quickly.

activity

THE IMPORTANCE OF CUSTOMER SERVICE

1 **Identify the needs of spectators going to a football match.**

2 **What might be the effects of poor customer service at your event?**

Customer relations

Appearance, personality and even personal hygiene can play a part in customer relations. Good customer service during the run-up to your event and on the day depends, above all, on one thing – attitude. Your team's attitude and individual members' attitudes will need to be positive (even when you don't feel like it!). Here are some aspects which you might keep in mind for your event needs:

- Use surnames with adults and first names with children.
- Never chew gum when dealing with customers.
- Don't be afraid to take the lead and strike up a conversation.
- Maintain eye contact.
- Keep calm with difficult customers.
- Don't break confidence on personal details or how you feel about customers to other customers.

At the planning stage it is important to know who in your team will actually establish what your customers' needs are – and how. You might have to use some selling skills to persuade people to buy a ticket or to take part, so identify who would be best for this. They probably need to be individuals who are enthusiastic, friendly and knowledgeable, at the very least. The whole team will have to work at 'raising customer awareness'. In the industry this would probably be done with the aid of an event manual. You may not have a manual at this stage, but a 'facts sheet' would suffice.

Your team needs to have a strategy for assessing customer needs, particularly during the run-up to the event and on the day. 'Can I help you?' is still the best way of finding out customer needs in conversation. You need to follow this up with more detailed questions, and then find a way to match their needs to what your event has to offer. If you cannot persuade someone to buy on the day, try reserving a place for them and following up later with a call.

Dealing with customers

Communicating with customers (internal and external) needs a simple strategy too. Discuss what your needs will be for the following, if appropriate:

- Appealing to children
- Answering the telephone (speak and explain clearly, take notes, get a name and contact number, listen carefully)
- How you will tackle written communications (letters, posters, flyers, menus, price lists, bills, signs, notice boards, emails, texts, faxes – maybe even your own website)
- Using a microphone, talking on the radio, giving press interviews, body language
- Relaying and taking messages for others
- Communicating changes in plans or giving feedback on poor performances
- Recording transactions, complaints, accidents
- Communicating at the opening ceremony, winding up the event, thanking contributors
- Writing up your inputs, efforts and evaluations for the assessment.

It's likely that as young amateurs you will make some mistakes, which might in turn lead to customer complaints. With this in mind, you should plan a strategy to deal with customer complaints. Dissatisfied customers might report you, and you could soon gain a bad reputation. Leisure businesses recognise that complaints arise so they all have a customer complaints procedure (see below).

Customer complaints procedure

For a minor complaint:	For a major complaint:
Member of staff deals with it on the spot according to preset parameters in line with company policy	Facts and details are gathered from the customer
Member of staff calls manager to oversee process or a make a decision	These are compared to those held by the organisation
	All details are sent to head office for evaluation

Assessing customer satisfaction

At this planning stage you should also agree how you will assess customer satisfaction and the quality of your event. Leisure organisations value any quality awards they can gain because they say a lot to customers about their service, and 'benchmark' the leisure provider as one of the better organisations. Examples of industry awards and certificates (which you learnt about in Unit 1) include:

- Quest
- Charter Mark
- Investors in People
- ISO (The International Organisation of Standardisation).

Your event team won't be able to attain any of these, but you can follow some useful guidelines.

1. Set some good standards for team members to follow, using some of the methods described in this topic. Perhaps check out an event management company website for their standards.
2. Devise a customer satisfaction survey with appropriate questions.
3. Prepare some illustrative methods of presenting the results of the survey, such as bar and pie charts.
4. Decide what criteria you will use to assess: yourselves, the team, the event, communication, customer satisfaction, value for money, friendliness, standards being met, complaints, enjoyment, safety, access, etc.

Gathering feedback needs to be done constructively too. Leisure event organisers tackle this in a number of ways:

- Informal feedback – anecdotal stories or comments and conversations overheard amongst customers.
- Surveys – through questionnaires and comments sheets.
- Focus groups – feedback from small groups of participants or customers.
- Suggestion cards or expert opinions.
- Observation.
- Appointing a mystery participant or visitor.

activity

IN THE CUSTOMER'S SHOES

Recall any occasions where you have been an external customer at a leisure event. Were *your* needs met as a customer? Share your experiences whilst considering the following questions:

1. Did you experience any rudeness, delays or ambiguous information?
2. Did you feel valued as a customer?
3. Was there an identifiable 'team' at the event (perhaps using a dress code)?
4. How did you rate communication?
5. Did you need to complain about anything? If so, how was your complaint handled?
6. Did you notice any industry awards or certificates at the event?

Topic 4 Marketing your event

Marketing is one of the key planning aspects you will have to tackle, because if you cannot attract participants, spectators, sponsors or customers, your event will fail. As we have seen in the last topic, a lot of planning needs to go into the process of identifying and meeting customer needs. Professional event companies compete against each other through websites, glossy brochures and networking with managers. You won't be able to match those aspects of marketing, but you can borrow some of their practices to guide your own. It is advisable to carry out some preliminary research on your plans before you 'go to print' and communicate your event to the target market you have chosen. Finally, deciding on how you will evaluate your work will be a crucial aspect. This flow gives us our headings for this topic:

- **Developing a marketing plan**
- **Factors affecting the plan**
- **The marketing mix**
- **Market research**
- **Evaluating marketing activities.**

Developing a marketing plan

Due to the importance of marketing it is probably best you allocate a small team for this aspect of the event. They will have much to do in the run-up, and different jobs during the event, as the emphasis shifts to customer care on the day. This team can work out more details and the format of the plan – while other teams develop their own responsibilities – then they can all report back at a suitable meeting for everyone's approval.

The structure of the plan needs to include:

1. Aims and objectives
2. A SWOT analysis of the event and team
3. A PEST analysis of external factors
4. Identification of customer needs
5. A marketing mix of the four Ps
6. Marketing communications proposals
7. Evaluation criteria.

Where necessary, the ideas should be backed up by research.

activity

HOW ACTUAL MARKETING PLANS WORK

Try to get hold of and assess a real leisure organisation's marketing plan. Evaluate how closely it follows the above structure.

Factors affecting the plan

Factors affecting an event plan can come from internal and external sources. Internal factors come from within the team – or from the event format itself. These factors are usually within the control of the organisers and can probably be dealt with by making minor changes. Most external factors, however, are not under the team's control at all, and can have a big impact, requiring major changes to be made.

There are different tools for analysing and assessing internal and external factors.

A SWOT analysis of internal factors

SWOT stands for Strengths, Weaknesses, Opportunities and Threats. When it comes to assessing these for your team and plan, you need to be honest. The diagram below shows a SWOT analysis for a team attempting to stage an outdoor orienteering event in a local country park, for fellow schoolmates. Participants have worked hard to gain sponsorship, with the proceeds going to a local charity.

SWOT analysis for orienteering event

Strengths	**Weaknesses**
• Three of the group are active orienteerers • The press have agreed to cover the event • A sponsor has been found • Park rangers have agreed to help	• Four of the group haven't done much orienteering • We only have one laptop for recording results in the field • Parking close to the venue is limited • Not all competitors are very familiar with orienteering
Opportunities	**Threats**
• 12 teams of three have entered • A local sports celebrity can attend to present prizes	• No wet weather alternative • We have overlooked the fact that the event is on Cup Final day

activity

YOUR TURN TO SWOT

1. **What recommendations would you make to help the orienteering event team overcome their weaknesses and threats, and maximise their strengths and opportunities?**
2. **Now perform a SWOT analysis for your team's event.**

A PEST analysis of external factors

PEST stands for Political, Economic, Social and Technological. These are the types of external factors which can affect your event. In other words, they form the environment and context in which the event is being run.

- **Political factors**
  Political factors can affect real event management companies, such as DTB International, quite markedly. The government may change taxation laws, add licensing regulations or tighten up on safety legislation, which will have implications for operators. For your event, you may have to have music licences, for example, or get police clearance for parking, or need permissions from the local authority or your institution. Getting these organised is a major priority in your planning process – otherwise your event may be illegal and unsafe.

- **Economic factors**
  Event organisers, such as Capital, are affected by several economic factors which will help to determine how profitable they are:
  - How much disposable income people have to attend events.
  - What company budgets are for these types of corporate activities.
  - The rate of inflation.
  - The level of taxes (business rate and allowances).
  - Employment levels.

You should consider the economic climate for your target group when deciding on your event pricing. A subsidy or sponsorship could go towards lowering the prices to make it more affordable.

- **Social factors**
  Social trends affect what customers choose to buy. Trends can be population-based (for example, the growing over-50s market) and can originate from fashions favoured by particular age groups. Trends might also be governed by the way we live today and the 24/7 leisure time clock. Event companies take a great deal of care to study social trends – it allows them to tailor their event formats to suit the changing tastes of customers. Social trends in the event world sometimes follow the sporting calendar, with attendance at key events being important for certain sections of society – the Boat Race, Royal Ascot, the British Grand Prix and the opening matches of the football season. For your event plan, be sure you know what trends your target group is likely to follow.

- **Technological factors**
  Event communications, themes and venues have all benefited from rapid progress in technology in the last decade. Companies like Accolade are able to increase their range, year on year. Companies who cannot compete on a technological level may well fall by the wayside. Event technology might include laser light shows, online betting, virtual reality – even transport to a venue could be a factor. The internet acts as a window on the event world and is perhaps the most important technological development. The use of technology at your event might not compare with these levels, but you must ensure that you take advantage where you can of electronic means. At the very least, technology can save your team time by speeding up communications. Having something special at your event – such as footage on a large screen – might well help to bring in more participants or customers, so do try to incorporate it in your plan.

activity

YOUR PEST ANALYSIS

Do a PEST analysis for your team's event.

The marketing mix

As you may recall, the marketing mix combines the four Ps – product, place, price and promotion – into a blend that will work towards achieving the event's objectives.

If we consider the following formulas they should make matters clearer for your planning.

PRODUCT

The product is the event – the features of the product and the characteristics of the event are the same thing. These characteristics should meet the customers' needs.

- If you have targeted a group of sports players, an event might need features that are competitive, fair and rewarding.
- If you are offering a visit for fellow students, then features will be safety, fun, and making the event memorable.

Your event should aim to be distinctive, to help make it unique and leave a lasting impression. The features that help to distinguish a product are often called USPs (unique selling points). For your event you might consider something like free fizzy drinks, a celebrity appearance, or a raffle. Use your imagination here, but keep your customers in mind. You are going to have to work hard to raise awareness of your event because it will have a very short product lifecycle. If you don't get the product right (the event) it won't matter how you promote, price or place – it won't sell!

activity

YOUR PRODUCT

Carry out a final review on your product (event) to ensure it is aligned with customer needs. Can you think of any suitable unique selling points?

PLACE

The place is the venue or location for your event. There should be a close fit between the characteristics of your event and the location chosen. Don't choose a hall simply because it is available for free – question whether it will suit your purpose, your customers' needs and the event image.

The decision as to where to locate a theme park is far more complicated than the question that you will be faced with, but it highlights some principles which you might consider for your event:

- Catchment zone – How many people live within an easy drive of the event location?
- Access – Is it easy to access the venue by car, bus or rail?
- Support facilities – Is there accommodation or are there complementary facilities such as catering and parking nearby?
- Respect – Does staging the event at the chosen location interfere with anyone else's concerns? If your event is to be staged in the evening, are there any people living nearby who might object?
- Infrastructure – Is there enough space to move large items around and accommodate any special resources?

activity

YOUR PLACE

Carry out a final check of your proposed venue using the criteria in the previous bullet points.

PRICE

This can be one of your more difficult decisions. Planning for pricing requires a lot of information to back up decisions. Two questions your team must consider are:

1. What factors will determine price?
   The factors determining price will vary from event to event, but common aspects of *cost* need to be considered first – venue/equipment hire, buying of raw materials, printing costs, hiring of staff, prizes, transport, insurance and licences. In most cases, the more costly your event is to stage, the higher the price you will charge customers.
2. What are your financial objectives?
   Most event organisers aim to make a profit. If you set a profit-making target you will have to price accordingly – by covering costs, plus a small percentage of profit. This percentage will be agreed when setting your objectives. Remember that chasing a profit may force your price beyond what prospective customers can reasonably afford.

You may wish to stage a free event, but not all resources will be free. Assess how you can create income – through donations, sponsorship, secondary sales or grants – to balance any costs.

If you only wish to 'break even' (balance your income with your costs), then the break-even point will have to be calculated in terms of a measurable objective – tickets sold, seats sold, items sold or fees paid (see diagram).

Break-even diagram: tickets sold

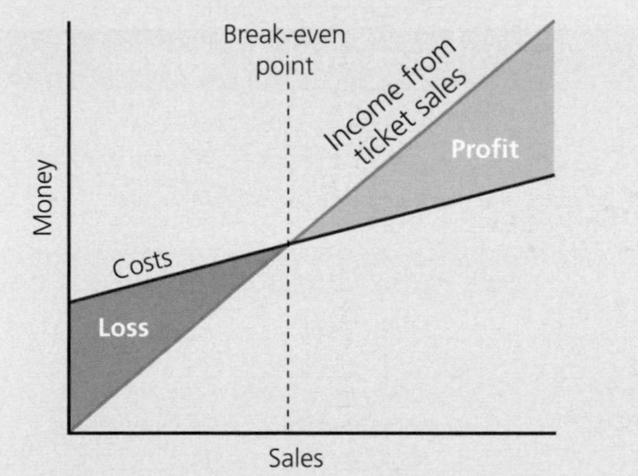

With low sales, income costs cannot be covered. Only once costs are covered is a profit made. The point at which costs are covered by income = break-even.

Event companies have several strategies for pricing in the leisure industry, which you might consider:

1. A price to help them 'penetrate the market' – setting the lowest price they can to attract the maximum number of people.
2. A price to help them cover costs plus a small profit, maybe 25–30%.
3. 'Competitive pricing' means adjusting their prices to those of other event companies. This can be a risky strategy if event companies try to keep lowering prices to undercut each other. However, it would be unwise to stage an event in direct competition with any other group – professional or classmates.
4. You may well consider 'discount pricing' by setting different prices for different types of customers. Many events charge a lower price for students and pensioners.
5. 'Variable pricing' may be selected to suit different buyers – higher prices for better seats, for example.
6. A 'price-skimming' strategy can be used to skim off at the highest rate when price sensitivity is not an issue. Certain sports fans will buy their team's shirts and tickets to games whatever the price, either through loyalty or for a one-off event. The bidding prices on eBay.co.uk for large events – where status, quality and rarity are the key factors – reflect this attitude. You may not be able to create this type of pricing scenario for your event!

activity

YOUR PRICING STRATEGY

Your financial team should now calculate what the best pricing strategy will be for your event. Remember these three things:

- **Keep the customer in mind**
- **Give value for money**
- **Pay attention to what other groups are charging.**

PROMOTION

You have already looked at promotion on page 19 in Topic 2, but you will examine it in more depth here. Promotion is all about communicating the message about your event so that customers will want to come. One common term used by professional companies is AIDA.

AIDA means:

Creating **awareness**	**A**
Getting people **interested**	**I**
Creating **desire** to participate in the event	**D**
Encouraging **action** to book a place for the event	**A**

Ideally, with an ongoing event, if customers enjoy the experience they will book again and you have created some loyalty to the event which will help make it sustainable in the future.

The challenge for your team is to plan how to promote and to decide what types of promotion (see events promotions table below) you will use for each of the stages of AIDA. Before you do this consider:

- what the costs will be
- how to match the types of promotion to the event and the customers (your target audience or participants).

Applying the marketing mix

Once you have selected suitable types of promotion for your event, your team must decide exactly what techniques to use and when. Professional organisers use a 'launch technique' well in advance, then various 'drip feed' techniques during the run up, with a final 'splash' close to the actual day. It's a case of matching your efforts to the timescale, the budget and the customers.

Market research

Research is always worth doing because it means you can plan more effectively and in a more informed way. This is an ongoing task for many leisure organisations as they search for the competitive edge. Market research is increasingly regarded as a requirement.

Much of your research will have been covered at the feasibility stage and in assessing customer needs (see pages 26 and 27) but a few reminders are necessary to help final decisions or establish if further data is required.

Choose your final research technique carefully because it could affect your budget and time, and unless done carefully, give you inaccurate information. Make sure you have covered the points in the checklist opposite.

Events promotion table

Techniques	*Strengths*	*Weaknesses*	*Possible uses for your event*
ADVERTISING	• Can give wide coverage. • Dynamic. • Can create impact.	• Could be expensive.	Inclusion in radio slots or TV reports, websites, electronic boards, intranets, large posters, magazines.
PUBLICITY MATERIALS	• Provides significant opportunities. • Can be targeted.	• Needs good sales techniques.	An event leaflet, tickets, information packs, press releases, pre-event T-shirts sales.
PUBLIC RELATIONS	• Can attract a lot of attention.	• Needs dynamic delivery.	Small-scale displays, interviews, stunts or shows, newspaper stories, freebies, prize draws.
DIRECT MAIL	• May only be glanced at, but more targeted.	• Can have low response rates. • Impersonal.	Letters, leaflet drops, flyers to target groups, emails, texts.
SPONSORSHIP	• Can help to cover costs. • Association with important company.	• Sponsor's aims or products have to have synergy with the event.	Ensure your sponsor gains maximum exposure on all promotional material.
PERSONAL SELLING	• Direct. • Personal.	• May not attract genuine interest. • Needs good communicators.	Telephone calls, presentations, casual conversations, talks, lobbying.

✔ All objectives and customers' needs have been matched through research (perhaps through sampling, surveys and segmentation).

✔ Any changes to the event or target market have been identified by checking the event format and lifestyle factors of target segment (perhaps through focus groups).

✔ Promotional activities are being finalised (see following activity).

✔ Some secondary research has taken place on the type of event being offered, including previous successes, through reading reports or magazines articles, looking online or contacting real event organisers.

✔ Any primary research has been checked for validity and reliability.

activity

MARKET YOUR EVENT

Using the event promotions table, the research checklist, information you have collated through customer research from Topics 1 and 2 and the feasibility study material from Topic 3, have your marketing team plan the marketing mix. You might also refer to professional event materials for ideas.

Evaluating marketing activities

Suitable questions for assessing how effective your planning and execution was:

1. Were customer needs met?
2. Was the event appropriate for the customers?
3. Was the venue effective?
4. Did marketing communications work well?
5. If used, was pricing acceptable?
6. Were the attendance/participation levels as expected?

The marketing evaluation will only be one part of the overall event and team evaluation. So the collecting of data and information can be done using the same techniques – observation, surveys, samples, questionnaires, scales, scores and ratings – which are mentioned in customer service (page 28) and again in event evaluation. Take care when analysing your information to avoid ambiguity, bias and unreliable data or statements. Always try to present your data or findings graphically, in charts and tables, for clarity and ease of use.

Examples of data presentation techniques

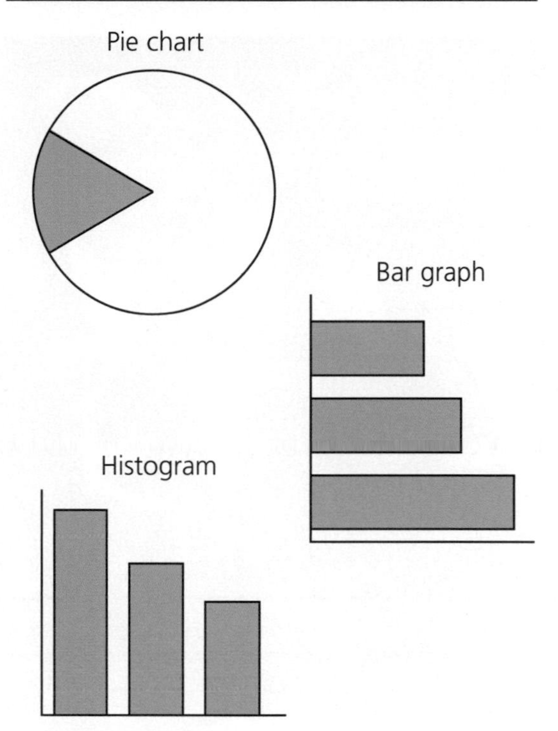

Topic 5 Resources, finance and staffing

You will now turn your attention from the planning process to focus on how the following will be organised:

- **Resources**
- **Finance**
- **Staffing.**

These are the three key areas of the planning process, and likely to occupy the time and efforts of at least three people in your team.

Finding your resources in the first place will be a challenge as they may be hard to come by. How you use them will affect the smooth running of the event, so effective use of resources is important.

Finance is also normally tight for your type of event. Any income will have to be used wisely, and expenditure and costs will need to be kept low.

The people involved in delivering your event (staff) are probably the most important commodity you will have to manage. Effective teamworking skills will be addressed in Topic 7, but external staffing relationships will be covered here.

Your team will have to combine these three areas to make all things work smoothly.

In the following sections you will explore ideas, good practice examples and, at the same time, consider what *does not* work well.

Resources

Resources are supplies that you will need for your event. They are sources of aid or support that will contribute to the overall success of your event. Resources might range from pin badges for your staff to a fridge for keeping drinks cool. There are three stages to the process of using resources effectively:

1. Identifying what is needed.
2 Finding the resources.
3. Using the resources effectively.

Identifying what is needed

Identifying physical resources for an event can begin at the brainstorming and feasibility stages, so that you have an idea of what you are going to need. When final decisions have been made, the teams or individuals with responsibility for resources can plan out the details more specifically.

This can be done by carefully listing all the requirements for each stage of the process you are involved with. Checklists similar to the ones illustrated below can be created to help record the detail.

A whole range of needs might be identified, depending on the type of event your team chooses. Therefore it would be good planning to have a range of checklists, with headings to classify resource needs under each. Examples might include those shown below.

Resources checklist 1

Type of resource	*How and where it will be applied*	*Source*	*Quantity*	*Comments*
Chairs	For seating audience	School dining room	80	Try to get the best type of chairs possible

Resources checklist 2

Sports equipment	*ICT resource needs*	*Catering needs*	*Safety materials*	*Venue/ Premises*
Basketballs Play tops Whistles Scoring kit	Computer Laptop Radios Mobile phones	Tables Plates Cutlery Barbecue	Fire extinguishers and blankets First aid kit	Seats Signs Toilets Rubbish bins

If you wish to plan this in full detail, allocate the finding of specific resources to individuals who then have to account for them by a certain date, as illustrated below.

Resources checklist 3: Resources action plan

Type of resource	*Person finding*	*Likely sources*	*By when*
Water feature	Lucy	Garden Centres, hardware stores	30 April
Scoreboard	David	Local sports centres	5 May

Before you can finalise your list of resources you need to settle on quantities. This will require those responsible for these decisions to set a target for numbers of physical resources. Depending on the resource, try to acquire a few more than you actually need so that you will have some in reserve. When considering quantities you might need to consider:

- Numbers of participants and spectators
- Parking spaces needed
- Catering levels.

Quality may be an issue too – getting the cheapest of any given item may mean that vital resources break or fall apart at key moments in the event.

Premises and facilities may come under the resources team remit, so check out your venue – what can it supply and what do you need? Other venue characteristics might be important, such as roof height, security, ventilation or fire exits. If you are creating a temporary venue – in a marquee, for example, or outdoors – you will need to ensure that all resources comply with legislation and are built by experts. The same applies to lighting and sound systems and for disability access: call in the professionals.

activity

YOUR RESOURCES – WHAT ARE THEY?

Set target dates for each team or individual who needs resources to report back with their list of requirements. Gather as a team and ensure that all angles are covered and that no duplication exists. Then set a deadline for the resource 'agents' to report back with sources, costs and quantities. Resources checklists 1 and 2 will help you to organise this.

Finding the resources

Finding the resources which you have identified may not be easy. You need to plan carefully how you will find them at the lowest cost – be resourceful.

The cheapest way to get resources is if someone can be persuaded to give them for free. You might have to ensure that they are credited and acknowledged for their help in your leaflet, or perhaps even mention them as sponsors in return.

Where it is clear you are going to have to buy in resources, make sure you get at least three sets of prices so you can compare and select the best for value and quality.

Hiring may be a possible option. If you are staging your event for charity it is worth mentioning this – sometimes companies might lend you resources for the event for a short period at no charge.

Check that your resources are all suitable for the event and venue – for compatibility, size, make, specification and quantity. This needs to be done at a team meeting

Judging quantities of resources can be difficult.

to ensure that if any resources are shared it is done in a fair and planned way. The cost of resources will have to be agreed with the finance team.

activity

YOUR RESOURCES – WHICH AND WHERE?

Call a team meeting to finalise which, and how many, resources you will acquire. Try to come to an agreement on quantities, where to get them from, costs and alternatives. Create an action plan, as in checklist 3.

Using resources effectively

Once you have your resources you need to ensure you know how they will be used. For many types of resources this will be obvious. However, some will require special consideration in terms of their use. If you order a load of plates for a buffet lunch, are you going to hand them out or let customers take their own? How will you retrieve them? What if people take more than they need? These are the types of things you should consider.

Plan where you will store the resources, who will have access to them and how you will record usage, returns and manage repairs or shortfalls. Decide whether they will be centrally controlled or if each team will have their own.

The use and allocation of the resources is something which can be evaluated for assessment purposes, so records of quantities, costs and other factors are needed. You could evaluate the following:

- Was there enough to go round?
- Was there a shortfall anywhere?
- Was there much wastage?
- Was there any obvious lack of quality?
- Were you made aware of more suitable resources after the event?

activity

USE OF YOUR RESOURCES

How will you record usage and evaluate effectiveness?

Finance

In the events world there are many financial aspects which have to be covered. One of the key aspects of the successful London Olympics bid for 2012 was how well thought-out the funding of the games was, with income from lottery grants, sponsorship and TV rights, tickets sales and taxes covering the inevitably huge costs. Your event is not on this scale of course, but the funding and financial control might share the same basic principles. Your team (or, more specifically, your financial controller) will have to demonstrate how you will manage the following:

- 'Start-up' and resource costs
- Budgets
- Overall income and expenditure
- Payment methods
- Reporting after the event.

Common software packages can be used to record finance for your event, just as professional companies do. Assign spending to each person responsible for each aspect of the event (admin, transport, marketing). Companies often break down their spending by departments (referred to as 'cost centres') to help them keep track of the distribution of spending across the company.

Finance is another aspect that needs objectives set when planning, and evaluation criteria set after the event. You may also wish to keep records of your financial inputs for assessment purposes.

'Start-up' and resource costs

For your scale of event 'start-up costs' should be nominal, perhaps just enough to cover research and feasibility testing (bus fares, telephone calls or stationery). How you finance this will depend on what your college, tutors and team feel is possible and fair. Try to use your college's resources for initial stages to keep costs to a minimum. Or set a small budget limit for start-up costs which everyone must adhere to – like leisure professionals do.

Resource costs will have to be researched to inform the planning. The real costs will come later once budgets have been agreed and it is known what can be afforded. Your team need to remain realistic in financial terms – keep costs low and set achievable targets (remember SMART).

It is important that you keep accurate records and receipts for any costs at this stage.

Budgeting

Budgets are a mechanism for controlling spending – and you should use them. They are calculated by comparing estimated costs (the figures you have researched) against estimated expenditure (what you think you can afford, based on an estimate of your project income). The result will be a budget limit (amount which spending should not exceed). Budgets must be accurately calculated to the nearest penny. Your team must have someone to oversee this aspect of the event – someone who is good with figures and prudent when spending.

At this stage your team also needs to calculate the break-even point – the point in time at which income exactly covers your costs. From then on, any additional income will begin to contribute to any profit-target set. Refer to the break-even diagram in Topic 4.

It is always wise to have a small contingency fund set aside to cover unforeseen costs and for last-minute overspending, repairs, replacements and cost increases.

activity

DEVISE A SENSIBLE BUDGET

Hold a team meeting, once all costs and income have been estimated. Assess whether income will cover these costs, then make cuts or increase spending accordingly. This might have an impact on other plans for the event, so this is a key exercise for the team to go through. Re-plan and re-cost where necessary.

Payment methods

Assuming your team are going to be paying and receiving cash as part of the event, you need to decide how you will do this safely and how it will all be recorded. It may be possible to receive credit/debit card payments through your institution, thereby increasing the payment options for customers. It is sometimes possible for students to open up accounts at certain banks – accounts that could be used specifically for your event, with multiple signatories. You should explore these possibilities with your tutors, if necessary.

Using a cash box is wise, and your institution should have a safe where it could be stored. If your event is likely to collect a considerable amount of money, other aspects to think about on the day include:

- Having a float with plenty of change
- Having a receipt book
- Having a lockable place for the money (cash box, safe)
- Not leaving anyone alone with all the cash
- Not allowing anyone to travel to the bank unaccompanied with large amounts of cash.

Reporting finance after the event

For a number of reasons it is important to keep good records throughout your event, some of which we have mentioned already, but when money is involved particular attention needs to be paid.

If you keep good records whilst you are setting up the event, the team will be able to see if budgets are being kept to, targets met, or if over-spending is occurring. Use your records to show your financial position each week in the run-up to the event.

Within your evaluation you should show:

- the cash flow for the event
- if your budget was realistic
- where your estimates were most accurate/misjudged
- how sponsorship money was spent and any returns from it.

activity

RESEARCH FINANCE

Visit your library or go online to have look at some leisure companies' annual accounts to see how and what they record.

Staffing

Staff are considered to be the most important asset an organisation can have – especially with leisure, because it is an industry focused on people. For your event you will need the right people for each job.

Your team

At this final planning stage, roles and responsibilities will be becoming clearer all the time as tasks are identified. On the day, however, team members may have to take on different roles, even multi-tasking as needs evolve and deadlines approach. When allocating roles and responsibilities within your team, ensure that you consider:

- strengths
- weaknesses
- preferences
- constraints.

You might want to carry out a SWOT-type analysis on everyone in your team, under the headings in the bulleted list above. This will help you to develop your role allocation and identify gaps. Remember that everyone needs to be good at more than just one thing!

activity

HUMAN RESOURCES

If you select one person to oversee Human Resource management (sometimes called 'personnel'), make sure they have good people-skills. There are likely to be a number of potentially tricky situations they will have to deal with in the build up to – and on the day of – the event. Here are some scenarios for you to discuss:

1. **How would you deal with a personality clash?**
2. **What advice would you give to staff to help them deal with customer complaints?**
3. **How would you deal with a team member who is always turning up late?**
4. **How would you cope with an inept team leader, knowing you still needed them for the event?**
5. **How would you deal with a group of volunteers who feel they are being 'bossed' around too much by a certain person?**
6. **How would you deal with a complaint by a supplier or representative of a company about one of your team members?**

Other staff

Your team is likely to have to liaise with other groups of staff such as:

How you manage these different types of staff for your event can contribute to its eventual success. Each group needs a slightly different style of management and consideration, as shown below. Liaison with these groups may be delegated to other team members, so full information must be to hand. Other guidance is given in the customer service topics about behaviour on the day (see pages 27–28).

Assessing performance

Staffing is also an important area for assessment and evaluation, for both the team and individuals. A format should be agreed for peer and personal evaluation. Some suggestions are given below on the peer and personal evaluation charts.

Peer evaluation chart

Person being rated	Role being assessed	Grading and comments (1 = poor; 5 = excellent)
David	Greeting of guests and customers	**5** David was bright, cheerful and polite with everyone.
Gunjun	Announcements	**3** Gunjun's instructions were not always clear.
Leroy	First aid	**4** Leroy did a good job attending to a badly cut finger, but did flap a bit at first.

Managing different types of people

- Managing volunteers – Make sure they have clear roles, instructions and responsibilities. They should be able to enjoy some sort of perk if you can organise that (a free T-shirt, their picture in the paper, or food) and they should get a letter of thanks afterwards.
- Networking with professional people – Make sure you have exact details to pass on to them or clear questions, so that you do not waste their time or give a poor impression. The more seriously they take you, the more likely you are to get their assistance. They will not want to be associated with a disorganised or unsuccessful event, especially if it is on their premises.

Rewarding work for a volunteer litter patrol in the USA.

- Using suppliers – This will be a formal arrangement, perhaps with a contract or official order, so you need to understand the legal implications and be able to pay any bills on time. Ensure that your team are able to deal direct with suppliers. Again, a professional approach is best.

A bicycle courier provides a quick link between organisations and suppliers.

Personal evaluation chart

Situation being assessed	Comment (good/bad/ satisfactory)	Recommendation
Control of accounts	Satisfactory – Did not keep a tight control of spending at first.	More assertive and better record keeping

activity

FINALISE YOUR TEAM

Using an agreed team structure and set of tasks, make your final staff planning and allocation of roles and responsibilities. Create a structure chart to show the breakdown and allocations.

Topic 6 Administration, timescales, targets and evaluation

This topic will cover the key aspects of planning that will complete your event plan and allow your team to begin preparation:

- **Administrative systems**
- **Event timescales**
- **Target setting**
- **Legal aspects**
- **Contingency plans**
- **Reviewing and evaluation.**

We have covered all of these in part before, so you may have already done some groundwork on these aspects.

Administrative systems

A well-thought-out and functioning administrative system is needed to help the flow and recording of information, decisions and changes. The whole team should understand any procedures that are laid down, and the system must, in return, help staff and team members store and find information, check data, and proceed with work. Technical systems need to support the human efforts.

All administrative systems need a co-ordinator, budget, resources and location, but yours also needs to be:

- Fit for purpose (suited to your event needs)
- Value for money (fitting your budget or, ideally, free)
- Accurate (information will be what you need to evaluate and make decisions)
- Efficient (needing minimum time and effort)
- Secure (ensure confidentiality – Data Protection)
- Easy to use (both paper and electronic)
- Agreed and understood by all (after some training, perhaps).

Your personal logbook (diary) is an administrative system of sorts, so try at this stage to think how you want to record information in it and how to access and analyse it later.

There are two types of administration to bear in mind – for routine work, and for non-routine work.

Administration for routine work

These are the day-to-day operations you might do for the event, such as

- Financial transactions (selling tickets or ordering resources)
- Taking bookings (allocating seats)
- Taking minutes in meetings (so that decisions are recorded)
- Answering queries (email or telephone enquiries).

You need to have a system or procedure for each. If these procedures are paper-based, decide where the papers will be kept, in what format and by whom. If the system is electronically based, make sure that documents and systems are backed up.

Administration for non-routine work

These will link to your contingency plans for:

- Emergencies
- Accidents

- Lost children
- Staff problems.

For emergency situations, the authorities usually have a plan in place and run through it several times, so when the emergency happens for real, any potential situations can be dealt with quickly and appropriately.

activity

ADMINISTER TO THIS ACTIVITY

1. Design an accident report sheet for non-routine administrative records and a booking sheet for a barbecue in the park (with menu selections).
2. Choose a routine and non-routine function, specific to your event, and design forms for them – as either paper-based or electronic.

Event timescales

It is important for each individual to plan how to spend their time in the build-up to the event. It is also important to be aware of how much time you have, as a team, to plan. The biggest danger is that you won't have enough time, so what time you do have needs to be apportioned effectively. You may pick up some pointers from the London 2012 Olympics planning team. They had a two-year planning period, just to put the bid together, before the decision in 2005, with no guarantee of success. Seven years might seem adequate time to prepare for the Olympics, but if you look back to the Athens games in 2004, there was great panic that the facilities would not be ready on time – they were, but only just! Fortunately, you won't have to build any facilities, but you do need to plan how to use your time to best effect.

Timescale factors for the event team

A range of deadlines for the team to meet need to be set at the planning stage. These will be determined by a number of factors about what needs to happen leading up to the actual event. These deadlines might relate to:

- Publicity or printing
- Payments being made
- Order or delivery dates for resources
- Staff availability
- Health, safety and security checks
- Legal obligations.

Delays are to be avoided, and key dates need to be mapped on to a planning schedule.

You can use simple calendars, a bar chart to show more detail, or a critical path analysis to define progress and key points (see examples).

- Calendars can really only show you the day by which something needs to be done.

Calendar-style timetable

WEEK	MON	TUE	WED	THU	FRI	SAT	SUN
1	First team meeting		Aims & objs decided		Bus. plan		
2		Marketing commences		Second team meeting	Fund raising days		
3	Third team meeting		Roles decided		Booking confirmed		
4		Publicity stunt					
5	Fourth team meeting		Final checks				
6	Project starts					Project finishes	
7	Evaluation						
8	Reports		Logs				

- Bar charts can show the length of something being done more graphically than a calendar.

Bar chart

Task	Week ending (Friday)										
	8 Jan	15 Jan	22 Jan	29 Jan	5 Feb	12 Feb	19 Feb	26 Feb	5 Mar	12 Mar	19 Mar
Agree plan for event											
Design layour											
Identify and book speakers											
Prepare publicity											
Allocate material an resources											
Agree contingencies											
Check arrangements											
Liason and exhibitors											
Final press releases											
Stage event											
Gather and evaluate data											

- A critical path analysis (CPA) groups tasks and shows the sequence in which they must be done.

Critical path analysis

Getting customers to an event

Month 1 Month 2 Month 3 Month 4 Month 5 Month 6

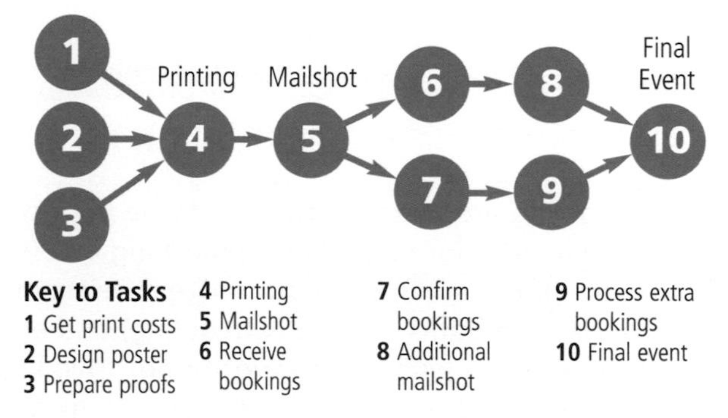

Ideally, you should use all three to avoid confusion and prevent delays – the calendar provides the overview, the bar chart shows the length of time and the CPA illustrates the group's network of tasks. This type of planning allows you to avoid (or minimise) delays by ensuring that if one aspect is held up, energy can be reapplied elsewhere. The most common delays are caused by:

- Lack of up-to-date information through poor communications
- A shortage of funds
- Delays in finding/receiving resources
- Waiting for a decision or approval to go ahead.

Delays cause a knock-on effect for event organisers, such as:

- Increased costs
- Wasted time
- Additional administration
- Frustration amongst staff
- A failed event.

Individual timescales

Individuals should have their own timescales for tasks and roles to be carried out. These can be put on a personal planner, as shown below.

Personal planner

Tasks	January 1 – 31	February 1 – 28	March 1 – 31
1			
2			
3			

Flowcharts can also be used for personal timescales. Whichever method you choose, ensure that you are able to prioritise tasks and place them in chronological order. Your personal planner should form part of your diary or logbook for assessment purposes. Even the best made plans can be delayed, so if you can, build in some spare time ('buffer time') and always plan to meet deadlines early. Just before the actual event your team should plan a final briefing.

If you have enough time and the location allows, you might consider doing a rehearsal, or a 'dry-run', depending on the complexity of your event.

Target setting

You have set targets for the type of customer you wish to attract, and objectives for the overall event. Now you need to arrange targets for the team and individuals within the timescale priorities and event parameters. By now you should have the exact date(s) for the event, so plan backwards to help identify other target dates.

Team and personal targets

The success of your event will probably depend on how well you meet your targets overall, so at this stage it is important to keep realistic goals. Suitable team targets might be to:

- Sell enough tickets several weeks before the event to break even
- Monitor the progress of all activities every week
- Avoid customer complaints before, during and after the event.

Typical personal targets might be to:

- Attend every team meeting
- Complete every task on time and on budget
- Stay motivated throughout.

activity

YOUR INDIVIDUAL TARGETS

Sit down and set out your own personal targets for the role(s) you have been assigned. Note these in your logbook for later evaluation.

activity

TEST YOUR POWERS OF SCHEDULING

The following are tasks which need to be prioritised and scheduled prior to an event launching a new range of leisure clothing in two months. Organise them into appropriate amounts of time (scheduling) and agree an order for dealing with them (prioritising). Two key tasks have been missed out – decide what you think they are whilst scheduling and prioritising them.

- set up stage and lighting
- check delivery of garments
- book photographer
- send out invites
- press release
- book models
- ?
- ?

Legal aspects

This is a very serious part of your work. You have a clear duty to ensure that nobody is put at risk during your event. You may not be experts in every aspect of risk assessment nor be aware of the details of regulations or legislation, but you will have to try and make sure that such considerations are covered in your plans. You need to investigate what laws might apply, what might happen, how you insure against it happening, and how to minimise the risk – or eliminate it altogether. Although not every aspect will be covered, the following ideas serve to highlight what you will need to explore:

- Health and safety legislation
- Risk assessment processes
- Security procedures
- Types of insurance.

For professional event companies, failure to comply with legislation or failure to set up measures to cover incidents can have serious consequences. Inadequate procedures can mean serious injury, prosecution, or loss of income/image and custom. A large claim for damages might even put a company out of business – it would certainly increase their insurance premiums. The box below shows some of the ways in which event teams and companies benefit from effective measures and plans.

There is a range of obligatory health, safety, security and insurance legislation which must be applied in the case of event management. You need to familiarise yourselves with this legislation to assess what plans and actions you need to take. You are not going to be experts, so you should seek guidance and advice from suitable sources, indicated in the following sections.

Health and safety legislation

Depending on the nature of your event, a number of health and safety considerations might need to be met, such as complying with fire regulations, observing selling regulations, the safety of children with adults, dangerous activities or travel. You need to have taken measures to follow health and safety regulations as closely as is practical. The actions that your event team take need to be balanced against cost, time, resources and the difficulty of applying them.

activity

PITFALLS IN THE PITSTOP

As a team, form ideas about dangers or hazards at an event by imagining that you are charged with the responsibility of identifying types of dangers at the British Grand Prix at Silverstone for the following groups:

- **Customers**
- **Event organisers**
- **Participants (drivers and pit crew)**
- **Suppliers or sponsors on site.**

Risk assessment processes

A 'risk assessment' underpins most health and safety legislation. Risk assessments identify hazards which might cause harm, such as fireworks, cables and wiring, and wet or slippery surfaces. The chance of a hazard causing harm or hurting someone is greater if you have not identified it and taken reasonable measures to minimise or eliminate it. We take simple health and safety measures every day. For example, we wear a seatbelt in a vehicle, we look both ways

Benefits of effective health, safety and security

For the organisation

- Work is carried out within the law
- Fewer accidents
- Increased productivity
- Compensation claims are reduced
- Prosecution is eliminated
- Company image and reputation is enhanced
- Insurance premiums are lowered
- Fraud and theft can be reduced.

For the environment

- Damage is reduced or prevented.

For the staff

- Morale and effectiveness can improve
- Hazards and risk are reduced
- Working conditions improve
- Stress or threat level can be reduced
- Awareness is increased about health, safety and security needs
- Training needs are identified.

For the customers

- Suppliers or workers on the premises are protected
- People with disabilities can have special provision
- A safe, secure environment is created for visitors
- Standards of service may improve.

when crossing the road – even just washing our hands after going to the toilet. A leisure event is not an everyday occurrence so care has to be taken to investigate matters in greater depth.

A risk assessment involves identifying hazards and making reasoned judgements about how dangerous these hazards are and what level of harm they might cause. The minimum legal requirement for event organisers is to carry out a risk assessment for each area of their event, and investigate the following:

- Transport or parking hazards at or around the venue
- Hazards which might occur inside the venue (fire, collapse or evacuation)
- Dangers to participants, customers and organisers
- Unsafe resources (sports equipment, seating, minibuses and electrical goods).

In the accompanying chart you will find six steps which are suggested for a risk assessment which you may remember from Unit 2. This will help guide your investigations.

Stage 1 Identify the hazards

Stage 2 Who might be affected

Stage 3 Likelihood of hazard occurring

Stage 4 Severity of hazard

Stage 5 Risk rating

Stage 6 Measures to minimise risk

activity

ASSESSING RISK AT YOUR EVENT

Design a risk assessment sheet specifically for your event. Write down all the information needed and present ideas for covering the hazards identified. Calculate how severe the hazards might be if they occurred, and what the probability of them happening is. Develop a suitable scale for both severity and probability (perhaps a rating out of 10). Finally, devise an action plan and timescale for putting these measures in place. Submit these proposals to your tutor and your institution's safety officer for feedback and amendment.

Security procedures

Security procedures at large events are very extensive and need intensive preparation. Try to think about the measures taken for Wimbledon, the Cup Final or the Glastonbury Festival.

Large-scale events at big venues will carry out risk assessments based on security hazards. They are able to rely on a range of sophisticated techniques to spot hazards, such as:

- CCTV
- Intelligence on known troublemakers
- Undercover police
- High police presence to segregate troublemakers
- Scanners and ID cards.

This helps them combat a range of potential security breaches or problems, such as:

- Violence and anti-social behaviour
- Theft of property or money
- Ticketing fraud
- Sabotage
- Vandalism or damage.

It is unlikely your event will be threatened by any of these hazards, but you should still carry out a risk assessment. You might be able to identify or stop lesser threats under the same headings.

Types of insurance

Professional event companies take out insurance to cover many of the hazards we have just described. It is likely that your institution will cover all your activities as part of the curriculum, but do check – there may be exclusions. Professional event teams can carry cover for:

- Personal accident – to staff
- Public liability – for customers, visitors and others on site
- Employer liability – for anything which the company might do
- Medical costs – above NHS provision
- Travel – for staff working abroad
- Special risk – activities which are out of the ordinary (bungee-jumping, skiing, stunts)
- Cancellations or compensation
- Damage and loss.

Neglecting this area of your planning could have dire consequences or cost you or your institution time, effort and money through compensation.

Contingency plans

A contingency is a possible, but not very likely future occurrence. By now you should be aware that your team has to cover a lot of potential problems. Some will be predictable, such as loss of possessions – others not so much, like a broken leg. You will need to plan for three types of contingency:

1. Foreseeable ones such as loss of money, shortage of resources or complaints.
2. Unforeseen ones such as accidents to people.
3. Emergency ones such as evacuation.

activity

ASSESSING CONTINGENCY PLANNING

You need to assess how well your team coped with contingencies. Create charts to capture and record this information under the following headings:

- **Health hazards – minor and major.**
- **Safety hazards – minor and major.**
- **Security hazards – minor and major.**
- **Other occurrences of any type not covered by the above.**

Reviewing and evaluating the event

The final phase of planning is preparing to assess your team's event and your performance. Evaluating is deciding whether you fell short of the targets you set at the beginning, or you achieved, or even exceeded them in the actual outcomes. Reviewing is identifying where things went wrong or well, and making recommendations for the next time.

How will you record all this? Professional event teams use methods which include:

- Film or video
- Digital photos
- Mystery participants/customers
- Customer questionnaires
- Contrasting what was planned with what actually happened – through records of meetings, decisions and plans
- Feedback from other agencies (suppliers/experts).

You might also use peer review, tutor observations, witness statements or feedback from colleagues.

All organisations have to review their performance and many will use 'performance indicators'.

Here are some reminders about assessing and gathering feedback that would be useful to note:

1. When collecting your data, make sure the information is clear and easy to collect.
2. Use several sources of evaluation so that you get a rounded picture – not a biased view from one source.
3. If providing feedback to classmates, do so sensitively and constructively, or it may hurt their feelings and ruin friendships.
4. Try to use scales or ratings as much as possible, so that you can illustrate the figures.
5. Cover all aspects of your event in some way.
6. Keep a diary or record for yourself, refer to the assessment outcomes for guidance and think through some recommendations.

activity

MEASURING YOUR PERFORMANCE

Performance can be measured in four main ways: quantitatively, qualitatively, effectively, efficiently. But what do these ways mean when put into practice? Find the definition for these words and show how you will measure performance under the above headings:

- **in your roles**
- **for your event**
- **by your team.**

Topic 7 Effective teamwork skills

In this topic we begin to turn our attention from planning to actually carrying out the event, with a focus on teamwork – the glue that holds the whole process together. You need to develop your team skills to be able to complete this event and the unit successfully.

Professional event management teams rely heavily on teamwork to get their work done. They usually have small teams of dedicated staff carrying out certain roles. At a wedding reception, for example, different teams would be used for erecting marquees, catering, greeting guests and entertaining – while, back at their office, administrative staff and marketing or sales teams would play their part in securing bookings. Smaller teams come together to produce the final event.

A team is defined as 'a group of people who work together in an effective way to complete a task', in this case to plan and run an event. To be effective, your team needs to have the following:

- **An overall purpose for your team**
- **Team structure**
- **Leadership and motivation**
- **Roles and responsibilities**
- **Communication**
- **Approaches to teamwork and problem solving**
- **Team-building and interaction.**

The success of your event will probably link closely to how well you all work together and what level of teamwork is demonstrated.

An overall purpose for your team

Your team's purpose is illustrated by the assessment criteria, which in summary are:

- A sound, realistic plan, based on relevant and effective research
- A significant and consistent contribution from everybody
- A successful event. Problems dealt with reasonably and effectively
- A sound evaluation of your and your team's performance, producing realistic recommendations.

In the previous planning section on aims and objectives, the final details of 'purpose' are set out for your team and the event. If any sub-teams are formed to carry out small tasks, make sure they know their purpose too.

Professional teams will want a result that will:

- more than satisfy customers
- be within the set budget
- be likely to lead to further bookings or recommendations.

Refer to these three points and the criteria to ensure your event is on the right track. You can illustrate the information in a checklist:

✔Research complete
✔Plan devised and known to all
✔Aims and objectives set
✔Roles and responsibilities delegated and accepted
✔Assessment criteria met
✔Evaluation criteria in place and recording process agreed

Less quantifiable factors which will have to be present are enthusiasm, commitment and motivation over a long period of time. Good teamwork doesn't just happen – as you will know from watching your favourite team play. They have practised, trained and been coached to complete a task on a weekly basis, not just for a one-off event. Maybe you can follow their example by making the best of your skills and supporting one another.

Team structure

Formal team structures

These are where team members have set roles and responsibilities and usually report up a chain of command. See the structure diagram in Topic 1 for an example.

Informal team structures

Roles and responsibilities are flexible and tasks are shared. A chain of command (or hierarchy) might exist, but it is not so rigid.

Leadership and motivation

This role can be handled by one person or a small team, depending on the people in your group and, to some extent, on who has demonstrated the necessary strengths in the work to date. Typical attributes of people who can lead or co-ordinate are:

- Good at decision-making and communicating
- Approachable and fair
- Knowledgeable and respected
- Able to motivate others.

A leader or co-ordinator's main roles are to:

1. Keep a clear overview of what is going on, so that they can keep work on target.
2. Maintain momentum and motivation amongst teams and individuals before and during the event. Getting to know everyone well is a key aspect here.
3. Be the spokesperson for the team, with other organisations or the press, so they must be aware of the need for good communications and a clear overview.
4. Try to bring out the best in team members in terms of skills, abilities and support for one another. They must help create team synergy.

Leadership is based on the ability to motivate others extrinsically (motivation from outside). Intrinsic motivation comes from within someone. Both of these provide the catalyst for success. A well motivated team will usually meet its targets or at least give themselves the best chance of success.

In terms of leadership we can use Herzberg's motivators and satisfiers diagram to illustrate where leaders need to put their motivation efforts.

Herzberg's motivators and satisfiers diagram

Motivators	Satisfiers
Status	Good policies and administration
Opportunity for advancement	Wages, salaries and bonuses
Gaining recognition	Quality of supervision
Responsibility	Quality of interpersonal relations
Challenge or stimulation	Working conditions
Sense of achievement and growth	Job security

It is possible that leadership may change during the course of the project as different people may prove to have more appropriate skills or abilities to offer. This is not necessarily a bad thing because it shows that you are using people to the best effect, and demonstrates flexibility.

The 'leadership style' – the amount of control a leader or group of co-ordinators exerts on a team – can often determine how well the team operates. For example, if the leader is too autocratic, people may be resentful and not work effectively. If the leader is too lenient, on the other hand, there might not be enough direction and control shown, and the event planning will suffer. We can use Tannenbaum and Schmidt's Continuum, a model of delegation and team development, to help us visualise just where the best leadership style needs to be pitched.

Tannenbaum and Schmidt's leadership continuum

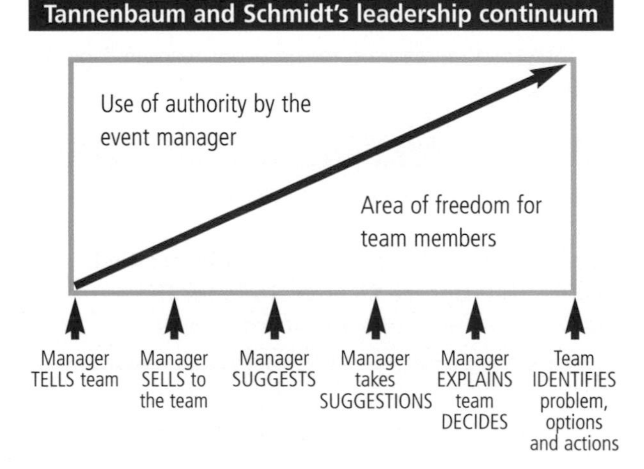

activity

CHOOSE A LEADER

Individually, write out six criteria that you feel your team will need to use to identify the best leader. Compare your list to those of others, and choose the best eight criteria. Now use these to decide who will be your best choice(s) for team leadership.

Roles and responsibilities

Roles and responsibilities (R&Rs) are allocated to individuals to cover the tasks that need to be done for the event. Many will probably have been given out already at the feasibility stage, but now you must refresh and reinforce them for the run-up to the event and the event itself. Roles and responsibilities must be:

- Clearly understood by each individual, but by others as well – try recording them in your logbook for evaluation later.
- There should also be a 'questions session' planned, so that team members can clarify issues surrounding their R&Rs.
- Nobody should be placed in a role or responsibility which they are not confident with or competent at – try reshuffling the roles or simplifying the tasks.
- Set good standards for people to meet – agree these as a team.

There are some problems which can occur with R&Rs which you need to be aware of:

- If someone has too many R&Rs they may become overloaded with work, de-motivated or make frequent mistakes.
- If someone does not take on their fair share of work this can lead to bad feelings – and de-motivation amongst others.

See the structure diagram for an event team in Topic 1, page 15.

activity

YOUR R&RS

Design a page which could be photocopied, which can capture all your R&Rs for the before, during and after-event phases.

Communication

Communication will occur on two levels when planning and running your event. First, you will have to communicate amongst each other as a team. Secondly, you will have to communicate with other parties and people outside of your team.

Good communication requires a smooth flow of information. Forms of communication are written notes, oral explanations, meetings, texts, telephone calls and emails.

activity

METHODS OF COMMUNICATING

List the methods of communication that you are likely to use for your event, in your team and with outside contacts.

Team communication

Good team communication allows decisions, discussions, new information and reports to be shared. You may have realised that you might need to communicate amongst yourselves at the event itself. Mobile radios are probably the most useful communication tool for members of large event teams communicating with each other.

Would your event benefit from mobile radios?

External communications

When communicating with the people that you are going to be relying upon for the smooth running of your event, make sure that your information is up to date, correct and easy to understand for the recipient. Ensure when you are composing messages or compiling notes that they express exactly what you want say. Your communications will have many different external recipients – staff, other team members, customers, suppliers and outside organisations – so the tone and style will need to differ to suit each one.

activity

WHO ARE YOU GOING TO COMMUNICATE WITH?

In teams, use a flip chart to draw a spider diagram of all the organisations you will need to communicate with at each of the four stages.

1. **Pre-event – feasibility, costing and planning stages**
2. **Immediately prior to the event**
3. **During the event**
4. **After the event.**

Discuss what problems you might encounter with communications at each stage, and plan appropriate ways to overcome these.

Approaches to teamwork and problem solving

Teamwork is one of the most common features of the leisure industry, especially in event management. Whatever the context, there are a number of aspects that effective teams share and display in the way they work. All team members share the same goal and work towards it, with enthusiasm and commitment and, as we have just covered, communicating effectively.

Event teams can be put together for a one-off event or they can stay together on a regular basis if the company stages regular events. When they stay together, the structure, tasks, leadership and communication are all re-enforced. Your event is a one-off and you have to create all of these attributes through your planning and teamwork.

Good teamwork doesn't just happen – it requires a cooperative effort and willingness amongst individuals. Many of the key requirements have been covered in previous sections, but the flowchart below provides a summary.

Teamwork flowchart

Clear purpose and shared goals

↓

An effective structure and leadership

↓

Shared roles and responsibilities

↓

Best use of skills and abilities

↓

Good communications

As teams develop, they go through certain stages. These have been described by Bruce Tuckman (see below) and you may recognise some of them.

Tuckman's forming to performing model flowchart

Stage 1 FORMING – people weigh one another up and get to know each other

↓

Stage 2 STORMING – a difficult time as people settle into a position in the group

↓

Stage 3 NORMING – relationships and roles settle down, group standards are set

↓

Stage 4 PERFORMING – things really come together and real teamwork is evident

↓

Stage 5 MOURNING – if it is a one-off team, sadly they break up and disperse

The process of getting from the 'forming' stage to the 'norming' stage of Tuckman's model reveals quite a lot about group dynamics (interactions within and outside the team). This aspect can be fraught with problems and conflicts, which can markedly reduce team effectiveness. Problems to look out for are:

- Personality clashes
- Disagreement on decisions
- Leadership clashes
- Underlying friction
- Lack of commitment.

In many cases, strong leadership or focusing on the

Case study: Ellen MacArthur

One of the most effective teams in recent years was Ellen MacArthur's sailing team when she took her B&Q trimaran on the fastest solo circumnavigation of the globe in 2005. There were three clear elements for the team involved:

- planning and organising the record attempt
- supporting Ellen whilst at sea and back on land
- working with the media.

The distinctiveness of this team was that they were not always together and had to communicate around the globe. Find out more at www.teamellen.com.

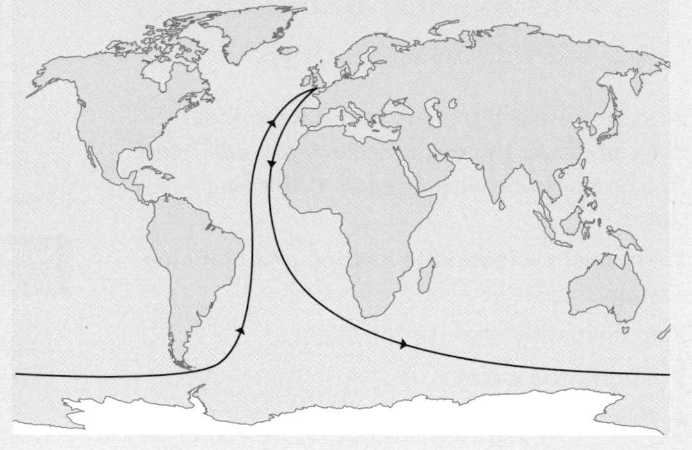

event goals deflect people's attention from conflicts and can solve such problems. Changing roles or moving people to other areas can also help. You should plan the composition of your group carefully, to avoid predictable people problems. Sometimes systems, rather than people, are at fault. You will look at these in more detail in the final section.

How teams tackle and solve problems with group dynamics is a key aspect. The standard approach is shown in the problem-solving flowchart below.

Problem solving flowchart

Identify the nature of the problem

↓

Find possible solutions

↓

Assess these solutions

↓

Plan how to implement solutions

↓

Evaluate the solution, re-plan if necessary

Team-building and interaction

Building up your team's motivation and ability to work together is an important aspect of developing effective teamwork. Companies operating in many sectors of the leisure industry spend a great deal of time and money on this, developing the way their staff work together. Staff are often viewed as the resource that gives a company its competitive edge over others. Fostering teamwork and good relations amongst team members is seen as a wise investment, as it provides the company with positive returns. The benefits of teambuilding and good interaction can be summarised:

- Good working relations are formed which are evident to customers.
- Leadership is easier because all team members are working towards the same standards of quality.
- Staff members know their roles and that of others and they can be flexible or multi-task.
- The atmosphere is conducive to a healthy working environment.
- Procedures are followed, resources are used well and processes are effective – resulting in smooth operations.

Team-building can be tackled in a number of ways:

- Small exercises (ice-breakers) can be staged to bring people closer together through interaction.
- Problem-solving tasks can be set on special team-building days or classes.
- Fun or social events can be organised to help people relax and get to know each other.
- Formal training courses for all.

Additional factors that may influence how your team works

In this final section you will need to look at a couple more factors that may influence how your team works – access to resources and the working environment.

Access to resources

By now you should have made very solid plans for your event and identified a range of resources that you will need, or would like. Make sure that everyone in the team knows which resources they are responsible for (you organised this in the previous topic). If one person is struggling to acquire a particular resource, they could involve other team members for advice. You may need to gather more team members together to physically transport a resource. The team will also operate more efficiently if everyone is aware of the current situation – it is no good if everyone finds out only days before the event that a vital resource could not be obtained. Good teamwork relies on sharing information.

The working environment

This is a very broad factor but, nonetheless, you have to ensure that the working environment for the different phases of your event suits:

- you as team members
- staff you may have as helpers
- suppliers on site
- customers at your event.

Here are a few considerations about working conditions and environment:

- Where will your administration be based? Make it accessible for team members, outside organisations and customers.
- Where will your base be during the event? Ensure it has space for staff to take breaks, change and clean up.
- Where will you hold important team meetings? Try to have a formal location so that it is easy to take notes and for everyone to contribute.
- Is the quality of your venue the best you can afford or find? Quality means space, ventilation, seating, access, toilets, parking, etc.
- There is nothing worse than a hot, smoky, cramped, smelly room to give people the wrong impression, and cause them to lose concentration and have headaches.

activity

IS YOUR TEAM READY?

Carry out a final check on team arrangements under the following headings from this topic. Make any last-minute changes you feel are necessary for:

- purpose
- structure
- roles and responsibilities
- leadership issues
- access to resources
- working environment.

Once you are all sure that the key areas are covered, ask each individual or team to carefully write out their part of the plan and submit it for inclusion in the 'event manual' which should form your team plan for the next phases.

Topic 8 Carrying out your event

By this stage in the unit you should have finalised all of your planning (keeping some aspects flexible). The advice and guidance given in this topic is aimed at helping your team carry out the actual event. You will be familiar with some of the themes and tools in this topic already. However, this topic will re-enforce those themes, acting as a quick reference which you can use in both the run-up to the event and the event itself. Professional event teams may well use a similar procedure as they refer to their manuals, colleagues, notes and plans when an unfamiliar requirement or situation surfaces.

The areas you will look at are both team-oriented and for individuals:

- **Completing the tasks allocated to you**
- **Dealing with customers and team-mates**
- **Supporting other team members**
- **Communicating effectively**
- **Reacting to problems**
- **Keeping to deadlines**
- **Seeking help.**

These also represent the way that people work, which – when done well – is highly valued by employers in the leisure industry. Indeed, following the practices and principles outlined in this topic will help you to become more employable.

Completing the tasks allocated to you

The roles and tasks you have undertaken mean that much is resting on your performance, not only in terms of achieving a good grade, but for the benefit of the event and the good of the team. You have responsibilities and are therefore accountable for seeing them through as competently as possible. You will now consider the many ways of organising yourself, which should help your performance.

Time management

Try to allocate adequate slots of time for your tasks each day and over a week, so that you focus on prioritising. A weekly diary or planner can help to plan your time around all of the other things to do when not working on the event (study, home chores, relaxing and maybe even part-time work). If you can, try to create an electronic time planner or look at the suggestion opposite for a format.

Checklists

Itemise your jobs on a checklist spreadsheet with details alongside, and tick these off as you make progress. Where changes are made or needed, make notes to ensure you remember what they are. Consider the format of the checklist opposite to see if it might work for you.

Action plans

These useful self-planners show the deadlines and targets you have to meet.

You may wish to have a version of an action plan just for the day of the actual event. Professional team members can carry these in pocket-sized plans for quick reference.

Time management planner

	Monday	Tuesday	Wednesday	Thursday	Friday
09.00 – 11.00	Class	Class	Event task phone calls	Class	Class
11.00 – 12.30	Event team meeting	Class	Class	Class	Class
13.30 – 15.00	Write up meeting notes	Lunch	Write up information found from calls	Lunch	Event team meeting
15.00 –17.00	Homework	Homework	Homework	Homework	Sports
18.00 –19.00	Part-time job	Part-time job	Part-time job	Set up event diary for next week	

Checklist

Task	Detail	
Design small business card for the team to use	Incorporate a logo and the team name followed by contact details – tel./email/address on white card with blue lettering	✔
Assess how much the card will cost to print	Visit local printing shop/ find out if anyone's parents could print them for free	✔
Buy 100 envelopes	Make sure they are decent quality	✔

Action plan

Task	How will it be done?	With whom?	By when?
Book a minibus and driver	Ring three hire companies for quotes	Check with tutor and finance person what the budget is	Week 3 before the event (20 March)

Contact database

You will have to build up a list of names of key people who you will need to contact to complete your tasks:

- Other team members
- Suppliers
- Sponsors
- Competitors
- Participants
- Expert helpers
- Volunteers.

A number of other records may need to be kept, including:

- Costs and expenditure
- Notes from meetings
- New targets
- Structures.

All of these would form part of your diary, logbook or portfolio of evidence, and would certainly help to keep you on track with tasks completed and those yet to do. Try to ensure that everything you do helps you and the team achieve the event objectives.

Dealing with customers and team-mates

In the customer care section you covered good practice with respect to the internal and external customer (pages 26–29). The key was to deal with everyone in a cool, calm and collected manner, giving the impression that you know what you are doing. If you don't, excuse yourself and find someone who does. Don't dig a hole for yourself and the team by 'muddling through' or losing your cool – it won't seem professional.

When dealing with colleagues, listen carefully, clarify any unclear facts or instructions, then check with them that you have done what is needed. Be patient when dealing with customers, try to understand their needs and try to meet them within the parameters of what you can do.

Project a positive attitude.

When dealing with people other than colleagues, operate at your best professional level, because these people are probably going to give you feedback on your abilities from a different angle, which may reflect on the employability skills mentioned earlier.

activity

EVALUATING YOUR CUSTOMER CARE

You will have to create a method of evaluating how you dealt with customers, colleagues and outside organisations and individuals. Devise some criteria and a scoring system around these key ideas:

- **Politeness**
- **Being responsible**
- **Listening skills**
- **Staying calm**
- **Being patient**
- **Getting the best results/right solutions**
- **Coping under pressure.**

Supporting other team members

If all your team look out for one another on the day, the more likely your chances of success. Support is essential, and recognising when it should be given and when it is needed is key. You can support other team members in a number of ways:

- Motivation – If another team member is having an 'off day', support them by cheering them up, sharing their tasks, or just listening.
- Meeting deadlines – If another team member is falling behind with their tasks and a deadline is approaching, ask what you can do to help.
- Completing tasks – If a team member has taken on a task where they subsequently find they really don't have the necessary skills, consider swapping with them or help them to tackle the job.
- Attitude – Always try to project a positive attitude which will hopefully rub off on others.
- Supporting volunteers – These are vital people for your event, but they will not know as much as you, so keep them informed and ensure they have the right resources for their role.

Support is all about sharing, and finding the right people to do each job so that skills are used to the best advantage. If you consider the case study above right, you will see how much support Charley Boorman and Ewan McGregor had on their ultimate leisure event – a motorcycling trip around the globe.

Case Study: Charley Boorman and Ewan McGregor – The Long Way Round

The Adventure Motorcycling handbook said they should take at least a year to plan their trip. They would need to plan all the logistics, map their route, organise visas, permits and other documentation. Then they needed to find the right motorcycles, find a sponsor to fund the whole event, learn basic first aid and survival techniques, know enough mechanics to do repairs, find camping kits, spares, learn some basic phrases in various languages, get fit and mentally prepare themselves for their 'long way round'. Both men were busy actors so they had to find a team of volunteers and professionals to support them. Friends, family, producers, agents, TV companies and fans all helped along the way. Over the 20,000-mile, 16-week trip Charley and Ewan had amassed a support team of over 50 people and at least 10 companies, which included BMW, British Airways, Mitsubishi, Stanfords and Pentax, to name just a few. Their efforts benefited the Macmillan Trust and UNICEF.

Communicating effectively

Much has been said in earlier sections about the principles of effective communication (see pages 50–51) so this section will focus on putting communication into practice for the event.

'Proper planning promotes perfect performance.'
By the time of the event you should have put in place a good system of communications to support the team, and inform the customers, thereby smoothing the proceedings. Questions to think about might include:

- Can all team members contact each other – in person, by radio or phone?
- Can all customers contact your team and venue for information?
- Can all volunteers, suppliers, sponsors and media contact you easily?
- Have you appointed a communications director for the event?
- Have you set up a suitable database of communications details and contact numbers for the event?
- Do you have a back-up system if your electronic/radio one fails?

activity

YOUR COMMUNICATION CHECKLIST

Create a checklist based on the ideas given, but tailored to meet your event communication needs. Discuss the consequences of poor communications in at least five of the points listed.

Reacting to problems

Your team have to be responsive to problems on the day. You may not feel they are your fault or that you can do much about them, but you do need to be seen to be tackling them. Problems have a habit of becoming larger and more complicated if left unattended. Ideally you will have some contingency plans for those problems that you can probably predict occurring, such as:

1. Complaints
2. Lack of information
3. Lost property
4. Confusion about locations, resources or running order
5. Team or staff absences
6. Changes in format
7. Minor injuries
8. Serious injuries
9. Power cuts
10. Evacuations

These problems are in descending order, from simple to extremely serious. You should have three types of plans to reflect the scale of problems likely to occur:

1. Plans for individual team members to follow if any of the first three problems occur.
2. Team-based plans for everyone to follow if problems 3 to 7 happen.
3. For problems 8 to 10 you are going to need outside professional help, such as electricians, the fire service, an ambulance or the police.

How you tackle problems will be a major part of your evaluation and create an impression with customers, who will also be evaluating you. You should not underestimate the importance of dealing with problems as quickly and efficiently as you can. The flow chart sequence given on page 52 may be used again, or use risk assessments if you feel they are justified.

Keeping to deadlines

Sometimes keeping to deadlines can be the biggest challenge for your age group, because staging an event requires a level of responsibility which may be above that which you are used to.

Deadlines are imposed by yourself, the team, and contacts external to the event. The key is to be organised, and to adopt strategies that make the deadlines possible:

- Map-out all deadlines in advance
- Identify the major priorities
- Re-plan deadlines where you foresee bottlenecks
- Always allow a little extra time for deadlines.

You will be evaluated on this aspect of your personal performance – as will your team on their overall performance. Keep records of what went to plan and what did not.

activity

FAILURE TO MEET DEADLINES MEANS...

List the possible consequences of failing to meet deadlines.

Seeking help

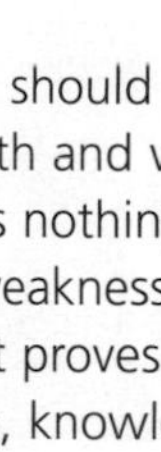

By the end of your planning phase you should have an idea of what your team can deal with and where you might need advice or help. There is nothing wrong with seeking help – it is not a weakness, but a strength of team-managing an event. It proves that you know when the limits of your skills, knowledge or expertise are putting the quality of the event at risk.

Event management is all about being safe – and certain that logistics and arrangements are appropriate for the job. You may well have to seek help from a range of sources, including, for example:

- The Emergency Services
- Health and safety officers
- Tutors
- Professional bodies
- Local authorities
- Event management companies.

You will want to seek help at the earliest opportunity, preferably at the planning and feasibility stages, when making contingency plans and part of a pre-event check. Hopefully you will not require too much help on the actual day of the event, because you will have forecast most problems already and be prepared to deal with them yourselves.

Topic 9 Evaluating your event

The evaluation is the 'litmus test' of success. It is not just about how *you* feel it went, but how it was for the customers (especially those you targeted) and the people who worked alongside you.

As you evaluate, you are trying to establish the true value of your work. To do this you will have to gather a wide range of feedback information and data. The performance will be judged, for the most part, against the criteria your team set out in the aims and objectives section of your plan, but also against other specific areas such as customer satisfaction and safety. Some of the data will be quantitative (measurable), some will be qualitative (relating to standards).

You will have set your evaluation criteria as you prepared, allowing time for the evaluation sheets to be devised and made. After the event, allow time for collation, analysis, associated recommendations and presentation formats to be agreed. To help you in this process, this topic will cover a range of aspects concerning evaluation:

- **Areas to evaluate**
- **Giving and receiving feedback**
- **Meeting objectives and targets**
- **Meeting deadlines**
- **The effectiveness of planning**
- **The success of the event**
- **The effectiveness of the team**
- **Making recommendations**
- **Preparing your findings in your portfolio.**

You will learn and benefit from the strengths and weaknesses that the evaluation reveals. Leisure event organisations continually evaluate their performance in order to improve service delivery.

Areas to evaluate

- Objectives
- Customer needs
- Marketing
- Use of resources
- Finance (handling and targets)
- Staffing and effectiveness
- Efficiency of systems
- Timescales (meeting deadlines)
- Health and safety
- Security
- Legal aspects
- Contingencies

How you evaluate these areas will be explored in this topic.

Giving and receiving feedback

You should gather feedback on your performance throughout the various event stages. Assessment for your objectives, meeting deadlines, progress with meeting targets and staffing can be done from as early as the planning stage. Customer feedback and general observations about the event can be carried out during the event itself. All of the other aspects – such as profit – can only be gathered once the event is over.

Sources of feedback

You need to be aware where your feedback comes from and in what form it will be acquired and received. Who provides feedback?

- Yourselves (team members)
- Your customers

- External individuals and organisations
- Your tutors
- Your event
- The media. (This is unlikely, but your event could be covered in the local press. The amount of publicity the event creates could be an interesting and valuable inclusion in your evaluation.)

Peer review

You will also be exchanging feedback about each other on your performance. Above all, this must be done in a sensitive and constructive way. Most people are uncomfortable hearing how they performed, unless they were exemplary. This session may have to be chaired by your tutor so that an independent person can move discussion on if tempers flair.

Your team needs to decide which categories to cover, but do check the assessment criteria for the unit because this provides the key words:

- Sound planning inputs
- Positive contributions
- Consistent involvement
- Good research and feasibility skills
- Relevant inputs
- Sound evaluation of self, team and event
- Realistic recommendations
- Some allowable weaknesses.

Feedback could be given confidentially, which helps reduce the tension that can arise. You may wish to devise some scales or scores, which give ratings for the various areas of evaluation. Here are some examples:

Peer review – roles and responsibilities

Took on all work in a positive way	5
Met all deadlines for roles	3
Coped with problems and responsibilities	4
Was clear about tasks	4
Was honest about difficulties	2

Key: 5 = excellent, 4 =above average, 3 = good, 2 = acceptable, 1 = poor

Peer review – communications

Politeness	***
Clarity	****
Level of information given	****
Responsiveness	*
Checking on outcomes	****

Key: * = Poor, ** = Room for improvement, *** = Satisfactory, **** = Good, ***** = Excellent

Peer review – personal ability

	1st choice	2nd choice	3rd choice
Contributions to planning and research	Jitesh	Rachael	Mark
Involvement and attitude	Claire	Jitesh	Kerry
Effort on the day	Rachael	Claire	Mark
Quality of inputs to problems or difficulties	Mark	Tom	Kerry
Leadership	Kerry	Tom	Claire
Teamwork	Rachael	Tom	Jitesh

activity

YOUR PEER EVALUATION

Discuss and decide as a team on the categories and scales you will use for your peer evaluation.

Personal evaluation

Personal evaluation is a difficult task because it needs you to make a comprehensive and honest evaluation of your own skills, abilities and attitudes. You will be a 'reflective practitioner' as you assess your efforts regularly to see where strengths and weaknesses lie and try to prescribe ways of improving weaker aspects. You can consult the assessment criteria to aid your reflective practice. For a merit, you need sound and consistent inputs, while a distinction requires comprehensive and significant levels of work.

You might be more specific, and consider assessing your employability skills such as competency, communication, leadership, politeness and customer care.

Gather your data from independent sources to avoid as much bias as possible.

activity

EVALUATING ... YOU

Compile a personal evaluation strategy, including:

- **The criteria you will use (for grading and employability).**
- **The sources you will draw from.**
- **The methods of presenting that data (SWOT analysis).**
- **An action plan for your findings (how you could build on strengths and minimise weaknesses).**

Meeting objectives and targets

Most objectives and targets are quantifiable, so they can be readily measured. To evaluate these, quantities will have been set at the objective stage, such as:

- Numbers – participants, customers
- Percentages – sales
- Volume – resources used
- Money – income, profit
- Ratios – expenditure to costs.

Ensure that your team and individuals all have the targets and objectives quantified in this way. Presenting data on this type of performance lends itself well to graphic illustrations through pie charts, bar charts and accounts.

Meeting deadlines

You will either have met your deadlines or not – there will be no ambiguity. Of course, there should have been some flexibility allowed at the planning stage for overruns (or even early completion). Consider the following suggestions for evaluating the meeting of deadlines:

1. Analysis of diaries, task sheets and calendars should provide the data for this evaluation.
2. Assessment of both team and individuals.
3. Percentages might be worked out to show efficiency ratings for both categories.
4. Draw on some feedback from outside organisations – did you meet their deadlines?
5. Evaluate whether deadlines were a key factor in getting you through the project efficiently – or did they disrupt the process?
6 What aspects of timescale and deadlines worked, and which did not work? State why in both cases.

activity

EVALUATING DEADLINES

1. **Decide how you might present this aspect of the evaluation graphically, with a narrative showing what went well and what did not.**
2. **Make some recommendations for what you would change in terms of deadlines, if you had to do it all over again.**

The effectiveness of planning

This area needs an in-depth analysis because you will have spent hours planning. It is probably best to go through each area at a time either as a team, in sub-teams or as an individual, so that you can summarise issues and findings rather than have an extended meeting which scrutinises every detail.

- **Complexity** – Was the complexity of the event just right, was it too complex or too simple?
- **Assessment criteria** – Did your planning ensure that you met the assessment criteria?
- **Venue** – Did the venue you chose work well?
- **Feasibility research** – How effective was the feasibility research – inadequate, satisfactory, good, spot on? Did it eliminate or avoid any obvious problems?
- **Aims** – Were the aims realistic and achieved?
- **Objectives** – Were all objectives SMART – if not, which ones were not, and why?
- **Satisfaction** – Did your planning provide for a good level of customer satisfaction?
- **Marketing** – Which parts of the marketing worked well and which did not (product, place, price, promotion)? Explain why.
- **Physical resources** – How well were physical resources planned? Did you find that any were underused at the event, or overused, abused, broken, ran out, not fit for purpose?
- **Finance** – Did you plan finance well? Was your budget realistic? Did the team meet financial targets, exceed them, or make a loss in any way?
- **The team** – How effective was the planning you put into your team structure?
- **Administration** – How did the administrative systems hold up? Did you plan enough for this when considering whether admin performed smoothly or not.
- **Contingencies** – Did contingency plans get made? Did they work, or were any needed at all?
- **Legalities** – Were all legal aspects covered? Did you miss anything?
- **Planning** – Was the planning phase itself inadequate, too long, just right in terms of timescale?

The success of the event

Success may be judged in many ways. You might judge your event as successful simply because you had fun, made some new friends, or learnt something new. Your team may judge it a success if they got on well, completed all the tasks and passed the assessment. Your customers may judge the event a success if it was deemed a good use of their leisure time.

In order to gain a true picture you need to 'triangulate' your findings (see below). This will help you to assess where success was strongest. A middling position would show success all round.

Triangle evaluation diagram

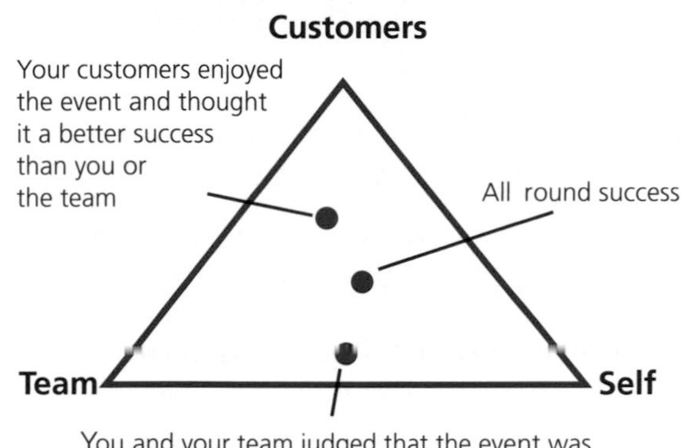

activity

Use your data and analysis to plot your final position within the triangle evaluation diagram.

The effectiveness of the team

The effectiveness of the team can be a difficult category to assess. Do not allow the after-event atmosphere, whatever it may be, to cloud your judgement.

The team

Take some independent opinions here from tutors, from individuals who worked with your team and from the venue staff. Select suitable evaluation criteria, collate the information into a workable format and rate your team's effectiveness.

It is useful to try and identify factors which affected team performance. Examples might be:

- Lack of effective leadership
- Adverse weather
- Illness or absence
- Poor rewards.

Making recommendations

Throughout this unit you have been made aware of the need to make recommendations for improving the team, yourself and the event. This section simply asks you to draw all of those aspects of evaluation into one area for your records.

Don't be over-ambitious. Do identify where factors intervened to prevent you from being as successful as you might have been – factors beyond your control. You might also identify constraints which were imposed, restricting your success (as a team or for yourself).

Preparing your findings for your portfolio

After the event, it is likely that you will have a lot of data which is paper-based and on a computer. This will need to be brought into a tidy format suitable for submitting for assessment (see below). You should have organised a folder at the outset, both for papers and electronic data, which can hold all your information.

You can probably include information, documents, raw materials and supplementary evidence in appendices so that they do not clutter up your work for assessment – but remember to refer to them in the report.

You should also show charts, photos, diagrams and tables which complement your written work in an illustrative form, but try to avoid excess. Examiners prefer quality to quantity.

Assessment requirements

Your work must include evidence of:

1. A plan of your leisure event which you completed with the rest of your team, giving details of your contributions.
2. Your involvement in the running of the event and a detailed record of your individual contributions.
3. The relevant research and analysis you completed when carrying out the feasibility and management stages.
4. Evaluation of:
   - your own performance
   - your team's performance before, during and after the event.
5. Recommendations for improvement in all areas identified.

industry focus

Q What type of events go on at the Spa and what facilities are there?

There are a huge range of events that regularly take place at the Spa Complex, such as conferences, exhibitions, weddings, theatre performances, rock and classical concerts, a jazz festival, dance events, large catering functions, boxing, and even chess and bridge tournaments. I also organise outdoor events such as a '3 Tenors' concert in Peasholm Park.

The facilities at the Scarborough Spa Complex include the Grand Hall (1,920 capacity), a theatre (620 capacity), banqueting suite (900 capacity), suncourt enclosure for outdoor events, restaurants, bars, car park, box office, reception and numerous other multi-functional rooms suitable for three to 300 people.

Q What is your role and what sort of skills do you need to have?

As General Manager I am responsible for all aspects of the effective running of the complex and have ultimate responsibility for the delivery of successful events. Crucial skills include staff management, operational expertise, financial acumen, sales and marketing, effective planning and strategic vision.

Q What sort of team(s) do you have to support the events?

Teamwork is absolutely critical and I have to rely on specialist skills from the whole of my management team. Within the events sphere I have support in the areas of catering, operations, technical, marketing, administration and box office. Some of these areas are obviously quite complex in their own right.

Q What special logistics have to be undertaken to host the events?

Special or unusual logistical issues are ideally determined at an early stage between my team and our client (if there is one) – this enables us to fulfil our customers' requirements either through our own infrastructure or through the hire of additional equipment or staffing.

Q What typical problems can you identify and how do you solve them?

There are many typical problems which occur during event management. Two examples immediately spring to mind. The first is where the numbers attending have not been calculated correctly. This can cause a lot of problems, such as a lack of seating or other accommodation. We may have a lack of staffing in certain areas such as catering which can cause queuing and ill feeling; or there may not even be enough food prepared. The reverse principle can apply where there is an overestimate of numbers. It is important to have contingency plans ready. The second problem is when a client changes their mind about something fundamental at the eleventh hour. It is important to maintain a dialogue with clients on a regular basis right up to and even during the event, to limit the possibility of last minute changes.

Q How do you plan for the events and how do you evaluate them?

I operate from the standpoint that every event is different and every client has different expectations, so we need to establish what those expectations are. The key here is to plan as early as possible and as comprehensively as possible, through checklists and extensive discussions and site meetings.

We evaluate events by sending out evaluation forms, through customer feedback/debriefings and through our own in-house debriefing meetings.

Effective pre-planning is probably the most critical component of any event.

Mike McCarthy, Events Manager

The Spa Complex, Scarborough

Sources of event information

This section of the topic provides you with many sources for information on organisations who stage events. This will help your planning phase, and it offers links to sites to help your evaluation phase. Leisure events are staged not only by private companies, but by local authorities and voluntary sector clubs too. Below are some examples you may wish to follow or use as prompts to find our own local examples.

Local authorities

- Thames Leisure
- Aberystwyth
- (Isle of) Wight Leisure
- Huntingdon
- North Ayrshire
- Spelthorne.

Voluntary sector

- Sports clubs
- Arts societies
- Youth groups
- Special needs groups
- Trusts and charities.

Event companies

www.passport2sport.co.uk – Sports gift vouchers for participants and spectators

www.eclipseleisure.co.uk/ – Organises stag and hen weekends

www.quantumleapevents.co.uk – Specialise in event management

www.rbaevents.co.uk – Specialist party planners, themed events, corporate team building and conference organisers

Links to events

www.eventweb.co.uk – Database of events companies, event management, corporate events and event organisers

www.entsweb.co.uk – A directory of entertainment, music and leisure

www.whatsonwhen.com/leisure.asp – Worldwide events guide

Event venues

This list is indicative of the range of leisure venues around the country.

Lea Valley – the site for the 2012 London Olympics. The 500-acre Olympic Park will contain the Olympic Stadium, the Aquatics Centre, the Velodrome and BMX Track, three sports halls, the Hockey Centre and media facilities.

The Apollo Theatre, Shatesbury Avenue, London – 796-seat venue staging plays and comedy.

Crowtree Leisure Centre, Sunderland – Busy indoor sports and recreation centre.

North Wales Indoor Athletics Centre at Deeside College, North Wales – Two large sports halls allowing for large competitions and events.

The Life Science Centre, Newcastle – Bringing together science and biotechnology, research and education, entertainment and ethics.

Thorpe Park, Surrey – One of the first theme parks in the UK.

The Leisure Exchange, Bradford – Includes a multi-screen Cineworld, a Hollywood Bowl complex, a range of restaurants and a casino.

Portsmouth Historic Dockyard – Home of the Royal Navy and many historic ships

Burghley House in Stamford, Lincolnshire – Elizabethan country home.

Extreme sports centre, Aberdeen – Proposed huge indoor alternative sports complex.

More examples can be found in the list of useful websites (p164) and list of organisations (pp8–9).

How Unit 4 is assessed

Unit 4 is assessed by coursework, where you produce evidence of a plan and your involvement in carrying out a real event. A portfolio format would be most suitable for capturing and displaying your work. It could be divided into the following sections, but this might depend on the nature of the event.

You can normally obtain more specific and up-to-date information on the exam from the Edexcel website: **www.edexcell.org.uk**, your tutor or school.

1. Choice of event. This should cover 'how you' aspects such as:

1.1 came up with ideas

1.2 short-listed your suggestions

1.3 made a final decision

1.4 made the event complex enough to involve everybody in your team

1.5 checked it would meet all the assessment criteria.

Another sub-section should show the relationship of the event to the leisure industry and give the reader an overview of the nature of the event.

2. Feasibility of the event. This is the section which will give the details of your event plan. These need to cover:

2.1 The aims and objectives of the event

2.2 Who your target customers were, how you identified their needs and planned how these would be met

2.3 Marketing for the event

2.4 Physical resource needs – equipment, location/venue, materials

2.5 Financial resource needs – budget plans, start-up costs, income from sales, transactions and payments

2.6 Human resources – staffing for the event, your team, a SWOT analysis or skills audit, other volunteers or specialist help

2.7 Administrative systems – for bookings, record keeping, both paper and electronic

2.8 Event timescales

2.9 Targets set – for the event, for individuals and the team

2.10 Legal aspects of the event – health and safety, risk assessment, security, insurance

2.11 Contingency plans

2.12 Plans for evaluation and review.

3. Teamworking skills – to be documented to show how effective you were together. The following need to be covered:

3.1 The purpose of your team

3.2 Team structures (formal and informal)

3.3 Roles and responsibilities

3.4 Communication methods

3.5 Actual teamwork in problem solving

3.6 Team building and interaction

3.7 Other (variable) factors which may have had an effect – leadership, poor communication, personality clashes, access to resources and the working environment.

4. Carrying out the agreed plan – to run the event efficiently and according to plan. Your evidence should show how:

4.1 completion of tasks allocated was done

4.2 dealing with customers, colleagues and other people was carried out (hopefully politely and responsibly)

4.3 support for other team members during the event was delivered

4.4 communication went on between all team members

4.5 your team reacted to any problems

4.6 sticking to timescales went

4.7 getting help and advice from others helped your planning and execution

5. Evaluating performance – targets and objectives. Gathering feedback from start to finish, i.e. give evidence that you have:

5.1 met aims, purpose and objectives effectively

5.2 met deadlines

5.3 planned thoroughly, resulting in perfect performance

5.3 completed a successful event

5.4 evaluated what went well and what did not go so well for you

5.5 evaluated how the team worked together

5.6 evaluated how working in a team suited you

5.7 given constructive feedback to others

5.8 produced some recommendations for future reference.

Additional guidance

If you are aiming to obtain a good grade some of the following advice may prove useful. Ensure you:

- have a clear plan which does nor gloss over logistics
- try to consistently contribute to a high level – don't be a passenger and allow others to do all the work
- meet all your deadlines, timescales, targets and objectives well
- research and carry out your role and input thoroughly
- be honest in your evaluation, but sensitive in feedback to others
- make realistic recommendations.

It is frequently said that the leisure industry is a people industry and good people skills are needed amongst staff who work in leisure. You probably judge the value of an experience or visit by the friendliness of the people who serve you, often without realising it. In many cases, employing good staff may give a company the competitive edge over other similar operators. It is a key issue for leisure providers.

Good staff do not simply exist, they grow within productive working environments and after careful selection. They also require motivation to remain in an organisation because tempting offers or conditions may come their way from competitors. Companies in the leisure industry must work hard to recruit and select the right people at the start and continue to train and develop them.

This unit will help you to understand and prepare for work as a member of staff in a leisure team. The topics will cover:

- Employment practices
- Recruitment and selection
- Employment issues
- Motivating staff
- Employment law.

This unit builds on the knowledge gained in earlier units, but especially Unit 2: *Working Practices in Leisure*. You may want to refer to this unit when revising and to refresh your memory.

The assessment for this unit is externally tested. You need to understand a broad range of contexts and situations as you need to practise assessing, explaining, and analysing case studies or scenarios to prepare for the test. Good use of appropriate terminology will help you achieve a higher grade.

The scenarios may well trace the pathway of a young person seeking a career in the leisure industry and the processes required. The scenario might develop to cover aspects of obtaining a position and settling into the organisation. Questions are also likely to be posed about conditions, motivation, reward and promotion. You will also be tested on your understanding of how staff development and training evolves in a leisure organisation and what discrimination might occur. Responses will need to include how to be aware of legal aspects in employment.

How well you respond will determine your marks, for example:

- If you only give a brief description this is likely to gain pass level marks (grade D–E).
- If you give more of an explanation and maybe an example, merit level might be achieved (grade B–C).
- If you are able to give in-depth responses with sustained explanations and evaluation you are more likely to be in the distinction mark band (grade A).

Generally you will do better with answers that show understanding and knowledge, use appropriate leisure terminology and, of course, good English.

The scenarios will cover a range of employment contexts, so when revising do not skip any topics and remember as many appropriate examples as you can.

Unit 5

Employment in Leisure

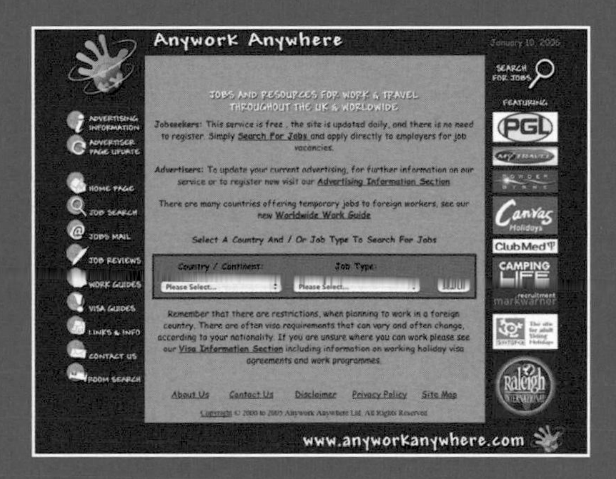

5.1 Employment practices in leisure

Topic 1 Different types of employment in leisure: Part one 68

Topic 2 Different types of employment in leisure: Part two 74

5.2 Recruitment and selection in leisure

Topic 3 Effective recruitment processes 80

Topic 4 Effective selection processes 84

5.3 Employment issues in leisure

Topic 5 Orientation and working practices 88

Topic 6 Organisational working practices 94

5.4 Motivating staff in leisure

Topic 7 Motivating staff 98

5.5 Employment law

Topic 8 The law and discrimination 104

Topic 9 The law and working conditions 108

Industry focus 114

How Unit 5 is assessed 116

Topic 1 Different types of employment in leisure: Part one

The leisure industry, perhaps more than most industries, provides a huge variety of employment opportunities. As one of the fastest growing industries in the UK, it accounts for over 10 per cent of total employment. There are many websites where you can search for leisure positions, such as www.leisurejobs.co.uk.

Leisure businesses are there to meet customer needs around the clock – this is very much a 24/7 industry, with both day and night time economies. They operate at locations around the globe, in the air, at sea and on land, whether organising lunchtime catering in the city, early-bird swims on cruise ships or weekend work-outs. Different age groups are served across the world in any number of ways and in many types of venue. As you will learn, the various jobs in leisure differ depending on the needs of both the business and the employees.

Perhaps the variety of locations and opportunities represent why you might want to work in the leisure industry.

Today's employers prefer staff who are flexible, willing to work in various locations and unsociable hours. But employers also appreciate that staff need to be rewarded for their flexibility.

In this first topic you will investigate some of the more 'conventional' types of employment in the industry.

The main sections in this topic cover the range of hours in which leisure time is taken to suit the lifestyles and work preferences of those benefiting from and working in the industry. Sections for this topic include:

- **An overview of work in leisure**
- **Full-time work**
- **Self-employment**
- **Part-time jobs**
- **Seasonal work.**

An overview of work in leisure

In Unit 1 you will have learned of the three sectors in the industry who supply leisure opportunities – commercial, public (local authorities) and 'not for profit' (amateur and voluntary clubs and bodies). Each has their own set of aims and objectives such as profit, community service or governance. Each business, local authority or leisure organisation will operate in a different location, probably have similar customers to some extent, but provide varied leisure opportunities, all backed by administrative, maintenance and marketing processes.

Employment opportunities in leisure also move with trends and developments, such as the boom in health and fitness and electronic gaming since the late 1990s and the increase in 'grey market' leisure interests of the same period.

The opportunity to enter the industry or gain promotion at better paid levels often depends on qualifications. Although you are studying at A2 level, there are opportunities to go on and study for degrees in leisure management at Bachelors and Masters level, to boost your career prospects. Experience, training, skills and abilities all count for a great deal too, as competition for jobs in the industry can be fierce.

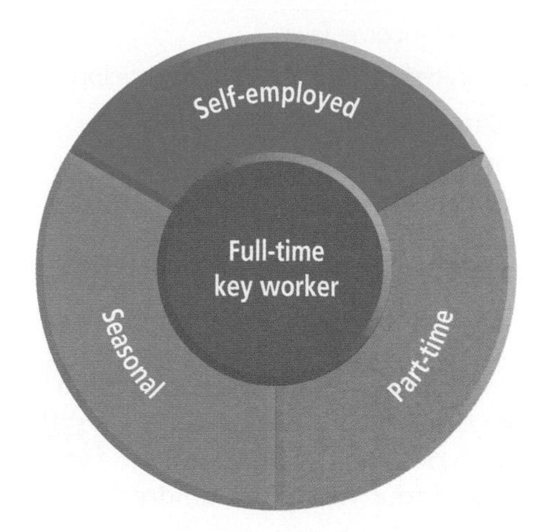

Much of what you will cover later in the unit will help you prepare for a career in various sectors of the industry, as you become familiar with the types of work patterns discussed.

The table below gives an idea of the various jobs within the industries and how the numbers employed have changed in recent years.

Numbers employed in core occupations

	2001–02	*2003–04*	*change*
Restaurant and catering managers	141,164	162,683	+15%
Publicans and managers licensed premises	51,255	67,710	+22%
Waiters, waitresses	221,017	231,830	+5%
Hotel and accomodation managers	51,099	52,950	+4%
Conference and exhibition managers	11,646	11,504	–1%
Travel agency managers	10,693	9,803	–8%
Travel and tour guides	16,945	16,004	–6%
Leisure and theme park attendants	25,070	22,914	–9%
Hotel porters	14,502	11,874	–18%
Travel agents	58,060	50,401	–13%
Chefs, cooks	261,467	245,352	–6%
Kitchen and catering assistants	416,136	399,730	–4%
Bar staff	277,859	261,418	–6%

Source: Labour Force Survey 2003/4, Office for National Statistics

Full-time work

One hundred years ago there were few opportunities to work anything other than full-time, but as economies, products, demands, lifestyles and personal priorities evolved so did work patterns. Full-time work usually means those who work on a daily basis for eight hours a day, doing just under 40 hours per week and usually around 9am to 5pm a day. This is a conventional work pattern. Some examples might be:

- The marketing manager at a health and fitness club.
- An administrator for a sports governing body, for example, The English Basketball Association.
- An assistant in a leisure goods retail outlet such as JJB Sports.

Increasingly, organisations are 'down-sizing' or 're-engineering' their full-time staffing needs to keep wage bills to a minimum, so full-time staff are often only those vital key workers who are decision makers and keep an organisation moving forward, while other types of staff do the everyday operations and delivery work.

Full-time workers usually carry quite a bit of responsibility because they are at work regularly and know the details of how the organisation runs and can respond to problems more easily than others. Typically they would be at managerial level with good qualifications and be able to multi-task.

In a modern multi-activity complex such as Center Parcs, Guildford Spectrum or Doncaster Dome, full-time staff have to work in closely communicating teams to keep each department functioning smoothly, and will tend to be run by full-time staff. Full-time staff usually enjoy certain benefits from their employers:

- In the private sector this might be a car allowance.
- The public sector may offer good pension plans.
- Voluntary sector workers may well get discounts for events.

Other general benefits might be a uniform, canteen vouchers or annual bonuses. (There will be more on bonuses and incentives in Topic 7.)

The second category of full-time staff is those who work a shift pattern to achieve a 40-hour week. Examples might be:

- A leisure centre receptionist who works from 7am until 3pm to be relieved by a colleague who takes over 3pm till 11pm.
- An outdoor pursuits instructor who starts at 8am and works with groups till 8pm for a number of days before having some days off.
- A swimming pool or multi-activity centre duty manager who works a flexible, but full-time shift, e.g. starting and finishing at variable times to complete a 38-hour week.

Job advert for a full-time position

Source: The John Lyon School Sports Centre

There are many other examples of full-time workers in the leisure industry who the customers do not always see because they work in support roles, such as:

- Maintenance engineers at a large complex
- Factory workers manufacturing outdoor sports equipment
- Suppliers and traders in leisure goods marketed through catalogues and the internet
- Ground staff at stadiums and golf courses
- Corporate event organisers.

Full-time work does not suit everyone and often it is a challenge to juggle work and family commitments. This is called the work/life balance as parents working shifts juggle getting children off to school and picked up by childminders, till they return home.

Work/life balance

The European Working Time Directive is meant to help to set standards and control hours that staff work, but in the UK many leisure staff opt out of this in order to earn more money. The benefits of full-time employment tend to be:

- An assured income level
- Opportunities for promotion and development
- Prestige and recognised achievements
- Guaranteed paid holidays
- Satisfaction and social gains.

activity

DISCUSS AND INTERVIEW

1. Discuss which method of working you feel is more desirable in today's world – a shift pattern or a 9am to 5pm pattern, for a family of four where the children are still at school.
2. Interview someone you know who works full-time in the leisure industry. Assess the merits and difficulties of their type of work pattern.

Self-employment

Working for yourself is sometimes referred to as 'freelance' and is an alternative to working for someone else. In recent years there has been a resurgence in this way of working. It still often means working full-time (sometimes more than usual, because the business is one's own), but it is distinctly different in what it offers the individual.

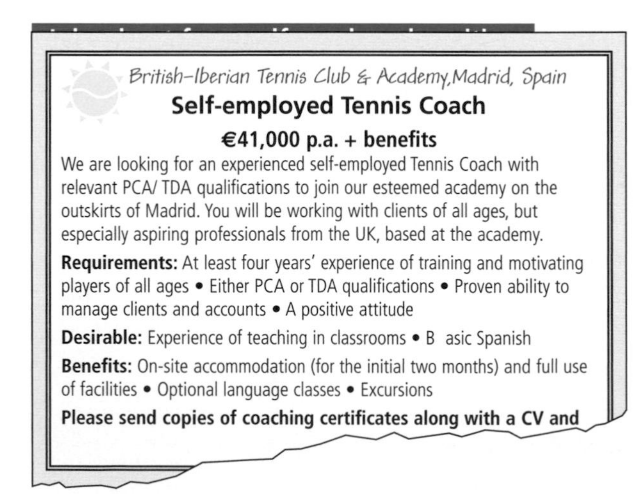

First of all, there can be tremendous satisfaction gained from working for yourself. Anything achieved is down to your own efforts and not that of a team of work-mates. For example, if you are a self-employed sports coach, the success of your athletes will be down to your efforts in conjunction with theirs.

Secondly, you are often able to control the hours you work, who you work for and the type of work you do. Some people who work in the leisure industry take on short-term contracts or jobs because they like to move on and enjoy change – a DJ, for example.

The third main benefit is the freedom not to work when you do not wish to and to choose your own days off. Agency work allows for this work pattern. There are many people working like this in hotels and catering in the UK.

If you have scarce skills, such as in computing or creative talents, you may find that this level of independence suits you.

Those with the highest specialist skills can often ask for much higher rates of pay than full-time employees because of their scarcity. Professional sports players will often employ an agent to secure their contracts and rates.

Working for yourself does demand a lot of dedication and self-discipline, but offers the greatest flexibility in return. This paints a rosy picture of self-employment, but there are many pitfalls, which are worth pointing out:

- There is no company safety net if you are ill or unable to work, so you have to budget for those eventualities.
- You often have to find your own work or pay an agency to find it, which can be a lengthy and uncertain process.
- You need to check the credentials of any companies you seek work from and the terms of your contract (which will probably be short-term).
- You need to complete your own business plan, tax forms, organise insurance, pay someone to keep your accounts and ensure you have all legalities covered.
- You still need to market yourself and your services in an appropriate way and maintain good customer service.
- You are not automatically part of a large team – you are the team and you need to be good to survive – and many don't.

Employers in the new 'flexible working' labour market do like to use the self-employed because they offer many leisure businesses staffing flexibility to cope with peaks and troughs in demand and busy periods like holidays and Christmas.

Many self-employed staff are taken on as what is called 'peripheral workers' – not at the core of the business, but needed for regular periods of work, such as at theme parks or holiday firms in the summer.

activity

WHERE DO THE SELF-EMPLOYED WORK IN THE LEISURE INDUSTRY?

1. Decide what types of job are best covered by working on a self-employed basis in the leisure industry.
2. Why do leisure businesses use this type of employment?
3. Why do so many leisure businesses use a set of core workers and employ freelance people too?
4. Discuss whether working freelance would suit a young person with A levels trying to get into the leisure industry.

Part-time jobs

In Britain, a part-time job is usually defined as one which involves less than 30 hours per week. This type of work has increased steadily over the last 20 years. As the economy has shifted towards a dominance of service industries, part-time work now represents perhaps as much 30 per cent of the workforce in the leisure industry.

Part-time work is more common amongst women than men in the leisure industry. Jobs such as sports centre receptionists, organisers of children's play activities and secretaries are typical.

Job advert for a part-time position

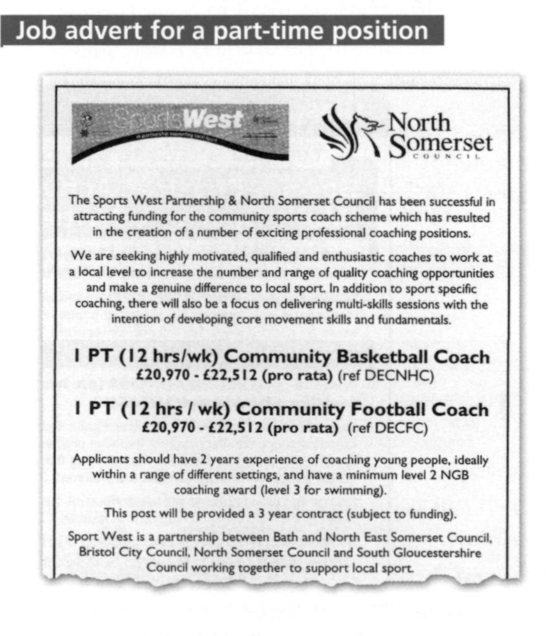

Source: West of England Sports Partnership, Sports West.

Part-time staff earn the same hourly rate as full-timers, for similar work, but often in leisure (and tourism) you will find they take on the lower-paid jobs, which are often unskilled or require little specialist knowledge, such as clerical work in a leisure company's admin division, or waiting on tables in a café or canteen in a pool complex.

Only recently has legislation (both UK Discrimination and EU Equality regulations) come in to help part-timers have similar benefits as full-timers, such as incentive pay, share schemes and pensions. Part-timers did not used to have the same rights in terms of holidays, sick pay, redundancy and unfair dismissal.

A shift can also be seen towards the use of more part-time staff in the retail sector of leisure. These changes include Sunday opening and the introduction of new technology, which facilitates exact planning of restocking (through electronic means) to suit the outflow of fast moving consumer goods.

There are a number of types of part–time contracts you may read about in this context:

- Zero hours – staff are given no regular hours, nor are they guaranteed hours, but are called in at short notice when demand is high, when an event is being staged or when cover is needed for sickness or holiday periods.
- Term time only – these are usually given to parents who can only work while their children are in school and need to be home for holiday and half-term periods. Some lifeguards, receptionists and sports assistants work these hours.
- Twilight shifts – staff are hired to cover quieter times, such as later in the evening when core workers are not needed.

Some people working in the leisure industry are able to hold down two or three part-time jobs at once to give them sufficient income and hours.

activity

PART-TIME WORK

1. Discuss why you think the distinction between women and men part-time workers is so striking.
2. Identify two pieces of current legislation, which helps protect the rights of part-time workers.
3. Identify three part-time positions in leisure at leisure facilities in your area.
4. Discuss 'job security' issues for zero hours contracts.

Seasonal work

Seasonal work is often evident in the leisure (and tourism) industry as summer and school holidays arrive. All three sectors offer seasonal work of sorts.

In the private sector
Some in the leisure industry only really operate fully in this period because their target market is young people looking for action in their holidays. PGL, Acorn Adventure and Camp Beaumont are examples of companies that provide for this market.

Source: PGL Travel Ltd www.pgl.co.uk

They take on many students as cooks, cleaners, drivers, handy men, entertainers, instructors and managers of camps.

This is a global feature – various American summer camps even recruit in the UK and it is great way to see the world, earn some money and travel.

Elsewhere, parks, hotels, holiday camps (e.g. Haven Holidays and Flamingo Land), all take on extra staff to see them over the busy holiday periods.

In the public sector
As local authorities open up more outdoor leisure facilities such as lidos, putting greens, crazy golf and boating lakes, and beaches fill up with holiday makers, temporary staff are needed as attendants, lifeguards and ice cream sellers in seaside arcades.

Ice cream sales are driven by holidays and the sunshine.

The night-time economies grow too, with outdoor and indoor concerts and firework displays.

In the voluntary sector

Many clubs, such as cubs, scouts, boys brigades, sail trusts and sea cadets will have summer trips and camps which require assistants, helpers, cooks and leaders.

Other clubs will run sports camps for under-privileged children or tennis and football camps for talented youngsters, all of whom need coaches with qualifications. With this huge range of temporary jobs exploding on to the leisure scene, there are bound to be problems and issues:

- Without a huge influx of students coming into the summer job market, these types of leisure companies would find it hard to recruit. Why are students ideal?
- Some positions, such as holiday camp managers are quite skilled roles with broad responsibilities. How can companies find, reward and retain high calibre staff to fill these posts?
- Companies have a relatively short time to recruit and train temporary seasonal staff. What issues does this raise for Human Resource Management (HRM)?
- Savings can be made on overheads. How do you think this happens?

activity

SEASONAL STAFF PROBLEMS

Why might issues arise in terms of commitment, reliability, loyalty, training and competence regarding seasonal staff?

Case study: Billy Jones

Billy Jones left college with a foundation degree in Sport and Adventure Management. He also took some activity leadership awards while studying at college, notably in canoeing, sailing and windsurfing. Billy has also been a keen skier since he was twelve and worked for a ski company as his work experience placement during his foundation degree. He has decided to work for a few years as a seasonal water sports instructor in the Mediterranean during the summer months and as a ski technician in the Alps during the winter. He wants to have some fun whilst gaining experience to further his career. To help him, he has prepared a CV to submit to several companies and made up a portfolio of experience and qualifications, to show at interview. Billy has signed up for a short course in first aid and is taking some French lessons to prepare for work aboard.

What advantages and pitfalls might there be for Billy by taking on two seasonal jobs abroad with different companies?

Case study: People 1st

People 1st (*www.htf.co.uk*) is the Sector Skills Council for the hospitality, leisure, travel and tourism industries. They also carry out research into trends in the sector.

Their website contains reports and briefs on the leisure industry and useful links for learning and skills in leisure. You might well use People 1st as a point of reference in Unit 6 when looking at policy matters and employment issues in the leisure industry.

The *Skills and Labour Market Profile Report (2005)*, available on the website, includes:

- a useful overview of the industry
- the size and growth of the workforce in various jobs within the industry
- information on the impact of skill gaps
- the types of skills required by employers
- skills shortages and gaps (by region)
- training, development and qualifications data
- the impact of the sector on the economy.

There are also reports

- by sector
- by geographic region.

Topic 2 Different types of employment in leisure: Part two

Many stewards are required at a large sports event and can be very difficult to manage.

You may have felt that some of the working patterns described in the last topic were less than conventional, but there are other types of employment – some which cater for special circumstances – for those who only want to work occasionally, have a reduced number of hours, or are in fact trying to find a way into the industry. We will look at these under the following headings:

- **Job share**
- **Temporary and casual workers**
- **Voluntary work**
- **Apprenticeships and training programmes**
- **Contracts of employment.**

A note on contracts

All types of employment in the leisure industry should have a 'contract of employment', although some employers feel it unnecessary for certain jobs.

Contracts are important to every employee because they represent a legally binding relationship with the employer and spell out the conditions of the service relating to the job, whatever hours might be worked. Staff have a legal right to know the terms of their contract under the Employment Rights Act of 1996.

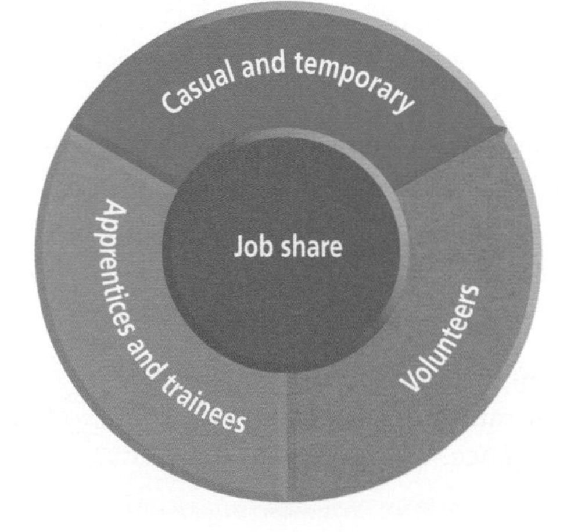

Job share

This is a relatively new type of employment, whereby two people share the duties and responsibilities of one full-time position and work effectively on half each. It requires both sharers to take joint responsibility for the whole, not just the duties undertaken individually. The salary and conditions of service are shared by the partners according to the hours worked.

If a company has a job share policy, those in a particular post could opt to job share their existing post. They would need to give a good deal of notice to allow the leisure organisation time to find their 'other half'. Examples in the leisure industry might include a woman returning to work after maternity leave, someone who wishes to study part-time as well as work, or maybe a member of staff approaching retirement who wishes to do less work.

If a post is being advertised then the advertisement may say 'open to job share'.

activity

ARE JOB SHARES A GOOD IDEA?

In the leisure industry, local authorities tend to lead the way with job share schemes.

Can you find any recent examples in *Leisure Opportunities* magazine, or similarly relevant sources?

Discuss what other issues might occur with job sharing in leisure contexts with the following in mind – gender, handovers, disability, flexi-time operations, promotions, training and development.

Temporary and casual workers

Temporary work is a broad category and includes casual and fixed-term contracts, seasonal and agency work. You have already covered the last two in Topic 1 and can learn more from the industry focus on page 114)

On the whole, temporary workers (temps) form only a small proportion of leisure employees in Britain, probably less than 10 per cent, with the greater proportion on fixed-term contracts. Job adverts in *Leisure Opportunities* magazine show various contract periods of six months, one, two and three years.

Temporary staff are usually paid the same rates or salaries as permanent staff.

Leisure organisations use this type of employment to give them flexibility for short periods of time.

Operational constraints have been a consideration for short-term fixed contracts such as:

- Budget constraints
- The need to reduce staffing costs
- Uncertainty of future funding
- Coping with uncertainty and peaks of demand.

Many leisure departments across the country have had to become more flexible with their working practices, depending more on temporary staff at peak times.

There are sometimes good prospects for being hired at the end of the fixed term for temps who have done a good job and in whom the organisation sees some potential.

However, temps do need a lot of training, quickly, to match the knowledge and competence of permanent staff. If trading circumstances turn for the worse, temporary staff can be paid off more quickly and at less expense than permanent staff.

Tour guides are often casual workers who cover peak periods.

Hospitality tents at the Henley Royal Regatta.

Casual staff

The hiring of casual staff is a great way to cover peak periods as long as no specialist skills are required. Casual staff are taken on for big events – to clean up, steward, park cars or clear tables, for example. They usually take on routine tasks. Busy holiday camps or hotels may take on extra casual staff to see them through two weeks in the summer when visitors are at their peak. During Wimbledon fortnight many casuals are employed, typically tennis-mad students. Hospitality tents at Royal Ascot (horse racing) and the Henley Royal Regatta (rowing, above) are staffed by casual workers.

Casual staff generally do not have much knowledge of the products or services on offer. They may not have well-informed customer care skills or much loyalty to the organisation. Because of this they can be a challenge to manage. But equally so, some are keen to be involved, just to be at an event they have a particular interest in. Supermarkets would find it very difficult to operate without casual staff stacking the shelves.

Hiring of casual staff is an area in leisure that offers very short-term prospects. Not all employers feel the need to draw up contracts. Hiring and firing can be done on a daily basis and conditions of employment might not be ideal, with a poor work environment, lack of supervision and long hours. There are no real long-term prospects with this type of employment, but it can provide valuable experience.

Casual work may be a possible way into the industry or a way to get to know certain parts of the leisure industry, but it will offer little security.

Case study: Greenwich Leisure Limited

One unique example of an organisation offering casual work is Greenwich Leisure Limited (GLL). It is one of London's leading leisure trusts, owned by its members and a non-profit organisation, managing 30 leisure facilities all over London. They boast over 1,500 casual jobs for people who are able to work daytime, evenings and weekends, with rates of pay around £5.10 per hour and up to 48 hours work per week. Benefits include staff discount, membership schemes and training for career prospects.

activity

ANYWORK ANYWHERE

Anywork Anywhere (www.anyworkanywhere.com) is one of many companies providing direct links to employers round the world with job vacancies. Imagine you have a year to do some casual work abroad.

1 Look at the jobs listed, choose examples from three different countries and pick the one you would most like to do. It might depend on location, pay, hours or specialist skills. You might find that some voluntary positions offer the most exciting challenge and would be worth the additional expense.
2 Compare your choice with classmates – you might be surprised at the range of job type and locations available.

TimeBank and Sport England

TimeBank offers a chance to be registered for volunteer positions. Once a member, you can search for local sports governing bodies and other national organisations who require volunteers for events and ongoing activities. Further information is available on their website at www.timebank.org.uk.

Other volunteering information can be found via a Sport England publication called Sports Volunteering in England 2002, researched by the Leisure Industries Research Centre in Sheffield. You can find further information at www.sportengland.org. Research in this report proves that volunteers are a hugely important resource for sport in England. It identifies the breadth and depth of contributions made, estimating the value of sport volunteers to be over £14 billion.

Voluntary work

You may have noticed a range of voluntary positions on the Anywork Anywhere website. These have become more popular in recent years as competition for work has increased. Most advertisements ask for around two years experience. For some people, the only way to achieve that is to work voluntarily in the sector in which they wish to carve out a career. Volunteering can be very rewarding if chosen carefully, and it demonstrates a large degree of intent on behalf of the volunteer. Most university campuses now have volunteering offices or services to help students bridge the gap. Some independent organisations offer voluntary opportunities, such as Raleigh International, and many local groups are set up to provide voluntary work experience through volunteering, such as Community Volunteers.

Volunteering benefits not only self-advancement, but others too. Some examples of personal benefits include:

- Confidence and self-esteem
- Meeting diverse people and making new friends
- Providing new opportunities and challenges
- Providing others with a sense of fun and adventure
- Making a difference
- Some claims have even been put forward that it improves your physical and mental wellbeing.

Feedback from leisure employers seems to indicate that they would look more favourably upon potential recruits with experience of volunteering. Networking opportunities often arise as you meet new people and leisure professionals who can steer you or just make you aware of other opportunities you did not know about. If you are going on to university, it may even count towards your acceptance. There will be many opportunities to volunteer at the 2012 Olympic Games.

activity

WHO WOULD YOU VOLUNTEER FOR?

Carry out some research, either locally, in your library or on the internet to find three organisations you could volunteer for if you wished to gain some experience.

Select one organisation to find a bit more about and assess whether they would help you in your preferred career. Compare your findings with those of others in your class.

Apprenticeships and training programmes

For people who may not wish to go on to further or higher education there are modern apprenticeships and many training programmes offered in-house by the larger organisations or externally by independent providers.

Apprenticeships

Partly funded by the Learning Skills Council and set up in conjunction with SkillsActive, (the Sector Skills Council for Active Leisure and Learning) and Connexions (the careers advice organisation) a range of apprenticeships relevant to leisure is available. There are many apprenticeships under the heading of 'Recreation and Travel'. There are opportunities to learn skills for jobs such as coach, activity leader, administrator or assistant manager.

Training programmes

These can be offered by colleges, independent training organisations or in-house by leisure organisations. They are mostly based on National Vocational Qualifications (NVQs) which are competence-based at several levels. NVQs and training in leisure cover a vast range, as you can see, and attainment at any level is going to enhance career and promotion prospects. They can be taken instead of, or in addition to, the A2 level you are studying. NVQs are described by the DfES as being based on National Occupational Standards (NOS). NOS are statements of performance standards, which describe what competent people in a particular occupation are expected to be able to do. They cover all the main aspects of an occupation, including current best practice, the ability to adapt to future requirements and the knowledge and understanding which underpins competent performance. NVQs are achieved through assessment and training, which is normally through on-the-job observation and questioning.

Businesses also have an input about what skills and qualifications they will need in the future, to inform what goes into training programmes.

There are over 4,000 qualifications recognised by the three regulatory bodies and designed by 114 different awarding bodies – so there is a large range-offering currency, validity and recognition for those undertaking the training and courses for a qualification.

You can check out more details on the SkillsActive website at www.skillsactive.com. SkillsActive also work with a range of providers who offer leisure-oriented training programmes.

Contracts of employment

As mentioned earlier, all types of employment require that a contract be issued. These written documents are evidence of a legally binding relationship with an employer, and should cover things like:

- Organisation and employee names
- Start dates and job title
- Details of pay and payment periods
- Hours of work and holidays
- Sickness and pension rights
- Reference to any internal procedures such as grievance, disciplinary or discrimination.

Contracts usually contain clauses that state:

- that the employee will faithfully serve the employer – sometimes called duty of trust and confidence. If an employee fails to keep to the obligations this could be deemed a 'breach of contract'. Examples of breaches might include theft, fraud and lack of co-operation.
- that the employee should at all times obey lawful and reasonable orders.
- that the employer will treat the employee with mutual trust and respect and provide suitable support for them such as a healthy and safe working environment, reasonable resources and also not to treat them unfavourably.

- that the employer will make payment of wages or salary clear. If staff are available for work they are entitled to pay whether the work is there or not. For example, if some extra staff were taken on for spectator control in anticipation of a large crowd arriving at an event and no crowd turned up – so that staff were standing around – they would still have to be paid.
- the employer must make good any out-of-pocket expenses as a consequence of undertaking duties which are part of the job, such as travel and subsistence.
- something should also be mentioned about what happens if a contract has to be amended (changed). The basic principle is that the amendment should be mutually agreeable.

Most job advertisements give the basics of what will be in a contract, and questions can be asked at interview to clarify any points, so really the contract is an affirmation of what has been laid out or agreed.

activity

DISHONOURING A CONTRACT

Significant breaches of contract make the news frequently. Carry out some research in your local or national newspapers to identify reports of breaches of contract (from any industry) and assess which category from those above was breached, and by whom.

activity

DRAFTING A CONTRACT

Design a simple contract with basic clauses for two of the following posts (you can use some recent jobs adverts, or download a template for a contract and use the guidance given above to help you construct the contract):

- A full-time sports development officer for football or netball.
- A part-time fitness and exercise lecturer.
- A self-employed health guidance officer to work for a hospital trust (limited hours).
- A job share post for duty managers at a leisure centre.
- A temporary contract for a membership secretary for one year.
- A voluntary play development helper.
- A seasonal climbing instructor.

Topic 3 Effective recruitment processes

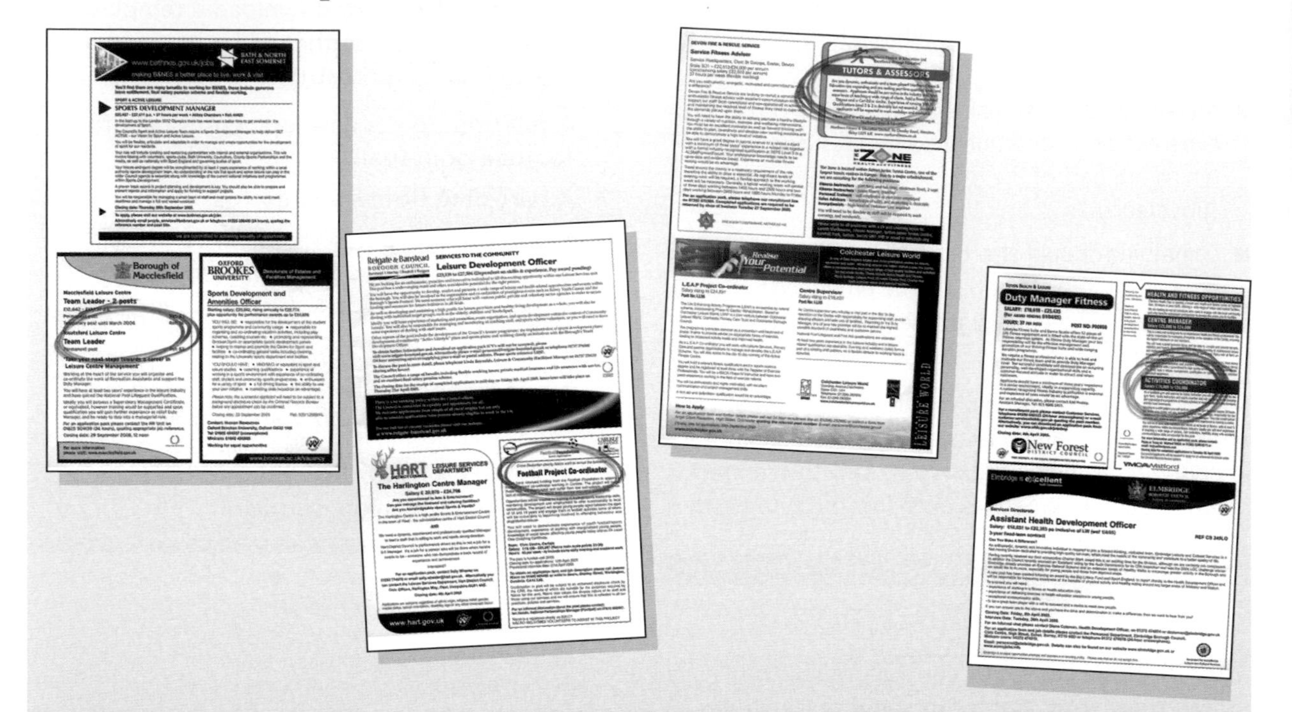

For your assessment and for your future in the leisure industry it is important that you understand the purpose and processes of recruitment for leisure jobs. Recruitment is where the employer identifies what they require for the position before selecting the person to fill it.

Leisure organisations need staff that will assist them in moving forward with their aims and objectives.

Recruitment and selection are expensive processes in terms of time and money, so organisations must strive to keep the process effective in terms of cost and making the best appointments.

There is a natural progression of stages for recruitment which will help your investigation. The stages for study are:

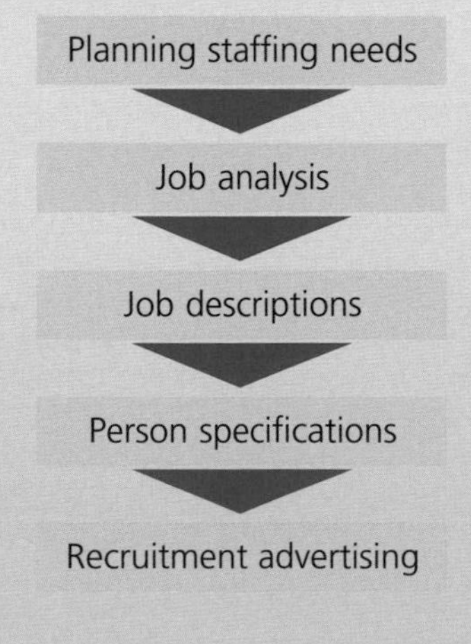

This may seem like a lengthy set of processes, but getting the right person for the job can mean the difference between success and failure.

The process of recruitment is part of what is called Human Resource Management (HRM), an increasingly important factor in organisational success in the leisure industry. The term is usually shortened to HRM and covers many processes concerned with employee relations and management.

Whatever the type and size of organisation, the starting point in HRM is to have a plan for staffing.

Planning staffing needs

Leisure organisations need to systematically plan for their staffing needs – whether they are permanent, part-time, temporary or seasonal. They have to somehow predict demand for their product or service and match that to the supply of staff at different times of the year.

The principle which is often used to describe this is 'getting the right numbers and kinds of capable people to the right places at the right times, to complete tasks aimed at meeting organisational objectives'.

The first stage of planning is to estimate overall numbers and types of people required for certain periods of time. This of course has a knock-on effect for issues such as recruitment, selection, training and development .

A four-step process suitable for leisure organisations could be:

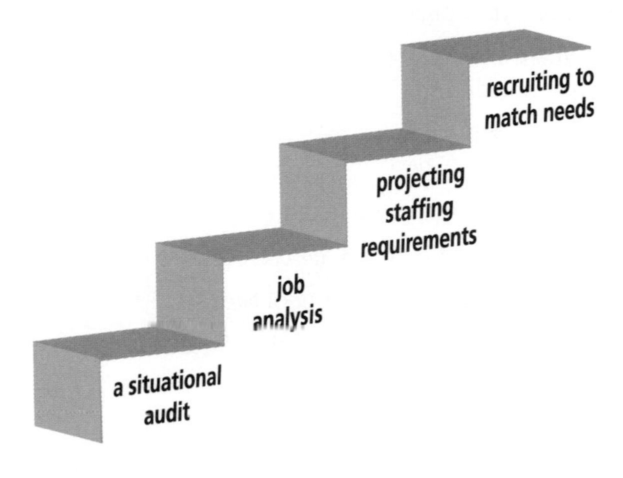

An audit is usually compiled from two sources – environmental and organisational analyses.

An environmental analysis might be based on a PESTLE analysis – Political, Economic, Social, Technological, Legal and Environmental factors. Understanding the impact of relevant changes on a leisure organisation helps the planning process.

An organisational analysis helps to focus on the specific nature of the leisure organisation which might have an impact on staffing. Each organisation will have different characteristics and therefore personnel needs. To explain this further, consider the following examples:

- A sports equipment manufacturer may well need researchers and engineers.
- An adventure holiday company will need highly qualified instructors who may have to be able to speak foreign languages and be competent drivers.
- Some organisations may be quite 'organic' in the way they work, such as in theatre or drama, while others may have a strict 'hierarchy', such as a local authority.
- Sports clubs with a range of teams will need players who fit into team positions and also have the right kind of mental attitude.

activity

IDENTIFY STAFFING NEEDS

Working in small groups:

a) using the PESTLE analysis, identify and discuss some factors that could affect staffing needs for three of the leisure organisations listed below

b) identify what organisational characteristics make them have different needs

- a theme park
- a swimming pool
- a camping and caravan park
- a sports centre
- a cinema
- a museum.

Compare your suggestions with those of other groups in your class

Job analysis

Before the complete picture is known about staffing requirements, the process of job analysis needs to be undertaken. This is a simple process of obtaining information about what a job entails and putting it into a job description:

- The duties, roles and responsibilities
- Specific job characteristics – for example, depth of knowledge and pressure points
- Specifications, such as education needed, training required, skills advisable
- Performance standards with criteria, such as national occupational standards (see page 78, Topic 2)
- Any performance criteria applied, such as targets.

Such information is highly valued because it feeds into other HRM processes – recruitment and selection.

- It communicates the job requirements to new staff and their managers
- It helps show the parameters of roles, responsibilities and duties for an individual
- It can assist in the setting of salaries and promotion criteria
- It provides a basis for negotiations, grievances or disciplinary issues.

What is important to remember is that if any of the PESTLE factors change, this should be applied to the job analysis as well, so that specifications or performance criteria can be adjusted.

At this stage of the staff planning, with job and person descriptions, specification, environmental and organisation audits complete, it should be possible to project the need for personnel over at least the short and medium term of the leisure organisation's delivery cycle.

Job descriptions

The data gathered in the analysis is used to produce a 'job description' which is used for advertising and selection purposes, so it is important that the content is accurate.

Generally, if you look at a leisure job description you should see:

- The nature of the employment, employer and a title for the post.
- The reporting structure – to whom they report or who reports to them.
- Responsibilities made clear in the description.
- That some responsibilities are not given in too much detail because they may only occur occasionally, such as when events are being run or at peak and holiday times.
- That some job descriptions are more comprehensive and show virtually all the roles and responsibilities.

Where responsibilities are not spelled out clearly much clarification is needed which can be costly and time-consuming.

By this stage you have the complete picture of what you want for each job, but not who you want, so next you'll explore how that is built up ready for recruitment purposes.

Person specifications

This involves building up a picture of the skills, abilities and characteristics needed to fulfil the job position in addition to the job description data.

The following are commonly used:

- Qualifications – both academic and professional such as A levels, national diplomas, degrees or NVQs.
- Personal attributes and qualities such as enthusiasm and drive.
- Experience and competence such as previous work and performance standards.

Employers in the leisure industry also want to know where staff have previously worked, for how long and how successful they were too. This may give some indication of their worth and potential. Some specifications are divided into essential and desirable aspects which helps to short-list candidates.

Key questions for a staffing plan

You might consider the following questions which relate to the balance of the workforce, timing and costs:

- What employment periods are best?
- What types of contract are required?
- Where should emphasis be placed – more in sales or marketing?
- Is there a need to increase the minority working groups?
- What gender balance issues are there?
- Over what time period are the changes needed?
- What is the likely labour pool like?
- Are we overstaffed and need to freeze or lose posts?
- How long will the recruitment drive take?
- Could we just ask staff to expand their roles to save on costs?

These types of questions need to be analysed carefully, often before a staffing plan is devised.

Finally, you can also visit the Chartered Institute for Personnel Development (www.cipd.co.uk) and Advisory Conciliation and Arbitration Services (www.acas.org.uk) websites to see what their views are on any of the processes described above.

Recruitment advertising

There are a number of factors which must be taken into consideration when advertising for positions within leisure organisations:

1. Design and layout – it is important that the advertisement format is clear, of an interesting style and shows the company in a good light with a logo displayed. There may even be an agreed 'house style'.
2. Composition – the wording needs to convey a clear message about the position, the organisation, the role and conditions of service. It can be difficult to squeeze all of these into a small advertising space.
3. Contact details – prospective applicants need to be able to get in touch with the right department (usually HRM), and know what to send and who to request further information from.
4. Placement – the right magazine or newspaper to

get the message to the target market of applicants and placement on the page.

5 Timing – organisations must calculate when they will need the new staff and work backwards to allow enough time for composing the adverts, placing them, responding to applications, short-listing then selecting and inducting. This can be quite a lengthy period for full-time senior staff.

6 Effectiveness – adverts need to attract just the right number and type of applicant, so that thousands of applications do not flood in for one post, which then have to be sifted through, sorted and replied to. The wording, qualifications and experience described in the advert should have done this already.

7 Cost – a successful appointment is an investment in the company, but the cost of the process must be justified in terms of composing and placing the ad, short-listing candidates and the costs of the selection processes.

8 Evaluation – adverts can be monitored to discover who generates the most enquiries, generates the most applications, generates the best quality applicants and offers the best value for money.

9 Compliance with legislation is a major issue and the Advertising Standards Authority Code provides guidance at www.asa.org.uk.

10 Online recruitment. This makes the process quicker and more accessible. Online recruitment forms can be automatically sorted, and types of jobs can be filtered by the candidate.

Advertising is not restricted to trade magazines, newspapers and the internet. There are many recruitment channels to choose from. They depend on budget, type of position advertised, breadth of selection and start date, to name some factors. The table below shows different ways of reaching possible applicants.

activity

MAKE AN ADVERT

Working in small groups and using all the guidelines given in this topic, compose your own recruitment advert and choose which channel to use for one of the following positions. You could ask your tutor to judge the best effort:

- An operations manager for a museum
- A sauna and spa assistant
- A gymnastics coach for girls
- A sports development officer for ethnic minorities
- Children's summer camp directors
- A lecturer in leisure management with a speciality in disability.

Advantages and disadvantages of job advertising channels

Channel	*Advantage*	*Disadvantage*
Internal search	Easy and cheap to do, good for staff morale, applicants already know the organisation	Limited scope of recruitment, may create jealousy and perceived favouritism
College or university visit	Can reach large groups easily	Usually only for lower levels Can be time-consuming
Use of Job Centre	Free and readily available national network	Limited use by people looking for higher positions
Private agencies	Are able to head hunt over a wide network of credible people	Expensive – best for senior positions
Newspaper advertisements	Wide distribution, possible to target certain desirable groups, quick process	Can be costly
Advertisements in professional journals or magazines	Direct to best group	Can be expensive and needs long lead time
Conferences and Job fairs	Attracts large group of potential candidates	Not selective
Internet	Quick, automatic and accessible	Technical problems

Source: Slack, Understanding Sports Organisations (1997)

Topic 4 Effective selection processes

You have learned that the recruitment process should identify and attract applicants capable of filling job vacancies, based on a staffing audit, organisational analysis and future needs.

Once this stage is complete and the recruitment channels chosen, advertisements can be launched and preparations begun for the next stage – the selection process.

This needs to be just as effective as the recruitment stage. A number of techniques can be used to assist those making the selection, to see find the 'best fit' candidate.

In this topic you will look at:

- **Methods of application (selection techniques)**
- **Short-listing**
- **Interviewing**
- **Making an appointment.**

Methods of application (selection techniques)

It is important to note that there are quite a few factors which influence the methods that can be applied.

From the outset it is important that the recruiter only selects methods which are appropriate to the criteria specified in the job description or person specification. Techniques used must be:

- valid for the job context – for example, would ICT competence need to be tested for an assistant sports coach?
- reliable every time in their predictions for candidates and at different times.
- cost effective. Sending receptionists to an assessment centre for a day would be over-elaborate and costly.
- able to be administered easily. Some psychometric tests need training to administer and evaluate.

The following methods are the most common in the leisure industry for lower and middle posts.

- Application forms
- Letter of application
- CV.

Application forms

Almost every leisure organisation will use an application form – either electronic or paper-based. Some will have a fairly straightforward format – others are more elaborate, depending on the type and amount of information they wish to capture. It is important that suitable job descriptions, or person specifications are prepared for posting out to applicants or on a website. These will detail requirements, roles, desirable qualities and qualifications, salary and hours. Candidates can then assess how well they match up with what is specified and can prepare their letter of application and/or presentation with those details in mind.

Application forms can be quite effective at gathering biographical data as well as the obvious personal details such as name and address. The information is also verifiable (it can be checked), such as the authenticity of their qualifications. Most background information can be checked by contacting the referee provided by the applicant, the institution from which the person gained a qualification or their previous employer.

PGL application form

PGL APPLICATION FORM

First read through the details and then complete all sections as fully as possible even if you have attached other information such as a CV. If you require assistance in completing this form, for example if you have a disability, please contact the PGL Recruitment Team who will be happy to help you. This will in no way be detrimental to your application.

➤ PERSONAL DETAILS
SURNAME
FORENAMES (underline used name)
DATE OF BIRTH
NATIONALITY
NATIONAL INSURANCE NO

➤ ADDRESSES (at which you can be contacted between now and your given start date)
HOME BETWEEN THE DATES OF
ADDRESS
DAYTIME TEL (including STD Code)
EVENING TEL
MOBILE
EMAIL
TEMPORARY BETWEEN THE DATES OF
ADDRESS
DAYTIME TEL (including STD Code)
EVENING TEL
MOBILE
EMAIL

➤ LEGAL ELIGIBILITY
Under the Asylum and Immigration Act 1996, it is unlawful for PGL Travel Ltd to employ anyone who does not have permission to work in the UK or the country they are applying for. All successful staff will be required to produce proof of identification on arrival at centre, e.g. passport, work permits or other legal documentation.
DO YOU HOLD A VALID EU PASSPORT? Yes ☐ No ☐
Passport Number: Expiry Date:
DO YOU HOLD A CURRENT WORK PERMIT
Yes ☐ (please send a photocopy with your application)
No ☐
Are you in the process of applying for one? Yes ☐ No ☐
PGL is unable to apply for a work visa/ permit on your behalf.

➤ PRESENT OCCUPATION
JOB TITLE
STARTED ANTICIPATED FINISH
NOTICE PERIOD REQUIRED

➤ AVAILABILITY
Dates between which you are available for work (please give precise dates). If you can give the widest choice of dates it will increase our ability to place you.
FROM TO
Preference will be given to applicants able to start work between Jan-May

POSITIONS PREFERRED (For list of positions see PGL Recruitment brochure)
1ST CHOICE
2ND CHOICE
3RD CHOICE

PREFERRED LOCATION OR CENTRES
1ST CHOICE
2ND CHOICE
3RD CHOICE

GENERAL
Are you applying with a friend? Yes ☐ No ☐
Friend's name
Will you accept the job without them? Yes ☐ No ☐
Have you worked for PGL previously? Yes ☐ No ☐
If Yes, what year?
Have you applied to work for PGL before? Yes ☐ No ☐
If Yes, what year?

OFFICE USE ONLY
C/REF GRADE
P S

www.pgl.co.uk/recruitment

Source: PGL Travel Ltd

LA Fitness application form

SITE MAP | HOME

LA fitness

JOIN LA
MEMBER BENEFITS
Offers LA SHOP
CURRENT OFFERS
FIND YOUR LA CLUB

online application form

*Please complete the online application form below, or alternatively **click here** to download a copy of the application form.*

What position/s are you applying for? (hold down CTRL to select multiple positions)
Club Administrator
Club Manager
Deputy Club Managers
Fitness Instructor
Fitness Managers

Preferred Location: (hold down CTRL to select multiple locations)
London clubs...
Aldgate
Bayswater
Edgware

Salary Required (Basic):
Salary Required (OTE):
Do you require a Full time or Part time position? Full ○ Part ○

PERSONAL DETAILS
Title: Mr
Forenames: *
Surname: *
Address:

Source: www.lafitness.co.uk

Letter of application (covering letter)

Many organisations will ask for a covering letter of application as well as a form or CV (see below) to help assess other factors about the person, particularly how they communicate in writing if that is important for the job. Content can be analysed for clarity, matching the job description and person specification. Presentation may give an indication of their ability to compose a letter, which might be especially important for an administrative role. A scruffily handwritten letter is hardly likely to impress anyone and may be one of the first to find its way into the bin.

Curriculum vitae

A curriculum vitae, or CV for short, is the common name for someone's 'life history'. Normally these would show personal and contact details, education history and qualifications, employment record, other achievements or skills and names of referees. A CV needs to be a true factual record with no exaggerations or fraudulent details. It should also be only a summary (no more than two sides of paper) and laid out clearly so that information can be digested quickly. At a later stage the employer should ask to see all the certificates and records of achievement listed, which might well be kept in another folder for ease of display and access.

PRACTICE APPLICATION

Using the advice given here and any other guidance available in your institution:

1. Compile or update your own CV
2. Compose a letter of application for a position in a leisure organisation of your choice using their recruitment advert.
3. Ask your tutor for feedback on your efforts.

Short-listing

This really means screening all the applications and selecting the most feasible candidates, or those that meet a pre-determined criteria or score in the first place, before shortening this initial list into a select few. If the advertisement has been effective, there will be a reasonable set of applications to sift through. In reality, many leisure organisations do not pay enough attention to the advertisement wording and fail to use this as a selection process in its own right. As a result too much screening has to take place, which is time-consuming and may end up being done arbitrarily or in a rush.

Different people should be involved in the process of short-listing. For example:

Applications

HRM
(using suitable criteria to eliminate applications)

Immediate supervisor
(line manager)

Department heads

Short list

Time should be set aside for the interview day(s), letters sent out and a proper plan made to host the candidates.

A short list is usually 3–5 candidates. Most leisure organisations will try to ensure that there is a balance achieved between the candidates, such as:

- Internal (from within the organisation) and external candidates
- Males and females
- Ethnic groups
- The disabled
- Local people.

This helps employers to meet cultural and diversity needs within the organisation and serve any equality factors required. Before letters of invitation go out, the interview panel need to agree upon their assessment process and set-up for the day. Once the format is agreed and questions compiled, notification of the interview date and format needs to be sent out to candidates and confirmation of attendance requested.

Interviewing

It is safe to say that almost every leisure organisation uses interviews as a means of selecting staff, and most would say that this method of selection works best.

Interviews have a number of purposes:

- To allow the organisation to assess whether a candidate meets the criteria set for the post
- To see how candidates compare to one another
- For candidates to present themselves and ask questions about the organisation.

Interviews are popular because they are flexible so that the employer can see the candidates in several different contexts.

As mentioned at the short list stage, the interviewing person or panel do need to make some proper preparations so that there is a consistent and fair sequence to be followed and sufficient time to read through each short-listed candidate's CV and letter of application.

A suitable venue will be needed, and interviewing staff given a note for their diaries well in advance. Tours may be appropriate, as might informal discussion with future colleagues so that feedback can be gathered from diverse sources.

The questioning process needs to be planned, with a logical sequence that puts the interviewee at ease and

allows the candidates to express why they think they are suited to the job. The sequence should also move from simple to the more complicated types of questioning.

When assessing applicants, the interview panel might also consider:

- How well prepared and presented the person is e.g. quality of answers and suitability of dress.
- Body language and listening skills.
- Confidence and speaking ability.

There are some broadly accepted models which can be used to guide the interview session:

Attributes	*How they are assessed*
1. Impact on others	Appearance, speech and manner
2. Qualifications and experience	Education, training, work experience
3. Innate abilities	Aptitude for learning
4. Motivation	Consistency, determination and success in achieving goals
5. Adjustment	Ability to get along with other people and cope with pressure

Despite their popularity, research has shown that interviews are not always entirely reliable, so all the more reason to keep the questions standardised and consistent.

It is important that the interview is concluded politely and the candidates are told when they will hear a decision.

activity

PLAN AN INTERVIEW

Plan an interview day for the following position:

Leisure Facilities Administrator to assist with the operation and development of a range of facilities, including two swimming pools, two dry leisure centres, a golf driving range, a small athletics stadium and a tennis centre.

The candidates must have experience with:

- Leisure facilities and their development
- Budgetary control
- Computerised operating systems.

Desirable qualities:

- Able to work as part of a team and with outside partners
- Good communications skills.

Your plan should include:

- **Format and contents of the information pack for the post**
- **Method of application and format**
- **Short-listing criteria**
- **Letter of invitation**
- **Location**
- **Schedule for the day, including a tour of facilities**
- **Set of questions for all candidates**
- **Set of suitable tests or assessment activities.**

To extend this activity you could have colleagues role-play.

You can also visit the Chartered Institute for Personnel Development (CIPD) and Advisory Conciliation and Arbitration Services (ACAS), the Government's employment service websites to see what their views are on selection processes:

www.cipd.co.uk

www.acas.org.uk

www.employmentservice.gov.uk

Making an appointment

Interviews should be followed up with offers of employment as quickly as possible to those successful, and notification sent to those rejected. The offer of the appointment may not be possible immediately for a number of reasons, so this should be made clear to candidates on the interview day. It may be dependent on:

- Time for the interview panel to discuss each candidate
- Reference and qualification checks
- Further tests or a medical
- The required standard is not met and position needs readvertising.

The method of notification of the initial decisions can be done in variety of ways – by telephone, email or text, but this should always be followed up by a letter confirming the following:

- Job title
- Salary or scale point
- Start date
- Where to report to and what to bring.

activity

'YOU'VE GOT THE JOB'

Imagine you are a member of staff in HRM and have been asked to contact one candidate by phone to confirm an appointment and two others who have been unsuccessful. Prepare what you will say to each one. Create a position in the leisure industry for this and role-play your efforts with a colleague. Experiment with different reactions from the candidates.

Topic 5 Orientation and working practices

When a new leisure employee starts work it is normal practice for them to go through a programme which helps settle them into the company and find their way around. This is usually called an induction.

In this topic you will take a more in-depth look at specific practices, which, although generally supportive, can throw up issues that are often a concern for new staff:

- **Induction**
- **Hours of work (including flexible working)**
- **Scheduled breaks**
- **Annual leave entitlements**
- **Sickness and absence.**

You need to learn about these practices and their issues, so that you will be aware of when and how to apply them, at least in principle. In general they are supportive practices used to help set parameters for employment.

Induction

The quality and costs of this type of programme will vary between organisations. The common approach is to have several induction stages and activities over a period of time to suit the organisation and the employee(s) – anything from showing them where the fire exits are to hearing about the company's strategic plan. The overall purpose of an induction programme is to reduce the levels of anxiety for a new person, to begin to 'socialise' them into the organisation's procedures, practices and culture and provide them with useful information about their role and responsibilities. Orientation and induction contribute a lot to a person's ability to settle in and feel a valued member of a team.

To achieve its aims, an induction needs to have a mixture of formal and informal information. It is also best to have a staggered approach over a period of days as a minimum – but probably weeks – to give new staff time to absorb material, ask questions and gradually pick up the pace.

The type of content will vary with the kind of leisure organisation involved and the type of job. For example, if a person has been taken on in a theme park as a ride attendant, then the focus will be on operational aspects such as safety and customer care. A newly appointed or promoted manager, on the other hand will need to made familiar with plans and objectives, staff teams and company procedures.

The induction also needs to cover introductions to relevant staff, so that they know who reports to whom and who makes what decisions. For example, the ride attendant will need to become familiar with their supervisor, safety officer and immediate colleagues.

The manager will need to be introduced to the organisation's director, the person responsible for

HRM, and other managers. Both our newcomers would benefit from having a 'mentor' appointed – someone who is easily accessible and who they can go to for everyday questions.

New staff need to have a health and safety talk, be given a tour of facilities and at least an overview of departmental objectives. Good leisure organisations will have an information pack or induction booklet, which is useful as a quick reference guide for staff. Some companies may also have a promotional video.

Practical demonstrations are also a great way to show new staff how certain things work, like computer software, safety equipment and machinery. Some time should also be allowed for them to practise using the equipment, under supervision.

Finally, talks from key personnel ensure terms of employment are clear, such as wages, leave, sickness and discipline, (see activity, below).

activity

THE VALUE OF INDUCTIONS

Complete the value column. Some answers are given to get you started.

Content	Value to new employee
Overview of the company	To see where they fit in and understand their role
Terms of employment	To clarify conditions, pay and leave
Regulations for sickness and absence	To have clear guidance on procedures
Disciplinary and grievance procedures	
Union information	
Health and safety guidance	
Medical, first aid and disability information	
Amenities and welfare	
Purchasing and ordering procedures	
Administration and ICT systems	

Towards the end of the induction it is useful to carry out a skills and training needs audit, so that any gaps can be filled in through further training.

Top leisure companies evaluate the induction process to ensure it is effective and to pick up on areas where new staff are still not comfortable or sure what to do.

activity

WHAT TO DO?

Working with a colleague, try to answer the questions that follow this scenario: A young person is selected to be an assistant with a company with a large role to play in managing the Velodrome venue at the 2012 Olympics. After her induction she has a number of issues which she is not clear about. Recommend what she should do or who she should speak to.

1 She is not sure whether to join a union or not.
2 She did not understand some of the terminology that the managing director used, such as 'strategic fit', 'economic benefit', 'development velocity'.
3 She hasn't mentioned to anyone that she is dyslexic and it hasn't been noticed yet.
4 There is a discrepancy between the salary quoted in her letter of appointment and that mentioned during induction.
5 She would like further training and practice on the computer system, but is too shy to ask.
6 She missed the health and safety talk.

Hours of work (including flexible working)

In Topic 1 the idea of working variable hours in the leisure industry was introduced. The hours expected of an employee can be clarified by checking:

- the hours advertised with the post
- the requirements for flexibility at interview stage
- confirmation of both once a contract has been issued.

EU regulations govern maximum hours of work in Working Time Regulations, 1998. The upper limit is normally 48 hours, unless someone 'opts out' in order to work longer and earn more by doing so. There are also some exceptions for those who run key services which are vital to the country, such as members of the police force and armed services, and those who choose to work for themselves – the self-employed.

A new employee must ensure that the hours worked are reasonable for the type of contract (part-time, casual, full-time). Where 'unsocial hours' are involved such as early or late shifts, Sundays or Bank Holidays, enhanced hourly rates are normally paid.

Flexible working is a system that leisure organisations use to try and adjust the size and mix of labour to match shifting demand and to ensure that they are not overstaffed at any times. This places quite a demand on departmental managers and HRM to make the requirements known for the staffing plan. Organisational flexibility like this means reshaping internal working patterns and changes to job specifications, which some people do not like because it raises levels of uncertainty about income and security.

Some leisure organisations have adopted a 'flexible firm model', which suggests four forms of flexibility that firms could try to use:

- Numerical – adjusting hours to meet fluctuations in output (selling ice-cream over the summer).
- Functional – matching skills to tasks and changing workloads (where a slump in demand for leisure holidays occurs).
- Distancing – outsourcing work (employing a contractor to clean and cater for a holiday camp).
- Pay flexibility – adjusting rewards and pay to respond to high demand (to produce leisure goods much in demand at Christmas).

activity

FLEXIBILITY ISSUES

Using the examples given above, discuss what implications and issues there would be for staff working in each of the flexible employment conditions.

Now that the Employment Act 2002 is in place, parents can actually request flexible working to help cope with child care and achieve a better balance between work and life.

Support has been given by Investors in People (IIP), a quality award, because they see the advantages of flexible working to help reduce absenteeism, improve recruitment and retention of staff, with an obvious benefit to customers.

The Institute for Employment Studies has produced a flexible firm diagram:

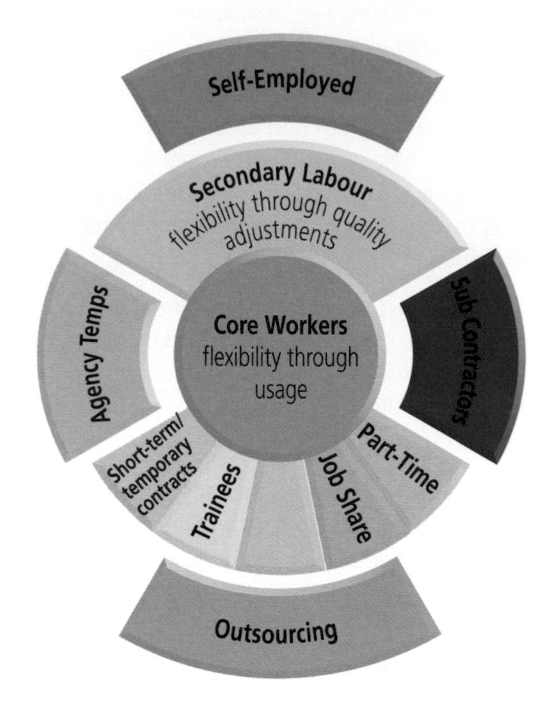

Case study: Bristol City Council

A project which piloted the use of flexible working was run in 2003 by Bristol City Council. This was previously a style of working more common in the private sector. After consultation with unions, local government employers and the EU Employment department, a scheme was launched, which mirrored those that had been run elsewhere in Europe. The system proved popular with staff who took more control over their work patterns and began to reduce the trend for the long hours culture. Many of the leisure facilities were actually able to open at more convenient times for customers, such as Sunday opening for museums and libraries. Some of the admin staff found they could get more done in quiet evening times than busy periods during the day.

People Management magazine October 2003.

Scheduled breaks

This will be covered in more detail under the EU Working Time Regulations in Topic 9. The extract opposite from the Department of Trade and Industry gives a broad overview.

WORKING TIME REGULATIONS

SECTION 6: REST BREAKS AT WORK

Employers must check:

- how workers' working time is arranged and whether they are able to take the rest breaks they are entitled to.
- whether any exceptions or flexibilities apply.
- the different rest break periods young workers are entitled to.

If a worker is required to work for more than six hours at a stretch, he or she is entitled to a rest break of 20 minutes.

The break should be taken during the six-hour period and not at the beginning or end of it. The exact time the breaks are taken is up to the employer to decide.

Employers must make sure that workers can take their rest, but are not required to make sure they do take their rest.

Mobile workers are excluded from the usual rest break entitlements under the Working Time Regulations. Instead, these workers are entitled to 'adequate rest'.

'Adequate rest' means that workers have regular rest periods. These should be sufficiently long and continuous to ensure that fatigue or other irregular working patterns do not cause workers to injure themselves, fellow workers or others, and that they do not damage their health, either in the short term or in the longer term.

Special rules for Young Workers

Different rules apply to young workers. If a young worker is required to work for more than four and a half hours at a stretch, he or she is entitled to a rest break of 30 minutes.

If a young worker is working for more than one employer, the time he or she is working for each one should be added together to see if they are entitled to a rest break.

A young worker's entitlement to breaks can be reduced or excluded in exceptional circumstances only. Where this occurs, the young worker should receive compensatory rest within 3 weeks.

You can check these in more detail on the DTI website at www.dti.gov.uk

From an individual's point of view, although it may seem of lesser importance than hours worked or pay scales, it is important to establish when and for how long breaks can be taken.

During the recruitment and selection phases this might be asked of a supervisor, because it might not be detailed in the contract or terms and conditions. Most leisure organisations will have set times, agreed between managers and staff.

Breaks are usually worked out to suit the organisation, staff and customers:

- For the organisation – to ensure that different positions are always covered. For rides, reception, and lifeguard posts, for example, breaks are usually staggered.
- For staff – to ensure that they can go to the toilet, have coffee, eat their lunch, or just have a break from a busy telephone or work station.
- For customers – staggered breaks ensure that there is no break in the service they might require or the enquires or purchases they might want to make.

The Trade Unions Council (TUC) issues guidelines called 'Know your Rights', for staff who are unsure about what their rights are or how to clarify issues. You can visit their site to read more at www.tuc.org.uk.

Annual leave entitlements

The Working Time Regulations of 1998 stipulate annual minimum leave entitlement in this country is four weeks paid leave, which can, if the employer wishes, include statutory bank holidays. Usually these are counted over and above the minimum four weeks. If a worker does a five-day-week, he or she is entitled to 20 days leave; if he or she does a three-day-week, the entitlement is 12 days leave.

If you consult the DTI guidance on paid annual leave it provides some key points:

- A week's leave should entitle an employee to be away from work for a week.
- Employers can set the time that employees take their leave.
- Calculations of pay will depend on the total weekly pay rate (excluding voluntary overtime or bonuses). For shift workers with varying rates of pay, the calculation will be made on the basis of an average week's hours and average hourly pay. For those working irregular hours, holiday pay is normally calculated over an average of 12 weeks.

Bristol City Council

Bristol City Council are reasonably generous because they provide:

- 30 days for senior leisure officers.
- Leisure administrators have 24 days plus eight statutory bank and public holidays rising to 29 and a further eight after five years' service.
- The Youth and Community staff have six weeks plus 11 statutory bank and public holidays rising to seven weeks and a further 11 after five years' service.

Some organisations have a fixed yearly period, into which everyone has to fit their holidays. Others have 'rolling programmes' based on an individual's start date, to help avoid compression of leave into the end of March period, which is traditionally the cut-off point for leave in some organisations. This also enables employees to carry leave over into the next year so it is not lost.

Part-time and job share employees' annual entitlement and statutory holidays are usually calculated on a pro rata basis. Notice of annual leave should be given to a employer so that it is agreed. This ensures that adequate cover can be planned and that fairness is applied in apportioning peak summer weeks amongst staff.

Should an employee become sick during annual leave, employers will normally credit the employee with the time, except where long-term sick leave has occurred.

Annual leave entitlement of employees leaving an organisation is proportional to their completed service during the leave year. Sometimes, if annual leave cannot be taken during the notice period, a lump sum payment may have to be agreed.

Any leave taken over and above annual leave can be 'clawed back' in monetary terms by an employer.

activity

ANNUAL LEAVE ENTITLEMENT

Select a few job advertisements (perhaps from *Leisure Opportunities*) with similar positions and evaluate who has the best leave conditions. Discuss what impact annual leave entitlement has when considering working for a company.

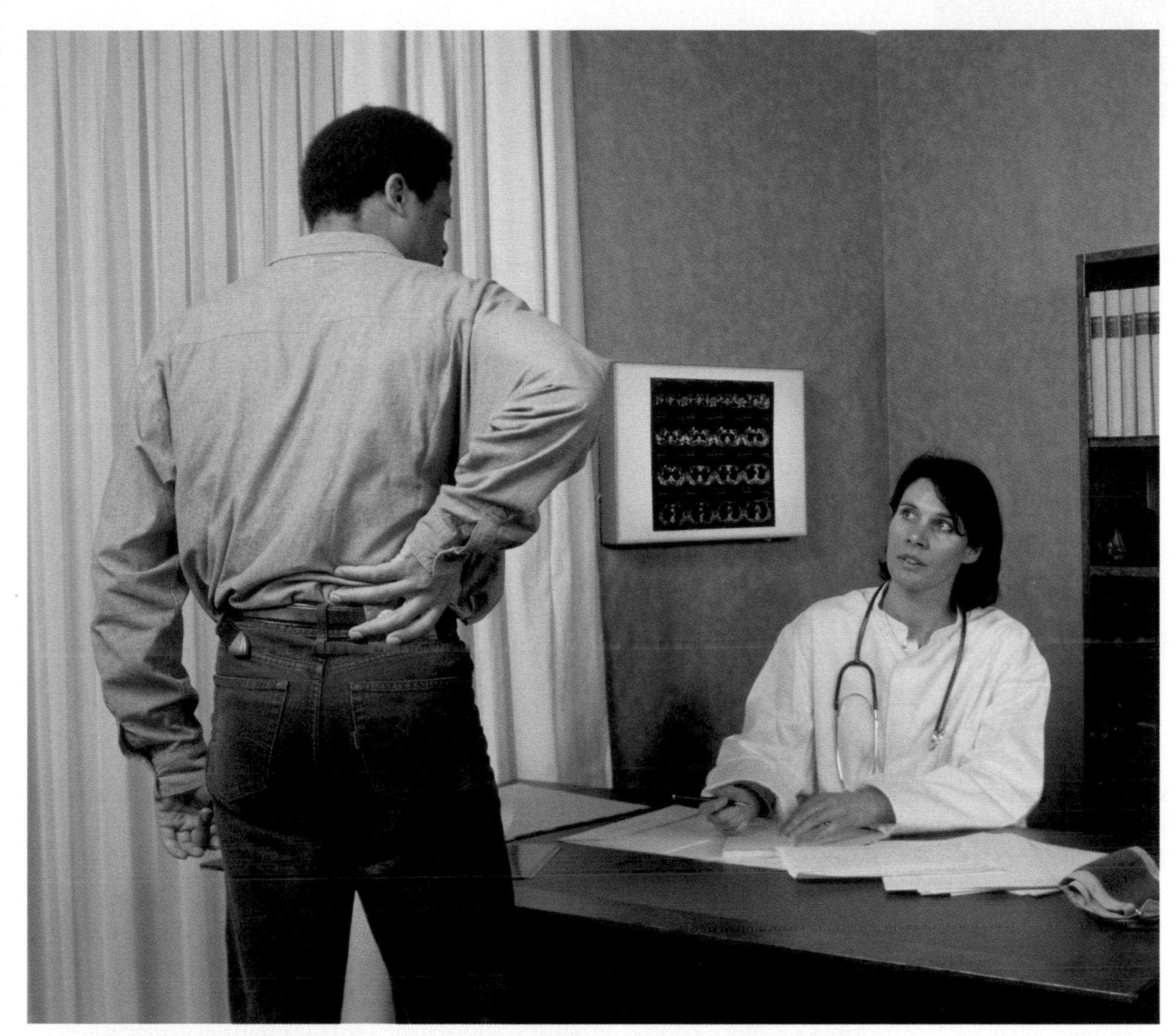

According to the Health and Safety Executive, back disorders are the most common form of ill health at work.

Sickness and absence

The majority of sickness and absence from work is due to minor ailments, colds and injuries. Most leisure organisations will have a sickness and absence policy with guidelines to be followed. Clauses inserted usually include notification of absence, (reporting) self-certification (for short illnesses) and medical certificates (for more serious illnesses or injuries) and statutory sick pay (usually up to six months maximum). Statistics show that absence from long-term sickness:

- costs UK business over £3.8 billion a year
- represents only 5% of absence cases, but accounts for 33% of working days lost due to sickness.

(CBI 2004 statistics)

activity

SICKNESS AND ABSENCE

Visit a local leisure centre and ask if you may have details of their sickness and absence policy. This may be more easily done with a local authority provider. Alternatively, carry out some research online to see what is required by some of the larger operators.

Topic 6 Organisational working practices

One in 3 Britons have thrown a 'sickie'

Working days lost in 2003 up 6% to 176 million

Government faces paternity punch-up

Employers awash with tribunal claims

Sacking or abusing workers prompts others to leave

In this topic you will investigate practices of employment. These can sometimes be awkward to handle, so it is important that systems exist to help managers and employees deal fairly with each other.

You need to learn about these practices and their issues, so that you will be aware of when and how to apply them, at least in principle.

The issues covered are:

- **Absenteeism**
- **Maternity, paternity and adoption conditions**
- **Notice periods**
- **Disciplinary and grievance procedures**
- **Redundancy, redeployment and dismissal**
- **Appraisals.**

Absenteeism

Absence from work due to sickness was covered in Topic 5, but 'absenteeism' describes someone's habit of being off work on a regular basis.

Absenteeism is a key indicator of employee morale and any levels over five per cent in a leisure organisation would be very serious – three per cent is the industry average.

Only a third of absenteeism results from health-related sources – the rest are personal.

Shift-work in the leisure industry is particularly prone to absenteeism – due to increased fatigue, the generally poorer health of shift workers and shifts that are badly designed. One way to reduce absenteeism is to redesign the shift schedule so that it fits both business needs and the wishes of employees.

Some people may have problems with elderly relatives or small children, or may be feeling under pressure due to problems with a difficult boss or colleague. Sometimes practical issues, such as a long commute, can play a role.

When people are absent:

- productivity declines
- knowledge is lost
- customer service suffers
- morale plummets among those left to cope with the additional workload
- reputations are put at risk.

If managers have at least some understanding of the nature of an employee's problem, they can make sure appropriate help and support is made available immediately. Keeping a record of the reasons staff give for absence can help companies identify common threads. Learning to reduce absenteeism is a team effort and it should not fall to just one person. Involving all relevant parties in the solution will relieve the burden.

Flexibility goes a long way to reducing the problem. As mentioned previously, since 2003 new rights have given over four million working parents in the UK the opportunity to consult with their employer so that they can effectively balance their work and home lives.

Maternity, paternity and adoption conditions

The Employment Act of 2002 introduced much more favourable conditions of employment to benefit those requiring:

- Maternity leave – All employees are entitled to 26 weeks ordinary maternity leave.

- Time off for ante-natal care – Pregnant employees are entitled to paid time off work to attend ante-natal classes and appointments in work time.
- Paternity leave – Fathers now have the right to take up to two weeks paternity leave at a rate of £106 a week.
- Adoption leave – Qualifying employees adopting a child aged 16 or less are able to take 26 weeks paid leave and 26 weeks unpaid leave.
- Parental leave – Employees with one year's service or more are entitled to 13 weeks unpaid parental leave for each child up until the child's fifth birthday. Special rules apply for parents of disabled children.

(Please remember that these conditions are subject to change.)

Planning for those requiring such leave gives any leisure organisation a number of advantages:

1. It helps to ensure that the remaining employees are not overloaded with work, which could encourage sickness absence, loss of motivation and increased labour turnover.
2. It provides more flexibility and time to plan for other implications.
3. The pregnant employee can leave on maternity leave feeling that she has been treated fairly. This will encourage her to keep the employer advised of her plans and return to work following the maternity leave.

Employees returning from ordinary maternity leave are entitled to return to the position, on the same terms and conditions they occupied prior to maternity leave. If the job has disappeared in their absence, they must be offered similar work.

A pregnant employee cannot be dismissed (or singled out for redundancy) because of pregnancy. Otherwise it would automatically be classed as an unfair dismissal resulting in compensation and/or reinstatement.

You can check out current legislation at various websites such as www.businesslink.gov.uk.

activity

ROLE PLAY

Plan some questions to be used in a role-play of an interview. The interviewer is trying to assess how the applicant was treated by her previous employers when she took maternity leave and then returned to work.

Notice periods

Notice is a formal statement that someone is going to leave a job. Notice periods vary according to the type of position and level of the job. For lower levels, a week is normal. For senior positions it is 3–6 months because it usually takes longer to find and replace a person with more responsibility.

The normal practice when handing in notice or resigning is to inform the organisation in writing.

Where notice is given by the employer to someone leaving over a misdemeanour it can be instant or by the end of the day.

The Department of Trade and Industry's website (www.dti.gov.uk) provides some basic advice for employers:

'The required notice period must be given in the employee's written statement or the statement must refer to the relevant legislation on notice periods. If for some reason there is no written statement, then generally the minimum statutory notice periods apply. To avoid disputes, most businesses specify that notice must be given in writing'.

Disciplinary and grievance procedures

It is important that any leisure organisation states its commitment to the elimination of any type of grievance or misconduct, such as racial or sexual harassment. Disciplinary procedures should be based on general principles of justice to ensure that everyone is treated in the same way and that any action taken or decisions made are fair and based on facts, not opinion.

Every leisure organisation should have a disciplinary and grievance procedure, which can be applied. There should be a set of guidelines for each side to follow.

Disciplinary procedures need to be applied if any of the following incidents occur:

- Misconduct – such as deliberately breaking a piece of equipment.
- Gross misconduct – such as accessing personal files, serious negligence, fighting or assault, theft or fraud, or being drunk or abusive at work.
- Persistent absenteeism or lateness for no obvious reason.
- Not conforming to standards or not following company policy and rules.

Grievances occur when someone wishes to complain about another member of staff for some reason.

Grievances are also likely to have an emotional dimension, which can complicate discussions and settlement.

The key to settling either a disciplinary or grievance situation is to get to the root of the problem, basing any judgements on facts. Carrying out an investigation into a situation can be both delicate and demanding – there a range of implications for those involved and anyone trying to settle the matter.

Here are some suggestions in the first instance, that might work well for a leisure manager having to take on the role of investigating either a disciplinary matter or grievance, set out in eight stages:

1. Arrange some interviews with relevant people, HRM staff or a union to gather facts.
2. Plan some relevant interview questions based on the facts gathered.
3. Allow informal discussion to bring in new information. Avoid being critical or judgemental. Always ensure the person knows their rights.
4. Try to build up an agreed version of facts and points.
5. Short-term action may be needed, such as suspension of the person involved (if a decision cannot be made immediately). Try to reach a decision quickly, however, as the stress and tension can be very damaging.
6. Record any verdict and penalty and let the person know that there is an appeals system or redress through an industrial tribunal if sacking is the outcome.

The Advisory Conciliation and Arbitration Services (ACAS) recommend for the first minor event that an informal warning is given to the person. For a recurrence, a formal oral or written warning needs to be given. Persistent problems beyond this would lead to a caution and threat of dismissal.

activity

NEWSWORTHY EVENTS

Carry out a search in local and national newspapers for stories of someone being disciplined or having a grievance settled and assess – as far as you can – whether the above principles were followed. Compare and contrast stories with your classmates.

Redundancy, redeployment and dismissal

These three categories of employment practice have the most serious implications for an individual and, as a consequence, there is legislation laid down to ensure that all organisations follow strict guidelines. Leisure organisations of any size need to follow Government regulations and notify the Department of Trade and Industry of any redundancies that are envisaged, at least 90 days before the event. Most large organisations will have a standing policy to cover the three procedures, which have been worked out in conjunction with unions. Smaller organisations may not have a policy, and might need help to comply.

Redundancy and redeployment happen as budgets are reduced, sales dwindle and job roles or companies change or disappear. Dismissal occurs when the individual is at fault.

Redundancy

This can take various forms. Ideally it needs to be a planned and consultative process. Where possible, other measures should be explored to help ease the process or reduce the impact, such as limiting recruitment elsewhere, considering re-deployment and reducing overtime.

Voluntary redundancy is a first step – some workers may be willing to volunteer for redundancy in return for enhanced rewards.

Compulsory redundancy is the worst scenario, and should not happen until all other avenues have been explored. The length of service, attendance and earnings should be a major consideration before taking this decision. Staff at risk usually have a skills audit carried out to assess who still has the most value to the organisation, especially if the redundancies are to be phased over a period of time.

'Constructive' redundancy occurs when a situation is deliberately constructed (perhaps over a period of time), where gradually all of someone's roles and responsibilities are intentionally eroded or moved to others, so that the organisation can make them redundant more easily.

Redeployment

This is an alternative to redundancy, but again, it needs planning to include retraining for any new jobs. Earnings and conditions may be affected, a lump sum payment may be awarded to compensate for the move. For some employees a 'protected deal' may be struck.

Common faults in the processes of redundancy and redeployment are:

- Insensitivity, vagueness and abruptness with announcements
- Lack of training amongst those involved in the process
- Lack of clarity of details and implications
- No alternative, counselling or support for individuals.

activity

THE IMPACT OF REDUNDANCY

Discuss with your colleagues what the material, physical, mental and social implications are of someone being made redundant at a museum.

Dismissal

An employee may only legitimately be dismissed in one of the following sets of circumstances:

1. Under circumstances where gross misconduct has been proved, such as stealing company property.
2. If appropriate work procedures have obviously not been followed or work standards have not been met.

However, cases of wrongful dismissal can occur. Many of these cases do not come before an industrial tribunal – the official organisation set up to decide whether dismissal was fair – because many people are not aware of their rights or are too intimidated to pursue their claim. Examples of wrongful dismissal are:

- a woman sacked for becoming pregnant
- unfair selection for redundancy
- sacking because someone belonged to an official union or went on official strike.

activity

DISMISSED FROM THEIR FIRST JOB

Being dismissed from a job can be very traumatic. Discuss what you think the impact would be for a young person dismissed from their very first job in the leisure industry, which is a children's play scheme. Where could they seek help to get them back into work?

Appraisals

Everyone should have an appraisal at least once a year to ensure that they are making progress and meeting the targets they have set themselves or that have been set by their leisure organisation.

An appraisal is an assessment of behaviour and performance of staff. Every leisure organisation should have an agreed system, carried out by trained appraisers (not just the line manager). It can be a crucial aspect of the job linked to financial reward and planned career progression. These are what staff require from an appraisal system:

- Good quality feedback on how they are performing (knowledge of any results that are recorded).
- Clear attainable goals
- Involvement in the setting of tasks and goals such as new qualifications to be achieved.

Leisure organisations have a choice in how they tackle their appraisals – who is appraised and who the appraisers are, and whether the appraisals include upwards feedback for senior staff and frequency.

There are some common problems that appraisal systems have:

- Decisions may be based on unreliable information – hearsay or opinion
- Reporting standards might be inconsistent
- Certain managers might not be very good at carrying out appraisals
- Feedback may concentrate on what has happened rather than looking forward – there needs to be a balance
- Appraisals might occur too infrequently, or too often.

As long as there is a transparent system, which everyone supports, including senior management, it should align personal and departmental goals to those of the leisure organisation and produce 'synergy'.

Topic 7 Motivating staff

If you speak to any manager of a leisure facility they are likely to say that one of the ongoing challenges they face is motivating staff. Good managers know that this is not always an easy task, but there is a range of methods available. In this topic you will investigate some underpinning theory, the most common range of methods used to motivate staff in leisure and how these are applied, under the following headings:

- **Motivational theory**
- **Management methods**
- **Staff development and training**
- **Working environment**
- **Remuneration and incentives.**

Motivation provides you with direction for your actions, but also affects the level of determination to see a task through.

Many questions are asked about the motivation of various sports teams – why do some players appear more motivated than others, when you could argue that all are equally talented?

It is a fascinating subject which probes the extent to which we want something and how much effort we are willing to put into getting it.

London's 2012 Olympic bid team were motivated by a great desire to stage the world's foremost sporting event (including Kelly Holmes, left).

Motivational theory

Motivational drives are unique to each person. For people in charge of staff in a leisure facility, the power and skill to motivate others are valued commodities.

An understanding of motivational theory will help managers in leisure organisations to direct staff in order to help achieve organisational goals and meet personal needs along the way.

The following motivational flowchart illustrates how staff behaviour is determined by their motivation, as they work to achieve a goal.

Motivational flowchart

- Motivation starts with needs and expectations
- Develops into drives and actions
- Develops into further drives and actions
- If goals are not achieved – the motivational cycle stops
- If achieved – encourages continuous motivation

Motivation at work

Motivation at work is usually classified as three types, although all three may be at work at one time:

1. Extrinsic – Coming from outside the person, seeking rewards such as a bonus, better contract or promotion. Often more tangible.
2. Intrinsic – More psychological and natural, often more personal, such as meeting a challenge or being recognised.
3. Social – Based on relationships with other people such as friendships, status, teams or work groups.

It is how we set about balancing these three angles that determines motivation, job satisfaction and work performance.

Triangle of motivational forces

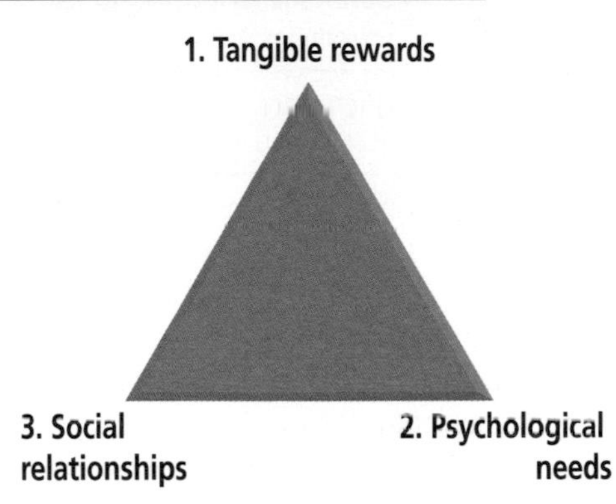

Actual performance levels will be determined by ability × motivation and, to some extent, the barriers that crop up to thwart us.

Strange behaviour in workmates can sometimes be explained by frustration or aggression, because something they are working towards is not going well. This might be evident at work in the form of arguing, being obstructive or just withdrawing from problems. These are very clear signs for a leisure manager that all is not well and some sort of remedy is required.

activity

WHAT MOTIVATES YOU IN CLASS?

What factors frustrate you as you work towards a goal, and what solutions do you (or your teachers) usually use? Identify which are intrinsic and which are extrinsic. Compare these with others in your class.

Ways of how to manage motivational problems have changed over the years in the leisure industry.

In the early days of motivational theory, high wages were thought to be the main motivator, but further experiments by behaviouralist researcher Elton Mayo showed that people worked for satisfaction too. This was expanded upon to show that many people were trying to be the best they could be. Eventually it was concluded that each person's motivational ingredients were different and that money is not always the main motivator.

Some writers say that the main problem is that we actually know a lot about what motivates, but don't really act on it enough. Why do you think this might be the case?

Motivation in the leisure industry can depend on a number of factors:

- Relationships and recognition, which have already been mentioned.
- The way the organisation is structured.
- The lifestyle or comforts attached to a job.
- The power that one wields.
- How a person is encouraged to be creative or extend themselves.

These may differ from company to company and even country to country. There is no single motivational theory that fits all situations, but it is agreed that two types exist:

CONTENT THEORIES – emphasise **what** motivates individuals.

PROCESS THEORIES – emphasise the actual process of motivation – **how**.

Even putting all of these together does not give a full and clear picture – only a framework with which you might understand certain situations better.

Management methods

In practice, leisure managers or team leaders apply motivational theory in everyday ways. The better they know their staff, the easier is becomes to know what motivates them. Examples might include:

- quietly praising someone for a job well done
- making a big fuss of someone for a job well done
- paying someone a good bonus at the end of the season
- telling someone they must try harder.
- offering incentives for high sales levels
- being consistently fair and unbiased
- setting SMART targets or achievable goals.

Staff development and training

Developing staff means helping to improve their personal skills, such as communication or confidence. Training staff means helping them to become more competent at tasks they have to perform. The advantages of training and development are:

- making the organisation an attractive one to work for
- aiding customer satisfaction
- meeting company goals
- helping to run the organisation more effectively and efficiently
- ensuring that staff are more competent and motivated.

There are quality awards associated with good training and development schemes – Quest, ISO 9002, CharterMark and Investors In People. These are used to show that the organisation cares for its staff and in turn serves its customer needs more effectively too.

Leisure managers have many means at their disposal to motivate through development and training such as:

- Putting on training days in a specific subject, such as health and safety.
- Staging team development sessions, initiative exercises or problem-solving tasks. Sometimes these are run on site, and at other times at an outdoor venue to get people away from their usual working environment.
- Bringing in a guest speaker on a topic, such as child protection or fire risks.
- Sending staff away to a training organisation to improve knowledge and skills.

All of these types of programmes make a huge contribution to motivation amongst the work force because they are evidence of the organisation supporting them and giving them a chance to improve themselves or their promotion prospects.

Of course, not everyone is comfortable being appraised or having to undertake further training – for example, older members of staff learning how to use computers. In these cases, these might be de-motivators.

Development and training in the leisure industry is usually required when new technology or equipment is introduced. The rapidity of technological change is particularly evident in retail (chip and pin) and ticketing (online booking).

Many leisure organisations have to regularly realign their strategies – it is often what keeps them competitive.

New skills and knowledge may have to be imparted if a leisure organisation is seeking to enter new markets with new products and services. Staff need to know how to promote these and be confident (and motivated) about doing so.

In the accompanying chart you can see the different types of training.

Training methods

On-the-job training	A co-worker teaches you how to do things
Job rotation	Employees move through a range of jobs to gain experience
Lectures, talks and presentations	By senior staff, other professionals or consultants
Case studies, videos or visits	Observational learning to see how things work elsewhere
Taking a short course (out of office)	Often gains an award or qualification and helps promotion
Job enlargement	Being given more or broader responsibilities

The key to having a motivated team of staff is knowing what type of training and development to use, when, and how often. Motivation of staff is an ongoing process with varied content to make them feel valued and enthusiastic.

Case study: Bourne Leisure

This case study highlights motivation and reward, but also relates to Topic 2, page 78, apprenticeships and training programmes. Bourne Leisure is one of the largest and most successful holiday businesses in Europe. One in ten people in the UK will take a holiday with Bourne Leisure each year with brands such as Haven, Butlins, Warner and British Holidays.

They offer apprenticeships in Customer Services to their 500 staff in their call centre in West Sussex. Fiona Johnston, Bourne Leisure's call centre HR Manager, believes that apprenticeships help keep staff focused. She is convinced of the benefits they have brought, including:

- improved staff retention by increasing job satisfaction among employees taking part in the scheme
- improved employee motivation by giving staff clearly defined personal goals to work towards.

Source: www.apprenticeships.org.uk

activity

DEVELOPMENT AND TRAINING PRACTICE

Carry our some of your own research on Human Resource Management or visit a sport and leisure centre to assess:

1. what benefits staff find in development and training
2. what benefits the organisation finds in development and training schemes
3. what barriers or problems occur for individuals or organisations trying to set up development and training for staff
4. which you think are most valuable to a leisure organisation – technical skills, interpersonal skills or problem-solving capabilities.

The working environment

One key area which deserves greater focus is the working environment in the leisure industry. This can be very varied compared to that of a typical office worker.

It is important to create a good working environment to maintain motivation The working environment should encompass:

- Levels of co-operation amongst staff, teams or departments
- Overall harmony between managers, staff and organisational goals (synergy)
- Growth, control and efficiency
- Management style
- The value of systems and operating standards
- Levels of staff comfort – changing rooms or equipment
- The way power is used or rewards are administered
- Attitudes to change or new working practices
- How legislation is applied
- The type of language used
- The 'culture' of the working environment
- The architecture of a facility

All of these aspects go into the melting pot of 'organisational culture' – the working environment. Every leisure organisation, whether it is a theme park, a fast food outlet or a sports facility, will need a different combination of motivational methods to make it run well. Football managers each have a certain philosophy about how they want the game played and the team run. This means changing the training, tactics and roles for players – their working environment.

Arsene Wenger motivates his Arsenal players from the touchline.

Larger leisure organisations (Nike, Disney or Virgin) will work hard to create a 'corporate culture' which they hope everyone will recognise and support. Ultimately it may determine how efficient they are in delivering their leisure services and products.

activity

WALT WHO?

What does Disneyland mean to you? What do you think of when you see the logo? Do you think Disney has generated an effective and/or positive corporate culture?

In most leisure organisations culture and motivation are the managers' responsibility to determine. This is achievable through five channels:

1 What, and how, they measure and control
2 How they react to critical incidents
3 How they model, teach and coach staff
4 What criteria they use to allocate rewards and status
5 The criteria they use for recruitment, selection, promotion, training and development (perhaps even who they fire).

activity

ORGANISATIONAL CULTURE

1 Discuss which of the five channels you feel are the most important.
2 Create a list of the factors most important in creating a 'positive work environment' based on the information given here.
3 Select a leisure organisation you are familiar with and try to describe its organisational culture or working environment.
4 What sort of organisational culture and management style will be needed for organisers of the London Olympic Games in 2012?

Remuneration and incentives

Remuneration and incentives are terms for the ways in which people are rewarded for their work. They are part of the reward system that leisure organisations operate, the idea being that payment is based on 'merit'.

You will need to understand the difference between a variety of monetary rewards including:

- Salaries and wages
- Piece rates
- Performance-related pay
- Profit-related pay
- Bonuses.

All these methods are used in the leisure industry, in one way or another, and although money is not always the top motivator, it certainly is an essential one. How people are paid and the rates they are paid are crucial to staff retention. If a member of staff feels overworked, undervalued and underpaid they will soon try to move to better conditions, creating a staff turnover problem for the organisation.

Many factors can determine the level of remuneration – age, length of service, loyalty, responsibility, qualifications and skills. As many factors determine levels of incentives paid – meeting (or exceeding) of targets, speed of work, customer satisfaction, return on investment, etc.

The method of payment chosen by an employer can greatly influence the labour force's attitudes and work practices.

Salaries and wages

Higher salaries tend to be paid to more senior staff and are fixed at an annual rate, so even if a supervisor works much longer hours, they will not receive any additional money. Wages are more commonly paid to hourly rate staff and paid weekly, either by cheque, cash or automatic bank transfer. The Government sets a national minimum wage (hourly rate) which is £5.05 per hour for workers aged 22 and over (2005).

Deductions are made to all payments to cover such things as income tax, pension contributions, national insurance, so although a salary or wage in a contract or job advert may look attractive, by the time deductions are taken off, the net amount will be significantly less.

A regular wage or salary offers stability and disposable income for spending, once bills are paid.

Piece rates

These are rates of pay for completion of a job, such as clearing a stadium of litter after a match. A contract is drawn up specifying what has to be done and a price agreed. The operator has to decide what tools and staffing will be required to complete the job. This style of payment is increasingly uncommon.

Performance-related pay

This is much more common amongst leisure operators. The principle of performance-related pay requires a judgement to be made of what is a fair and normal performance. However, a higher rate can be paid for better than average performance within a working period. This produces a mutually beneficial situation, so that if an employee is motivated to earn more, he or she can produce work of a particularly high quality and be rewarded for it.

Increasingly, groups and teams work together in a 'shift' and the reward is determined by the team's efforts. Sometimes smaller leisure companies may make a one-off payment to individuals if they feel they need to show appreciation for special work done, evidence of quick action in an emergency or the saving of costs.

Profit-related pay

This payment method follows on from the performance-related pay principle. It refers to when a portion of the organisation's profits are passed on to staff. Profit-related pay is usually linked to performance targets and can only apply to private sector leisure operators, not public or voluntary organisations who tend to provide a service and reinvest any profits.

Profit-related payments are sometimes supplementary to normal salary and wages systems.

Some sales teams are paid a basic salary and expected to make it up through 'commission' on sales.

Bonuses

In the leisure industry these can vary from an annual performance bonus, in the thousands of pounds for directors, down to an extra few pounds at Christmas for lower paid staff. Nonetheless, they are always seen as valuable and sometimes to be expected. Many annual bonuses are profit-related. Perks are usually bonuses in the form of additional goods or privileges given to staff. These can be very valuable, such as a discount on certain purchases, a subsidised canteen, or the ability to buy overstock at reduced prices. Others include:

- Uniforms
- Car allowances or loans
- Gifts
- Free access to events
- Prize draws.

activity

WHICH INCENTIVES?

Imagine you are a new small leisure company about to employ 10 staff for a season as mountain bike instructors. How would you pay them? What bonuses would you promise? What incentives might be appropriate?

Topic 8 The law and discrimination

All employers in the leisure industry must understand and apply a number of pieces of legislation when they are employing staff. You need to understand the key issues and underpinning principles of the legislation because they often have far-reaching implications for both employees and employers if either are guilty of non-compliance.

In this topic you will focus on laws that are in place to prevent discrimination – the unfair treatment of employees or potential employees. Four Acts of Parliament for consideration are:

- Sexual discrimination
- Equal pay
- Race relations
- Disability discrimination.

These acts were passed to prevent unscrupulous employers exploiting or discriminating against individuals or groups of people in working contexts. In a modern multi-cultural society with diverse leisure customers, knowledge of the main issues can be crucial for staff working in the leisure industry.

In your assessment for this unit you will be asked to analyse and evaluate case studies and scenarios. It would be particularly useful if, while you are studying this unit, you build up some case studies of your own to help give you practice material.

The principles of the discrimination acts are very similar and you will find commonality between the four we will consider, which should help reinforce your understanding. You may also find that some European legislation applies to UK law, for example, with some aspects of equal pay.

Sexual discrimination

This term means being treated unfairly (discriminated against) on the basis of gender. The UK has a long history of women fighting for their rights and you could argue whether an equal basis has been achieved today. There are many male-dominated societies and work environments around the world where progress towards equality is still very slow.

In the UK, legislation is still required to ensure that the rights of workers on the basis of their sex are not breached. The leisure industry is covered by this just as other sectors of the economy and society.

The Sex Discrimination Act of 1995 is the cornerstone of this legislation, but it has its roots in legislation which was introduced in the 1970s. It covers more than employment, but this will be the focus for you. Much legislation has been put in place since the late 1990s to ensure that part-time staff are also protected. The typical circumstances in which legislation might apply for pre-employment would be to prevent discrimination in:

- The advertising of posts
- Recruitment
- Job interviews.

During employment it could be applied to prevent discrimination in situations of:

- Training
- Promotion
- Dismissal
- Harassment.

Discrimination can happen in three ways:

1. **Direct discrimination** – treating someone less favourably on the basis of their sex or sexual orientation. For example, in the leisure industry not employing a woman for a post because the employer thought she was too weak for physical tasks in a gym would be discriminatory.
2. **Indirect discrimination** – where less favourable treatment is less obvious sometimes in more insidious conditions. These types of cases require evidence such as discriminatory clauses attached to a job contract preventing one sex from applying, perhaps by setting an age range which coincides with the ages women normally take breaks to have a family.
3. **Victimisation** – this occurs where an employee is treated less favourably because they have made allegations of discrimination or are making a claim against an employer on some other grounds.

activity

JUDGING DISCRIMINATION

What questions would you ask in order to make a decision on each of these cases?

- An older couple (both aged 62), Mr and Mrs James, wished to go swimming at their local pool which had a policy of allowing those over state pension age to use the pool for free. Mrs James got in for free while her husband had to pay £2.
- A female lifeguard was dismissed by her local authority as they felt she could no longer do her job after becoming pregnant.
- A shift system in a swimming pool that puts pressure on single-parent mothers.
- Refusing a job share for two receptionists at a theme park.
- Requiring married working staff with children to move areas and work in a different sports shop.

To make a claim on the grounds of discrimination an 'industrial tribunal' must be used. The claim must be made within three months of the alleged incident. If a claim is successful the tribunal will declare it upheld and make recommendations as to what should happen. Forms of compensation might include being paid for lost income, reinstatement or perhaps a damages payment to cover any physical injuries or emotional discomfort.

Equal pay

It is important for employee relations that people working in the leisure industry get along and are treated fairly. Wages are often a very apparent source of friction and disputes. The leisure industry has to adhere to general legislation which covers all sectors of industry.

The Equal Pay Act was originally brought out in 1970 to discourage discrimination on pay for different sexes. It works through the contract system, requiring a clause which says that, unless exceptional circumstances apply, men and women doing the same job, equivalent work or work of equal value, should have the same terms and conditions, including the same rate of pay.

Examples would include female chefs in a restaurant who should be paid the same as male chefs if they produce the same food or meals.

Work deemed equivalent should receive the same rate of pay (someone coaching one type of sport in a sports centre compared to another coach at the same level, but in another sport). A job evaluation exercise would need to be undertaken to verify work of equal value.

You need to remember that sometimes there are less obvious reasons which justify a difference in pay, such as seniority, level of qualification, degrees of responsibility and 'red circling', where an employee may have had to step down a level (in a reshuffle), but is allowed to keep previous conditions and rate of pay.

Race relations

In a multicultural society, race relations are very important. The extent of ethnic and cultural diversity in the UK makes this area even more significant. Unfortunately, the media often report stories of racial tension and hatred. The leisure industry is covered, along with everywhere else, by general legislation that helps to provide some level of control and prescribe standards that employers must adhere to.

Racial discrimination is covered by the 1976 Race Relations Act and its principles are very similar to the Sex Discrimination Act – including similar types of discrimination (direct, indirect and victimisation). Sometimes however, segregation can occur, where groups are treated the same and fairly but work separately on different roles. In a clothing factory, for example, female seamstresses of one particular nationality might work separately from packers of another. The legislation covers situations inside and outside of the workplace so that pay and holidays are taken into account.

Anonymous job applications suggested to beat racial prejudice

City council guilty of discrimination

French Muslims face job discrimination

Trust to promote racial equality

The term 'race' is broader than you might think because it includes differences in race, colour, nationality, and ethnic origins (but not religion). Racial discrimination can occur directly in the leisure industry when taunts and threats or disparaging comments are made at work or during sports matches.

Indirect discrimination can occur at work when an employer attaches a requirement for an 'English-speaking person' to an advert, for no practical reason.

activity

IN THE NEWS

Over the period of a week, carry out your own research in the national newspapers to identify cases of racial discrimination. Build up a scrapbook of these to further your learning.

Disability discrimination

Disability discrimination is the newest area to be covered by legislation, which only came into force in 1995. This has placed an enormous amount of pressure on leisure operators because it often requires them to redesign their premises (for access), reconsider who they employ and be careful of the grounds they might use for dismissal in the case of a disabled employee. Many pressure groups feel that the provision in the legislation is not as far-reaching as the other discrimination legislation, but with amendments in 2000, there is a clear improvement for disabled people at work and those who are active in sport.

You need to be clear about what a disability means – it is 'any physical or mental impairment, which has a substantially long-term adverse affect on a person's ability to carry out normal day-to-day activities'. Some conditions which are treatable with artificial aids or drugs come under the act, so employers in the leisure industry must avoid discriminating against people with artificial limbs, hearing aids and epilepsy.

Once a disability is highlighted, an employer must take care to provide for a member of staff who is affected by a limitation on any of the following:

- mobility
- manual dexterity
- speech, hearing, eyesight
- confidence
- physical co-ordination
- ability to lift and carry normal objects
- ability to concentrate, learn or understand
- ability to perceive danger.

A leisure employer must not treat a disabled applicant 'less favourably'. If a disabled applicant is clearly not going to be able to do the job advertised, then non-selection would be acceptable. However, if with some reasonable adjustments it might be possible to accommodate the person (for example, with the provision of a Braille keyboard) the disabled applicant might be able to fill the post. The key challenge is judging how far the 'reasonable adjustments' have to go.

Cases of unfair treatment also have to be referred to an Industrial Tribunal.

In the UK there are government-supported organisations to help monitor that equality is ensured. They are:

- The Commission for Racial Equality. Their mission statement reads: 'We work for a just and integrated society, where diversity is valued. We use both persuasion and our powers under the law to give everyone an equal chance to live free from fear, discrimination, prejudice and racism.'
- The Equal Opportunities Commission. Their mission statement reads: 'The Equal Opportunities Commission is working to eliminate sex discrimination in Britain today. If men and women had equal opportunities things would be different. We're working on it.' If you wish to visit their websites you can build up further information and investigate their activities in more depth. The websites are: www.cre.gov.uk and www.eoc.gov.uk.
- Disability Rights Commission. Their stated goal is: 'A society where all disabled people can participate fully as equal citizens.' Further information on disability rights can be found via the website: www.drc-gb.org/.

Tanni Grey-Thompson, Britain's most successful Paralympic athlete

activity

UNDERSTANDING DISCRIMINATION

1. **Create a set of five guidelines on discrimination in its various forms for leisure employers who run amusement arcades.**
2. **Make a list of five adjustments to accommodate disabled people in and around leisure premises that you are familiar with.**

Case study

Disabled discrimination results in compensation

A Barnsley mother has successfully fought a small case of discrimination on behalf of her Down Syndrome son. He was not permitted to take group swimming lessons with others, because she was not allowed to accompany him initially to give support and confidence. Compensation was paid and the boy joined the swimming group. The leisure company had to review its disability policy and agree to train staff to ASA level 2 which covers teaching disabled swimmers.

Topic 9 The law and working conditions

The legislation in this section focuses more on working conditions and protection of staff in employment. As before, you only need to understand key requirements of the legislation, but you do need to explore the implications and know what legislation might apply to different situations. As with the previous topics, you need to show that you understand the terminology used and can reflect this in your test answers. The four areas of legislation are:

- **Working time regulations**
- **The employment of children**
- **Health and safety at work**
- **Child protection**

All of these have keys applications and implications for leisure operators and employees. You may even have some experiences of your own that you can recall to help your understanding.

The information contained in this topic and Topic 8 may prove valuable as you look to enter into the industry. It will help to ensure you know your rights and understand your options if treated unfairly.

You may also be able to build up a picture of what is expected of you as a leisure employee, with regard to others, your employer and your job.

Working time regulations

The current legislation covering the hours we work and the length of time we do not work was introduced in 1998 and stems from European regulations, which apply to all EU members. They were brought in to prevent exploitation and a long hours culture, which many people had to endure, and which many people in the UK seem unable to avoid.

This can be the case in many leisure occupations, especially at busy times of the season, peak operating times or amongst those who are trying to impress management or meet targets by working longer and harder. Sometimes however, this can be counter-productive due to increased tiredness and errors. The globalisation of the leisure industry puts pressure on suppliers of leisure goods worldwide because there is always someone working in a particular time zone.

While London sleeps ...

Legislation exists to protect, as well as guide, employees at work as to what is acceptable in both their work and break patterns. Employees covered by legislation are:

✔ Anyone who has a contract of employment, is paid a regular salary, and works for an organisation, business or individual. The usual arrangement is that an employer provides the worker with work, controls when and how the work is done, supplies them with tools and other equipment, and pays tax and National Insurance contributions. This includes part-time and temporary workers and the majority of agency workers and freelancers. The legislation also covers an employee doing in-house training or a trainee on work experience. A 'young worker' is someone who is above the minimum school leaving age but under 18, where special legislation applies (covered in Unit 2).

Some aspects of employment are not covered, such as:

✗ Those who are self-employed

✗ Those running their own business

✗ Some freelancers working for different clients and customers.

This could represent a large portion of leisure industry workers, like freelance exercise instructors or coaches, sole traders, casual staff at a pool or leisure centre.

Certain leisure industry workers are not subject to the working time regulations because they are covered by sector-specific provisions. These are:

- Sea transport, as covered by the Seafarers' Directive (1999/63/EC) for those on Ferries and Cruise ships.
- Mobile workers on inland waterways and lake transport, such as barges and small pleasure steamers.
- Air transport, as covered by the Aviation Directive (2000/79/EC). This directive affects all mobile workers in commercial air transport (both flight crew and cabin crew).

Other workers are only subject to certain provisions of these regulations. These are:

- Mobile workers in road transport, as covered by the Road Transport Directive (2002/15/EC). This Directive affects EU drivers' hours, such as coach drivers, members of the vehicle crew and any others who form part of the travelling staff.

The armed forces, the police and emergency services who serve the leisure industry are outside the scope of the regulations in certain circumstances.

In August 2003, the working time regulations were extended to cover the following sectors:

- Workers in air transport, other than those covered by the Aviation Directive.
- All workers in rail transport.
- Workers in road transport, other than those subject to the Road Transport Directive.

You can see from this pattern of coverage that some services are considered essential and cannot therefore be tied down by regulations.

Cabin crew are exempt from working time regulations.

activity

INVESTIGATING WORKING TIME REGULATIONS

1 What reasons do you think governments have for bringing in working time regulations?

2 Workers need to have limits applied to working hours in many situations in the leisure industry. Discuss what the ideal upper limits should be for the hours worked in the week for
- lifeguards
- outdoor pursuits leaders
- instructors
- security guards at a theme park
- bar staff in a night club.

The legislation goes further than just regulating working time. It covers:

- Health checks
- Holiday entitlements
- Breaks while at work
- Annual holiday pay.

activity

GUESS THE ENTITLEMENTS

1 Do you agree that workers should have regular health checks? How frequently should this be done?

2 What holiday entitlements should staff have every year in your opinion (how many days)?

3 What would you consider was reasonable in terms of breaks during an eight-hour work period?

Once you have made your decisions and discussed these with classmates visit the DTI website (www.dti.gov.uk) or another detailing working time regulations to find out what the statutory regulations recommend and assess how close you were in your estimates.

The employment of children

The law says that children may work, but only to the extent that their health, development and education are not put at risk. The type of work that a young person may do depends on age, but also what regional laws apply (these are called local authority byelaws). Most would allow paper-rounds or light work on a farm, for example. The normal minimum age is thirteen, although in the leisure industry

Paper-rounds are regarded as light work.

younger children may work in entertainment, sport and modelling. In general, those over the age of thirteen can do light work in the leisure industry. This might include work in:

- a café
- a hairdressing salon
- a hotel
- riding stables.

The first official school leaving age is after Year 11, at which point students may obtain a National Insurance number and be employed. Children of this age are still prohibited from working in many areas of leisure, such as:

- Discos
- Cinemas
- Nightclubs
- Pubs
- Betting shops
- Hotel kitchens
- Fairgrounds.

Can you think why this is the case?

Working time regulations also exist for children, which employers must observe. This too is dependent upon age, but the most common rules are:

- All days – no work before 7am or after 7pm.
- School days – no more than two hours per day or 12 per week.
- Saturdays allow the most time for those aged under 15 who can work up to five hours paid employment and up to eight hours for those over 15.
- Sundays are limited to two hours paid employment.
- School holidays are set at the Saturday rates with a maximum of 25 hours per week for under 15 years old and 35 for over 15 years old (paid employment).

Break time regulations apply also, with one hour in five to be a rest period.

Employers must also observe health and safety regulations (which we shall cover in more detail later), but in the case of young people who may not be able to perceive the dangers so readily, be inexperienced or act immaturely, special care is needed when making risk assessments.

Leisure industry employers who wish to employ young people must apply to the local authority for a permit and have parents or guardians sign it.

For those working in the leisure industry between the ages of 16 and 18 (adulthood) additional considerations are made, the most notable being:

- Maximum 8-hour working days or a 40-hour week, with set breaks.
- Entitlement to two days off per week.
- Usually no night work, but in the leisure industry they are sometimes allowed to work for cultural, artistic, sporting or advertising reasons. Health and capability checks need to be made if night work is permitted.

Enforcement of these regulations and guidelines mainly rests with local authorities, though the Health and Safety Executive (www.hse.gov.uk) can be contacted for such matters.

activity

REASONABLE WORK

1. **16- and 17-year-olds are entitled to a national minimum wage. Find out what the current rate is. Also, try to find out if 18-year-olds with two years experience are entitled to redundancy payments, if a firm wishes to pay them off.**
2. **What is wrong with the following scenario?** A 15-year-old boy, about to finish school, works in an amusement arcade as a helper. He frequently handles money and moves machines in and out at the beginning and end of his shift. The owner leaves him alone while he has his dinner. He starts at 6pm and often locks up at closing time at 11pm if it is a quiet night. He has a half-an-hour break in the middle of the evening and gets paid £2.90 per hour.

Health and safety at work

This is a massive area of study, which you will have covered in greater depth in Units 2 and 4. In this section you will look at a range of legislation and cases most applicable to the leisure industry.

Legislation covers many aspects of leisure operations and locations – anywhere there are people and equipment. Risk assessment is the underpinning process which helps to predict potential hazards and take action to minimise or eliminate those hazards that could harm people. All staff have a 'duty of care' for others, whether they be colleagues or customers. If a problem is spotted, it needs recording and appropriate action taken. The bigger the danger, the faster and greater the measures needed to prevent it happening.

Risk assessments have six stages, applicable to any situation:

1 Identifying what represents a hazard, such as scaffolding, spillages, boxes in passageways.
2 Identifying groups of people who might be affected such as children, older people, customers.
3 Calculating the likelihood of the hazard occurring. This is done using an appropriate scale.
4 Evaluating how severe the hazard might be if it did happen, again using a scale.
5 Evaluating the risk by bringing together the two scales.
- Roof collapse – low likelihood, high severity.
- Bruises at a football match – high likelihood, medium severity.

6 Measures to minimise risk are then decided.
- Roof collapse – prescribe an annual engineers' check
- Bruises – provide first aiders, ice packs and medical treatment, referees briefed to keep control of the game, players required to wear shin guards.

European legislation has been made in Brussels since 1992 so you should find risks being minimised in many of the EU countries' leisure venues, such as Disneyland Paris or Port Aventura. However, in poorer EU countries the level of spending on health and safety may not be the same as in the UK, so there are many inconsistencies across the member states. EU legislation is meant to broadly cover staff at work in the following leisure contexts:

- Using visual display units (VDUs) – Display Screen Equipment such as computers or booking screens.
- In any place of work – Workplace Regulations apply to gyms, pools, theme parks and shops.
- Handling heavy goods – Manual Handling Operations, such as trampolines, table tennis tables and bouncy castles.
- Using specialist equipment such as plant and machinery – Provision and use of work equipment.
- Where staff require protective clothing, such as masks, overalls, helmets and gloves.

Case study: Girl saved from drowning

A newly installed safety system in Bangor pool saved a girl's life, when it spotted her unconscious at the bottom of the pool in four metres of water. Lifeguards were alerted by pager and dived in to save her. The system is called Poseidon and uses motion and sound-activated cameras to check underwater activities. There are fewer than 10 installed at the moment across the country, but with this level of safety cover they will surely become more popular.

In the UK we have had legislation developed over a number of years, which cover general leisure situations, such as:

1974 Health and Safety At Work Act – to cover all contexts.

1981 First Aid Regulations – to cover accidents at work.

1984 Occupiers Liability Act – to cover the renting or occupying of buildings.

1994 Control of Substances Hazardous to Health (COSHH) – to cover chemicals.

1995 Reporting of Injuries, Diseases and Dangerous Occurrences Regulations (RIDDOR) – to cover skin problems, contagious airborne diseases and accidents or near misses.

One final set of regulations apply to more specific situations in the leisure industry, some of which are featured below:

1968 Trades Description Act – Helps cover aspects of goods being used by consumers, making sure that they are fit for purpose and described accurately. Lifetime guarantees that are not honoured or a DIY tool which could not do the job it was advertised to do are examples of breaches.

1975 Safety at Sports Grounds – Covers aspects such as exits and entrances, seating arrangements, evacuation procedures and fire precautions at leisure venues. Venues covered would be stadiums, athletic tracks, arenas or temporary stands at events. These venues have to apply for permits.

1984 Data Protection Act – Protects the public from organisations revealing or selling personal details to other companies.

1987 Fire Safety and Safety at Places of Sport Act – Specific regulations brought in after several stadium fires and the need to seat and evacuate people effectively.

1990 Food Safety Act – Set up to maintain hygiene standards at many canteens and cafés attached to leisure venues.

1996 Adventure Activities Regulations – Brought out after many accidents to people on outdoor activities courses at commercial centres using poorly qualified and inexperienced staff.

2000 Disability Discrimination Act 1995 and 2000 – Designed to improve access to all facilities, but particularly for leisure venues.

activity

LEGISLATION IN THE NEWS

Carry out some further research to identify examples in newspapers which the above legislation covers and give two examples from the list of Acts.

Child protection

The final legislation worth knowing about is more recent than some, but was thought necessary due to more cases being uncovered through sport, leisure and the arrival of the internet. Child protection has become a big issue in recent times. There are cases of sports coaches abusing children while they are training, or youth leaders taking advantage of children. The Children's Act of 1989 began the process of protecting children. Staff working with young people in the leisure industry now have to obtain police clearance (a CRB check). Organisations hosting young children, such as at summer camps or nurseries, must apply for registration and have qualified staff. Many organisations exist to support young people who have been abused or who are at risk, like the NSPCC and Childline.

Abuse can take many forms:

- Physical – squeezing or hitting
- Sexual – fondling
- Emotional – lack of affection, taunting
- Neglect – failing to provide nutrition or care.

Organisations are advised to have proper supervision in place, a system of checks, training for staff and guidelines for staff and children to follow.

activity

... AT A SWIMMING POOL

Produce some guidelines for swimming coaches to follow:

1. **How to supervise children on the poolside.**
2. **How to check children are not showing signs of abuse.**
3. **Create a sequence that staff could follow if they suspected a colleague of abusing children.**

industry **focus**

The industry focus for this unit is a young leisure centre worker called Tanya who has first-hand experience of many of the employment practices in a leisure centre in London. She was recently made a permanent member of staff having had casual status before.

The centre is Brentford Fountain in Hounslow Borough, which offers a fairly typical picture of a local authority leisure centre, with activities and classes for all ages:

- Pool sessions
- A play/party centre for small children
- Trampolines
- Summer sports camps and courses
- Rackets sports
- Health suite and gym.

The local authority runs several centres, and a leisure card is available for all centres. Prices are affordable and opening times are 7am to 10pm weekdays and 9am to 6pm weekends.

We interviewed Tanya in the summer of 2005 when she had just been made a permanent member of staff.

Her job title is 'Receptionist'. Her duties are quite diverse as you can see from the following list:

- Controlling admissions and ticket sales
- Dealing with bookings and enquiries
- Arranging hire and sale of equipment and merchandise
- Accounting for monies taken
- Operating cash tills and other sales equipment
- Controlling lost property and valuables left for safe-keeping
- Undertaking clerical and other duties instructed by the manager
- Keeping the reception area tidy
- Promoting the Centre's image
- Helping to host functions, if required.

Her working pattern before her new permanent status was:

- Casual: she had to book shifts for every two weeks, with a limit of 48 hours per week maximum (regularly, but not guaranteed).

Now she works:

- Full-time, permanent: Working a four-week rota, averaging 36 hours per week.

Tanya, Leisure Centre Worker

Brentford Fountain, Hounslow Borough, London

Q How do others at the Centre work?

The majority hold permanent positions, but the Centre keeps plenty of casuals on the books, on call, so that all shifts can be covered during periods of sickness, annual leave, etc.

Q What type of contracts was used? What do others have?

One contract applies to core staff and a different one for non-core.

Q Was your job advertised and how did you get it?

The job was advertised (on posters) in the Centre and also in the local newspapers. Internal and external ads appeared at the same time.

Q How did you originally get the work there?

I knew people who worked at the Centre on a casual basis and so I applied for casual work.

Q Was there an induction process?

To some extent. I shadowed people working the shift for an indefinite period, until the manager was confident that I could do the job. (Roughly two weeks).

Q What does induction consist of?

It takes staff through Centre processes and health and safety procedures.

Q Can you say what your break entitlements, hours, annual leave and absence procedures are?

We are allowed half-an-hour break on a single shift. We have an annual leave of 23 days, calculated by hours worked. The absence procedure is to call the line manager before my shift starts to report sickness or other absence. Too many absences results in disciplinary measures.

Q What notice period do you have?

As a full-time employee this is one month.

Q Do you have appraisals? What goes into them?

The first is a probationary appraisal after three months with my line manager to discuss strengths and weaknesses. After that, training and development issues as well as performance might be discussed.

Q What are your development and training schemes or opportunities?

When your appraisal is done, you can request any courses that will benefit your work, for example, first aid training or life saving. There are also compulsory courses such as child protection and disability awareness.

Q What is the quality of the work environment like?

The Centre is due for refurbishment and upgrading, but is currently satisfactory.

Q What sort of reward scheme do you have – bonuses, incentives, discounts, perks?

Staff can use the Centre's facilities for free. Overtime offers a higher rate of pay.

Q How do they make you aware of disability, equal opportunities, race and sex discrimination legislation?

It is in the information pack when you start your job, but it is also reinforced through policies at work and sending you on courses.

Q Is there any child protection training or awareness?

Staff undergo a criminal records police check before commencing work. The Centre does not allow any photos or videos to be taken, the public are made aware of these policies through posters. In reception we have photos of people barred from using the Centre so that the staff do not accidentally admit anyone who should not be there. There is also a compulsory course that all staff must attend.

Q How are Health and Safety regulations covered?

There is a staff handbook on site. Staff are also informed in writing and talked through the procedures.

How Unit 5 is assessed

Unit 5 is externally assessed. The format will usually be a $1\frac{1}{2}$ hour written exam, using a question and answer style in a booklet format provided by the awarding body. Exams are usually set for January and/or June.

You can obtain more specific and up-to-date information on the exam from the Edexcel website: **www.edexcel.org.uk**, your tutor, school or college examination office.

The exam will use case studies covering the learning outcomes of the unit – employment law, practices and issues, recruitment, selection and motivation of staff.

You will need to be able to show that you could apply the knowledge on the subject that you have been studying in a practical way.

To prepare for your assessment you should create a revision portfolio to cover each of the learning and assessment outcomes so that you can refer to it regularly, and gradually cover all your likely needs for the assessment.

Sections should correspond to the following:

5.1 Employment practices in leisure

These differ greatly in leisure, depending on the employer and contract. You need to keep records which show how employees work in the following contexts:

- Part-time
- Job share
- Full-time
- Self-employment
- Casual and temporary work
- Voluntary
- Apprenticeships and training programmes

Under contracts, try to keep material for:

- Permanent
- Fixed-term
- Temporary
- Seasonal.

5.2 Recruitment and selection of staff in leisure

You need to understand the purpose, processes and importance of these in the leisure industry. So research and gather information on the following to help you become more familiar with these and understand the stage at which they are applied:

- Job analysis
- Job description
- Person specifications
- Recruitment advertising
- Methods of application
- Short-listing
- Interviewing
- Appointment.

5.3 Employment issues in leisure

You need to build up your knowledge of general working practices and more specifically the issues they sometimes raise, covered by the following:

- Induction processes
- Hours of work including flexible working practices
- Shift work
- Scheduled breaks
- Annual leave entitlements
- Absenteeism
- Sick pay
- Maternity, paternity and adoption benefits
- Notice periods
- Disciplinary and grievance procedures
- Redundancy and redeployment
- Appraisals
- Management style.

5.5 Employment law

You are not expected to be a legal expert, but you do need to be able to identify key legislation that might apply in different leisure situations. Your understanding of the implications will also be tested. As a minimum, collate materials for revision on the following:

- Sex discrimination
- Equal pay
- Race relations
- Working time regulations
- Employment of children
- Health and safety at work
- Disability discrimination
- Child protection.

5.4 Motivating staff in leisure

You will need to have materials on methods of motivation and you will also have to understand when and how these might be applied. Materials can be grouped under the following headings (some examples are included to guide you):

1. Management methods of motivation – style, target setting, awards and recognition systems, appraisals team-working approaches, job rotation and enlargement.
2. Staff development and training – on- and off-the-job types, courses, talks and promotion activities.
3. Remuneration and incentives – salaries and wages, piece rates, performance- and profit-related pay, bonuses and perks.

Guidance on collecting your materials, revising and preparing for the exam

1. Try to find some short case studies (which are similar to the ones the test may use) on the topics in the 'what you need to learn sections'. The media are a good source.
2. Practise understanding and analysing what is being described, so that you could readily pick out key points.
3. Make up and try out simple test questions on a partner to see how knowledgeable you both are.
4. Familiarise yourself with (or ask your teacher about) the test format and structure.
5. Make sure you have a strategy for tackling the paper – how much time to spend on each section and understanding the rules.
6. Know and understand the appropriate terminology, for this goes a long way to convincing the examiner that you do know what you are talking about.

This is a challenging unit in which you will research a topic of your own choosing. If done well, it should be of great value to those of you going on to either higher education or moving directly into the leisure industry.

This unit is best taken towards the end of your programme so that the full amount of your knowledge and understanding of the diversity of leisure can be used to complete your study. The research project will require you to work fairly independently. When covering the various issues to consider, however, there is plenty of opportunity for you to work in groups and share ideas.

Because of the diversity of the leisure industry, you can be sure of a good choice of subjects. Topics 2–7 give examples of suitable research topics or issues. While the scope is broad, you may choose something not outlined in this unit, from your teacher, class discussion, or your own reading. An example not covered in the unit is the issue of security at large events and a popular research project might look at the changes since September 2001. This unit provides you with the prospect of looking more closely at an area that already interests you, or the chance to study a topic which you have no previous knowledge about. In the course of this unit we shall try to give you enough information about an issue to make your mind up whether you want to pursue it further.

Simply being aware of each issue covered will be of benefit to you in the future. These are the topics that are discussed every day by leisure industry professionals.

As well as the issues themselves, this unit covers the methods for researching and presenting your project. Leisure research usually aims to uncover patterns of behaviour and can be used to explain them. It can also be used to evaluate events and shape policy. The purpose of research can be to find the best solution to a practical problem, or to test whether what is currently being done is valid. Research is regularly started before large projects are undertaken or management decisions are about to be made, so that the findings will 'inform decisions', such as a new policy or programme for a centre.

Topics 1 and 8 will help you with the structure of your project, but ultimately you have to choose the subject, identify the problem, devise the title, decide on what methods of research to use, carry it out and analyse the information gathered.

Unit 6

Current Issues in Leisure

6.1 Issues in leisure

Topic 1	Lifestyle and health	120
Topic 2	Equality, diversity and inclusion	126
Topic 3	Sex, gender and race	130
Topic 4	Events, festivals and traditions	136
Topic 5	Government and policy in leisure	140
Topic 6	The media and commercial issues	146

6.2 Leisure research project

Topic 7	Selecting and planning a research project	152
Topic 8	Final planning and writing of your research proposal	158
Industry focus		161
How Unit 6 is assessed		163

Topic 1 Lifestyle and health

In this and the following five topics you will get the chance to think about certain issues in more depth. Hopefully you will find an issue in which you can see some potential for your own work. In each of the topics some background will be given, and key issues will be signposted for you to explore further or take as themes for your research. The material will not be sufficient to complete your project, but enough to get you started, so additional reading and research will be needed.

In this first topic you will explore lifestyle and health-related issues:

- **Obesity**
- **Heart disease**
- **Drug dependency**
- **Eating disorders**
- **Balancing stress through leisure**
- **Special population leisure needs**
- **Healthy living campaigns.**

Obesity

The first topic you might choose to study in terms of leisure and lifestyle is obesity. Described here are the problems that obesity causes, but you might also research some of the remedies that active leisure provides.

Obesity is normally found in men when their body fat level exceeds 25 per cent. For women the level is 30 per cent. Obese levels of body fat increase the risk of contracting diseases and put many of the vital organs and body systems under pressure. It is a particularly important cause of heart disease.

For those with a tendency for putting on weight, it can sometimes be attributed to hereditary reasons (genetics), but also a lack of exercise and poor diet.

Mental and emotional health plays an important part in how healthy we are too. For many people who are obese, the challenge is often to try and overcome eating patterns and disorders that cause problems. It often comes down to will-power.

Measuring body fat can sometimes have the effect of persuading obese people to change their lifestyle habits. Five stages to this process have been suggested by experts:

The stages of transforming health and well-being

Pre-contemplation – getting some professional input about the condition

▼

Contemplation – thinking about how the change will affect one's life

▼

Preparation – making a positive move by assessing one's current state and making plans for a new approach

▼

Action – begin new activity and monitor progress

▼

Maintenance – plan how to continue

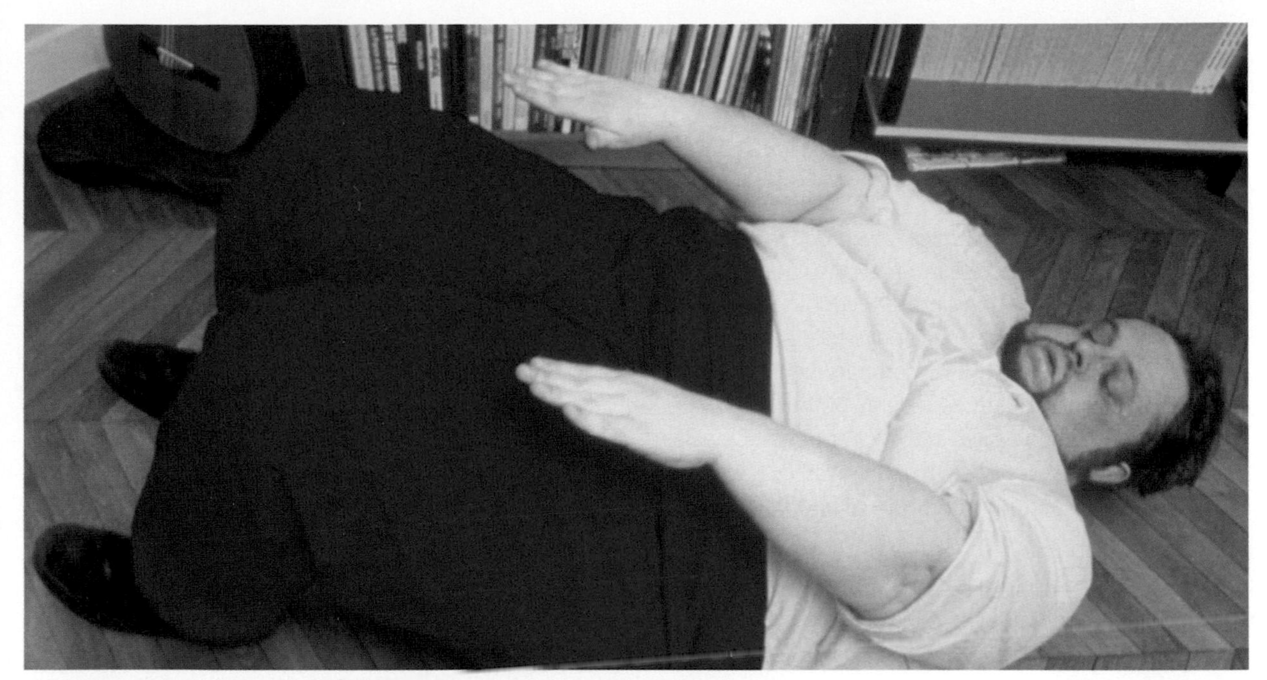

A programme of exercise and diet are necessary to combat obesity.

Obesity is an increasingly worrying problem in society as big a problem as smoking or drinking – which threatens to develop into an epidemic of startling proportions.

Statistics show that people are actually more successful at giving up smoking and reducing their drinking, than losing weight. Experts put this down to the emphasis on 'negative change goals' which means eating fewer dairy products or snacks, but without implementing 'positive change goals', such as eating healthily and exercising as an alternative.

Obese people are not always fully aware of calorific intake (levels of energy), or how much energy they need to expend to balance this. High intakes and low outputs will cause weight problems. To combat weight gain and the onset of obesity a programme of exercise and diet need to be combined.

Amongst the reasons for obesity (particularly in the developed world) is the abundance of food on offer alongside manipulative messages from food and drinks companies promoting relationships between happiness and consumption.

Consider the following questions:

- How effective are leisure providers and activities at combating this problem?
- What incentives are there for leisure operators to provide resources to help tackle obesity?
- How far does the media highlight the need for people to change their lifestyles?
- If the larger share of the solution comes down to an individual's determination, how important is availability of information and easy access to leisure facilities?

activity

TACKLING OBESITY

1. Visit your local leisure centre and identify if there are any programmes or facilities aimed – either directly or indirectly – at helping users tackle serious weight problems.
2. List TV programmes and organisations helping overweight people.

Heart disease

Heart or cardiovascular problems account for nearly half the deaths in America, while in the UK the British Heart Foundation says that heart disease is Britain's most common single cause of premature death.

Since the 1970s various studies have supported the benefit of vigorous exercise in protecting against coronary heart disease, and more recently it has been conclusively demonstrated that physically active people have a reduced risk of coronary heart disease. This can be effective with as little as 30 minutes of moderate intensity physical activity per day, such as walking. Heart disease costs the UK nearly £8 billion each year in lost earnings and formal and informal health care.

According to the British Heart Foundation, Coronary Heart Disease is still the UK's single biggest killer, taking nearly 114,000 lives in 2003. One in five men and one in six women die from it.

These might seem like horrendous statistics, but they are actually an improvement of over 30 per cent in the incidence of heart disease and an improvement of over 25 per cent in the number of deaths. The reasons for this are changes in lifestyle behaviours:

- Not smoking
- Getting regular exercise
- Eating well
- Maintaining a healthy body weight
- Managing stress better.

activity

GET ACTIVE

Active leisure pursuits have a role to play in recovery and prevention. What leisure-related activities do the British Heart Foundation suggest? List your own then visit their website at www.bhf.org.uk to find out what is recommended.

Drug dependency

Many people take their leisure activities very seriously and the most active may compete professionally, requiring peak performances to further careers. But in many instances the pressure to win overcomes a sense of fair play and concern for one's body. As a result some athletes and players take performance-enhancing drugs. Several issues could be explored under this heading both positive and negative. In an overview of each you may find something valuable and of interest to explore for your study in more depth.

Acceptable use of drugs

Herbal remedies can aid recovery from sport injuries or health problems. Thousands of inexpensive herbal remedies are available in a growing market. You might study how these are used in conjunction with active leisure for remedial purposes. More conventional drugs can also be used to help an athlete's recovery or simply to kill pain – allowing them to complete a match, for example. The immediate effects are evident, but the long-term effects of some herbal remedies are less well known.

Negative use of drugs

You are probably more aware of the issues surrounding misuse of drugs. These often attract a great deal of media coverage because accounts of fallen heroes make fascinating news stories. There are some moral and ethical issues surrounding allegations in the press prior to trial. In some cases sportsmen can have their reputation tarnished through sheer media attention before a case has been proven. You might wish to explore this as a topic – do you think the idea of drugs in sports puts people off pursuing a sport competitively? Is the problem more or less widespread than commonly feared?

Drugs are misused in many different ways:

- To boost energy
- To build muscle
- To enhance performance
- To improve stamina.

Athletes who take illegal performance-enhancing drugs (or illegal ergonomic aids) hope that they will not be tested, or that traces of the drug will have left their system before they are tested. Most sports governing bodies spend a lot of money on testing and the resources to do so, and in many sports testing for drugs is performed randomly and unannounced. It is an uphill battle to stay one step ahead of cheats as newer, undetectable drugs are invented. Common banned substances which you may have heard of are:

- Amphetamines, which increase alertness.
- Narcotic analgesics, which increase pain thresholds.
- Beta blockers, which control heart rate and anxiety levels.
- Diuretics, which help weight loss.

Recreational drugs are also a concern in leisure. Rather than for performance enhancement, these drugs are often taken socially.

For information on the steps being taken to combat problems of drugs misuse, you can look at the following organisations:

World Anti-Doping Agency **www.wada-ama.org/en/**

International Association of Athletics Federations **www.iaaf.org/**

Document on UK National Anti-Doping Policy from UK Sport **www.uksport.gov.uk** (This ties into Topic 6 Government and policy)

Drugs in Sport **www.drugsinsport.net/**

activity

THE DRUGS DON'T WORK

Consider the following questions:

- What are the ethical and moral arguments against taking drugs for performance enhancement?
- Which performers have been found out and what were the consequences for the image of their sport as well as the individual?
- What message do drugs scandals give to young people considering entering a sport?
- Why do governing bodies test for drug misuse? Is it effective?

Discuss with a colleague what the difficulties would be in looking at one or more of these areas as part of your research project. Make a list of possible sources and the difficulties you might face.

Diet

The next possible area for research is a healthy diet to support a leisure or sporting lifestyle and the dangers of an unbalanced diet. Few people have a good idea about what constitutes a 'healthy eater'. The basic constituents of any diet are:

- Carbohydrates (mainly found in bread, cereals, potatoes, sugar, pastry, sweets).
- Proteins (mainly found in meat, eggs, milk and cheese).
- Fats (mainly found in dairy products, meat, processed foods).
- Vitamins (Vitamins A, D, E and K found mainly in fatty foods, Vitamin C found mainly in fruit, vegetables and potatoes, Vitamin B complex found in meat).
- Minerals (iron, calcium, sodium, potassium).
- Water.

Food provides the body with energy for a number of tasks such as temperature control, building tissues, chemical reactions, and muscle movements. The energy from food is usually measured in 'calories'. Each gram of fat contains about twice the calories of a similar quantity of carbohydrate.

As a springboard for a topic in this area you might consider researching a healthy diet for mild recreational activities compared to those of Olympic athletes. You might consider assessing the diets of people who perform no active leisure. Recent documentaries have focused on how unhealthy fast food outlets and school dinners are.

activity

ARE YOU LOVIN' IT?

1 How ethically responsible do you think it is to build a fast food outlet next to a leisure centre?
2 How effective or genuine are examples of fast food chains giving something back to the community in terms of leisure activities? Look at McDonald's campaigns to promote active lifestyles under the 'Be Active' section of their website – www.mcdonalds.co.uk/. Were you aware that they sponsor the British Olympic team?

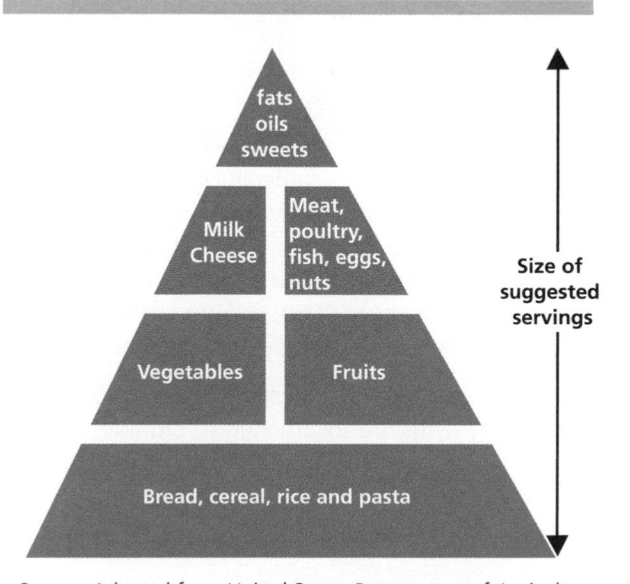

Source: Adapted from United States Department of Agriculture and Health and Human Services

With each area you think about, consider how it relates to the leisure industry, rather than simply being a study into health.

Eating disorders

Many young women fall prey to the image sold in glossy magazines and adverts of 'the perfect body'. Attempts to realise such images – and psychiatric disorders – lead to different kinds of eating disorders. The most common is Anorexia nervosa – where people have a distorted view of how fat they are and continue to see themselves as fat when they are in fact painfully thin. Bulimia is another 'thin fixation' which involves a ritual of overeating followed by vomiting to keep body weight down.

Dutch cyclist Leontien Zijlaard-van Moorsel (pictured) missed out on the Atlanta Olympics in 1996 as she dealt with anorexia and bulimia. But she overcame the eating disorders to win a gold and bronze medal at the Athens Olympics in 2004, making her the most successful woman in Olympic cycling history.

Do you think the leisure industry has a case to answer here? Many gyms use thin models to promote use of their facilities. Should leisure organisations be more realistic about the types of people who use their services, or is it fair advertising?

Balancing stress through leisure

Many people use leisure activities, both active and passive, to ease stress. Most research studies show that you can change a person's temperament from anxious to calm through physical activity. Whether because of higher self-esteem, enjoyment, an adrenaline rush or company, exercise lifts the spirits.

Although it varies from person to person, stress manifests itself through:

- Changes in skin conditions
- Upset digestion
- Muscular tension
- Faster heart rates
- Disrupted brain patterns and chemical imbalances
- High blood pressure
- Headaches
- Lack of sleep
- Ulcers.

You might be able to make a study of ways in which leisure activities can help relieve stress. Or the types of programmes which are available in leisure time through relaxation techniques or classes. Yoga, Pilates and Reiki are all popular forms of relaxation, provided for at most leisure centres.

Special population leisure needs

Special populations are groups of people who may have a disability of some sort or those who are not able to participate in exactly the same way as able-bodied people. Examples of special populations include senior citizens, ante/post natal women, those with learning disabilities and people with medical conditions such as asthma, arthritis or heart problems. Barriers to participation for these types of people include:

- Access
- Transport
- Suitable facilities
- Trained coaches
- Equipment
- Funding.

There is more inclusion than there used to be due to the role that helpers and volunteers play. You might wish to look at the impact of some organisations in this field:

- Mencap – www.mencap.org.uk
- PAMIS (Profound and Multiple Impairment Service) – no website
- RNIB (Royal National Institute for the Blind) – www.rnib.org
- Sense (UK Deafblind charity) – www.sense.org.uk/.

They have worked hard to help special populations overcome physical, sensory and organisational attitudes. In the past failure to recognise needs meant that the value of active leisure as opposed to therapeutic activities was never fully explored.

Now, with more choice and opportunity for people with disabilities, there is a range of potential study topics for you to consider.

Advances in science have provided many disabled people with prosthetic limbs which enable them to compete at the highest level. The Paralympics has become an important part of the sporting calendar.

This would not be possible without leisure provision for special population groups at grassroots level. Many sports development programmes are aimed at those who are normally excluded.

Accessing the Disability Sports governing bodies' websites should enable you to uncover issues and schemes, proposals and funding aspects which might prove a fruitful study. The English Federation of Disability Sport website is www.efds.net.

In 2005 the country's first Academy for Disability Sport opened in North Tyneside. This would make a great cases study.

Many charitable organisations (as listed above) support special populations and work hard to give them equality of experience in terms of leisure pursuits, such as trips to the seaside, theme park or museums. You might try to identify their worth and evaluate their efforts. You might study the numerous partnership schemes that exist or the work of the British Paralympics Association – www.paralympics.org.uk.

Healthy living campaigns

In recent years many more healthy living campaigns have been launched in order to raise awareness. This is increasingly high up on the Government's agenda and they have backed many campaigns. Local Health Authorities have teamed up with many providers to create local schemes targeted at various groups in the community who are considered to be at risk. Most of the campaigns have had active leisure at their heart, which would give you the opportunity to evaluate one or more of them, either locally or at a national level.

The Department of Health publishes an annual health events calendar which you could consult at www.dh.gov.uk. You might visit the BBC website for an update on their campaigns at www.bbc.co.uk. Weight Watchers UK may also give you some ideas to explore at www.weightwatchers.co.uk.

activity

A TRIP TO THE NEWSAGENTS

There are a huge number of magazines on sale which claim to give good health advice. Select two and consider the following for each:

1. **Who is it aimed at?**
2. **What type of leisure activity does it recommend?**
3. **Does it contain links to any leisure facilities?**
4. **What sort of organisations advertise in the magazine?**

Topic 2 Equality, diversity and inclusion

Opportunities in recreation and leisure are not equally available to everyone in communities around the world. The total provision of leisure opportunities and facilities is not always possible, and sometimes the best one can hope to do is simply maximise what is there rather than trying to provide for every single individual.

The concepts of equality and diversity will be explored in detail in this topic with a view to providing you with some possible research project areas. You will consider:

- **Providing equality**
- **Addressing diversity**
- **Inclusion schemes.**

Because of the role that policy plays in equality and diversity issues, a lot of the material in this topic will relate to Topic 5 Government and policy in leisure. Issues related more specifically to gender and race are discussed in the next topic.

Providing equality

In many countries there will normally be structures in place to help the less fortunate and the underprivileged – whether this requires providing basic things like food, shelter and jobs, or more developed things like public transport and leisure amenities. There is a moral and ethical obligation to attempt to make society more equal. Leisure provision may often be unevenly distributed by wealth, with a hierarchy of opportunities, but those countries that accept the moral obligation at least recognise that striving towards equality is desirable.

Many leisure organisations or departments will have their own policy on equality in place these days, and you will be able to research these on the internet.

Both the Institute of Leisure and Amenity Management (ILAM) and the Institute of Sport and Recreation Management (ISRM) are particularly active in supporting equality in leisure, as are most major organisations. There is a great deal of information about how these principles and policies developed, which you might choose to look at for your research project.

Policies and principles of equality in leisure concern:

- race
- ethnicity
- gender
- religion
- disability.

Such concerns can be implemented in a range of leisure contexts such as:

- facilities
- jobs
- services
- finance.

These are some of Manchester City Council's equality commitments – part of their parks strategy and general provision for the disabled:

Case study: Manchester City Council

Manchester Leisure are committed to providing access for everyone to well maintained and safe parks, play areas, woodlands, natural areas, recreational and sporting facilities and other open spaces, close to where they live and work. Parks are an important leisure, educational, historical and tourism asset to the city as well as providing the opportunity for social interaction, so provision is rather like a community service, which is at the heart of local authority services policy. The recommendations in the strategy recognise this, as well as providing commitment to the continued sustainability of open spaces through the development of environmental management plans.Objectives in terms of disability are also set to:

- improve physical access to buildings open to the public
- develop greater community consultation with disabled people on service delivery
- develop greater staff disability awareness and attitudinal change
- improve communication methods and provision of information to disabled people
- remove barriers to disabled people in transport provision across the city
- improve access to education and employment of disabled people.

Source: www.manchester.gov.uk

activity

ENCOURAGING EQUALITY

Working with a partner, select one of the objectives laid out in the Manchester case study, draw up a plan of how you would actually carry out the objectives set and evaluate if they had been met or not.

Although you have just looked at a local authority as an example to show how equality is being tackled, many other clubs in the voluntary sector, some private sector clubs and nearly every sports governing body will have examples of a policy or best practice, which you might investigate.

These principles are found at the highest levels in sport as well, with many international sports organisations leading by example and setting out standards of practice, codes of ethics and guidelines of how equality should be achieved – the European Sports Charter, for example.

Addressing diversity

The UK has one of the most diverse populations in the world in terms of wealth, religion, culture, nationality, jobs and ability. Meeting the needs of a diverse population is a challenge for leisure operators, particularly where wealth is concerned. (Ethnic diversity and race issues are looked at in more depth in the next topic.)

In medium to large towns there is usually a mixture of leisure provision to suit most needs – parks, pools, clubs and cinemas. It is a mix supplied by the public, private and not-for-profit sectors.

In most cases,

- the private sector will provide leisure opportunities at a cost to users (looking for profit), such as gyms, clubs and entertainment venues.
- the public sector will supply for general community needs, such as local residents and low income participants.
- the not-for-profit sector will supply for specific needs, such as youth and those with disabilities.

The more diverse the population, however, the more difficult it is for the leisure industry to respond to the variety of needs. The less response to increasingly diverse needs, the more inequality arises, including inadequate or an excess of leisure opportunities in some areas. The areas where there is a high concentration of leisure provision are usually found in more affluent areas, where residents have higher income and greater mobility. A leisure centre in the countryside without links to public transport Is unlikely to attract people without their own transport. Just as with planning for equality of opportunity and access, planning for diversity also needs to try to redress the balance.

Current practice in the public sector is to consult with local communities before they plan so that diverse leisure needs night be identified and incorporated where possible.

When more diverse groups are underserved, they are often forced to 'lobby', or protest to make their needs known and opinions voiced. This happens when leisure facilities may be closing as well as when something needs to be built.

Diversity needs in rural and urban areas represent three different challenges for leisure provision on the basis of:

- Efficiency – balancing cost, pricing and usage.
- Equity – maximising inclusion to tackle the gap in spending capability.
- Planned diversity.

Local authorities rely on community charges and government funding to fund local leisure provision and when these become 'tight' often leisure is seen as an easy option for cuts. Few local authority premises make a profit at all and many expect not to, but prices need to remain low to attract the right kind of leisure user and promote diversity in the industry.

Private sector organisation, however, must always make a profit if they are to stay in business so they must charge a high rate, hence the price of a cinema ticket may be twice that of a swim at the local pool.

activity

DO THEY REALLY CARE?

Do you think that private organisations consider many social issues of diversity and inequality when they allocate resources to provide a leisure need?

Many factors, other than economic, cause inequalities and highlight the diversity of leisure users:

- Finding time
- Age
- Having companions to share leisure time with
- Acquiring skills to do certain leisure activities
- Travel – method, cost and time
- Safety in a particular area
- Proximity to play area
- Access
- Social prejudices
- Image and pre-conceived ideas
- Gender and race (see Topic 3).

activity

IT'S NOT JUST ABOUT THE MONEY

Think which of the above factors might be potential problems or obstacles in terms of participation when joining:

- **a members-only golf club**
- **a fishing trip abroad**
- **a group of back-packers travelling round South America.**

Inclusion schemes

The drive for inclusiveness in society is a major government concern, so much so that there is now a Social Exclusion Unit aimed at 'Bringing Britain together' and helping with inclusiveness schemes. (Find out more at www.socialexclusionunit.gov.uk.)

You have already seen that the distribution of wealth is at the heart of exclusion from leisure. Over the last twenty years the gap between the rich and poor in the UK has widened. Poverty restricts leisure spending, highlighting the gap between rich and poor further. In the family expenditure survey of 2001 the top 10 per cent of the population were spending just under £190 on leisure each week, while the lowest 10 per cent were spending only £20.

Issues of leisure spending, poverty and opportunity could well be a fruitful research area, assessing whether any changes have been effective since the turn of the century.

Inclusion means more than simple access to recreational opportunities – it also means adapting what exists to help those with less opportunity, such as:

- Rescheduling programmes to suit work patterns and leisure times.
- Providing what is offered in a general way to each part of the community.
- Providing transport for distant users.

- Providing taster sessions for non-users.
- Developing staff to cope with users of low skills or disability.
- Facilitating access and use by grouping users by gender.

Planning for inclusiveness should be at the core of local leisure plans. Treating leisure time and activities as a basic human right and not a luxury has become more prevalent.

Ongoing huge social and capital investment is required as well as staff development and training to keep making progression towards greater participation of excluded groups.

activity

LOCAL INCLUSION

Working in small groups, visit or go online to investigate two local leisure providers such as a library, museum, theatre, community hall or arts centre and assess how they provide for the less able or well off in their programmes or activities. Make recommendations where you feel they could improve in terms of inclusion.

Examples of proactive inclusion schemes around the country:

- Highland Region local authority in Scotland provides cultural and leisure grants, available for a range of leisure and recreation amenities including village halls.
- Carmarthen Council in Wales. In order to boost rural transport schemes the county council has been looking at a number of projects to make it easier for people in remote parts of the county to get about.
- Westminster Council in London. All of Westminster's leisure centres are public facilities and most activities are available on a 'pay as you play' basis. Some facilities and programmes have to be booked in advance but there is something for all ages and abilities. Residents of Westminster can have a ResCard or a Concessions Card for discounts. The disabled, unemployed or those who are senior citizens can get free access to swimming by Concession Card use.
- The National Railway Museum, along with many other museums, now has free admission.

activity

WHAT DO THEY DO?

Have a look at the following organisations and schemes to increase participation and inclusion in leisure:

- The Private Finance Initiative (PFI)
- Sport Action Zones
- Arts Council funding
- Lottery funding for sport and leisure activity development.

1 What do they do?

2 How do they help inclusion and equality?

Topic 3 Sex, gender and race

As widespread and popular as sport and leisure pursuits are, not all include or offer everyone opportunities on an equal basis. You have already looked into general issues of inequality and diversity but this topic focuses on the more familiar, constantly evolving issues of sex, gender and race in leisure.

Historically, the close association between masculinity and more active sport and leisure pursuits has provoked much debate. This topic will tackle a number of related issues.

Race issues in sport and leisure are as, if not more, controversial. Britain is a multicultural society, with many nationalities. Despite a conscious effort to facilitate inclusion, particularly with regard to competitive sports, underlying problems still exist.

As in previous topics, a range of issues will be raised and examples given of where your studies might be undertaken.

This topic covers

- **Sex and gender issues**
- **Race and ethnicity**
- **Campaigns for leisure equality.**

FIFA president says pants to women's football

Soccer chief's plan to boost women's game? ... Hotpants

Football's most senior administrator attracted the wrath of the women's game last night by suggesting female players wear tighter shorts to promote "a more female aesthetic".

Sepp Blatter, the president of the world governing body Fifa, said women should have skimpier kit to increase the popularity of the game. "Let the women play in more feminine clothes like they do in volleyball," he said.

"They could, for example, have tighter shorts. Female players are pretty, if you excuse me for saying so, and they already have some different rules to men – such as playing with a lighter ball. That decision was taken to create a more female aesthetic, so why not do it in fashion?"

Blatter's comments outraged leading European female footballers, and have threatened to undermine the sport, which has 30 million registered players worldwide.

Pauline Cope, the England and Charlton goalkeeper, said the comments were "typical of a bloke". "He doesn't know what he is talking about," she said. "We don't use a lighter ball for one thing, and to say we should play football in hotpants is plain ridiculous. It's completely irresponsible for a man in a powerful position to make comments like this."

Marieanne Spacey, the manager of Fulham, said Blatter's views were harmful. "Surely it's about skill and tactical ability first and how people look second," she said.

Adapted from an article in The Guardian, Friday January 16, 2004.

Women's rugby – reshaping beliefs and stereotypes

Sex and gender issues

Traditional ideas of femininity and masculinity are constantly being challenged. Historically, female exclusion from all but the most passive and creative leisure activities was deep-seated in society. Leisure activities (especially sports) have been the main area in which gender discrimination has been most pronounced and well documented. The following points have been used to discriminate against female participation:

- The social argument – that the 'qualities' and 'behaviours' associated with femininity are not reflected in active leisure pursuits such as judo, rugby and boxing which involve physical contact.
- The aesthetic rationale – that women when engaged in physical activity are unattractive.
- The medical reason – that women are physiologically unsuited to some activities and may damage their child-bearing capabilities.
- Media gender reinforcement theory – images presented in the mass media reinforce stereotypes.

You may choose to counter one of these ideas as a research project. Nowadays increasing numbers of females are as successful as males in many leisure activities. This has caused a reshaping of some of our beliefs and stereotyping.

activity

A MAN'S WORLD?

Gender clearly shapes our leisure activities. Try putting the following activities into two groups – those you would associate with women and those you would associate with men. Some might be easy, others not so clear. Think whether this has always been the case.

- Ballet
- Kick-boxing
- Chess
- Shopping
- Yoga
- Hockey
- Gambling
- Cricket

This activity should also prove that gender issues arise concerning male participation in activities commonly associated with women. Prejudices can work both ways.

Female participation

Chauvinistic attitudes towards women and participation have been eroded since the early 1900s. Some feel that it is only because the activities were organised and regulated by men that women did not get an equal say in the activity's development. This means that in many sports there are no organised leagues or championships for women, so little to attract at amateur level.

In the UK, a difference in participation rates seems to begin to show at secondary school age – many boys continue to play certain sports while girls are much less likely to do so. This kind of pattern can be found in adulthood as well – lower frequency and less participation.

Visit the Women's Sports Foundation website at www.wsf.org.uk to find out useful facts and statistics.

In adulthood, women's participation is often replaced by childcare and household responsibilities. Women's participation is affected much more by social constraints, ageing, earnings and ethnicity. Even at the elite end of the spectrum there are far fewer women athletes and competitors. Recent sports strategies have tried to address many of these aspects. You can find a pdf of the report 'Game Plan – a strategy for delivering government sport and physical activity objectives' at www.isrm.co.uk, the official website of the Institute of Sport and Recreation Management (ISRM).

Studies of women who do participate in leisure show the enormous benefits to be gained in terms of self-esteem, personal development, fitness, shape and vigour.

Homosexuality

Sexism is not the only form of discrimination associated with inclusion in leisure activities. Homosexuality in sport is an increasingly debated topic in the news. Justin Fashanu was the only openly gay player in British football and many fear that the culture of the game, peer-pressure and the homophobia of the locker room makes it extremely difficult for any players to come out. It is easier to find openly gay participants in individual sports and there are more openly gay sportswomen than sportsmen. Why do you think this is? In tennis, Martina Navratilova and Billie-Jean King have successfully battled prejudices about their sexuality to rise to the top of their sport. Other examples include Greg Louganis (diving, USA), Ryan Miller (snowboarding, USA), Ian Roberts (rugby, Australia) and Billy Bean (baseball, USA).

The Premiership footballer Robbie Fowler faced criticism for alleged homosexual taunts towards another player.

Gender and sexuality are directly addressed in Manchester City Council's Sexuality Action Plan 2005/06:

- To proactively improve and develop services in Leisure for gay men, lesbians, transgender and bisexual individuals/groups within the community.
- To ensure monitoring, evaluation and review of this plan takes place on a regular basis.
- To ensure that Manchester Leisure regularly consults and engages with gay, lesbian, transgender and bi-sexual communities.

www.manchester.gov.uk

At local level in leisure organisations, inclusion regardless of sexuality is increasing and many have policies such as the one above. However, some hotels refuse to allow gay couples to share a double room and company policy doesn't always conceal individual prejudices. If you wish to pursue this topic further for your research project, there are many recent news articles to explore.

Race and ethnicity

Ethnicity relates to the characteristics of:

- Race
- Religion
- Language
- Cultural tradition.

An ethnic minority is an immigrant or racial group regarded by those claiming to speak for the cultural majority as distinct and unassimilated. Race is more simply defined as a group of people of common ancestry distinguished by physical characteristics.

Using another example from Manchester City Council, their leisure policy also addresses race:

Leisure's contribution towards achieving race equality is particularly reflected through the various programmes and activities, which are targeted at specific ethnic groups and the availability of all publicity material produced on behalf of Manchester Leisure, is produced in the community languages. Manchester Leisure is actively committed to managing diversity and providing and promoting racial equality, especially as a front line provider of services and is continuing to try and deliver best practice, integrating race equality targets within its performance, budget and service planning processes.

www.manchester.gov.uk

In 2001 the Office of National Statistics conducted a study on sports participation and ethnicity. The survey found that the participation rate for ethnic minorities – at around 40 per cent – was 6 per cent below the national average. The report concluded that though there is clear inequality in participation it may well not be related to racism.

Case study: Racial Equality Charter for Sport

In 1998 a body called Sporting Equals created the 'Racial Equality Charter for Sport'. It aimed to guide sports governing bodies for the new millennium in the following areas:

- Make commitments to challenge and remove racial discrimination and aim for racial equality.
- Encourage people from all communities to take part in sport, to coach, manage and help organise.
- Protect players, employees and spectators from racial abuse.
- Have equality policies and practices.
- Celebrate cultural diversity.

Increasingly, organisations cannot get lottery funding without these types of policy and practice in place which encourages widening positive policies for equality, not just in terms of race, but age, ethnicity and gender too.

Under-representation

Despite there being quite a number of successful black sportspersons in the UK in football, boxing, basketball and athletics, they are still under-represented in many other sports, such as golf, swimming, tennis and rugby.

These issues raise some questions which you might choose to pursue:

- Why is there an uneven distribution?
- Are access and inequality barriers to participation?
- Are some racial groups better suited mentally and physically to some sports and leisure activities?
- Are the roots of this non-participation based in PE at school?
- Do racial prejudices 'channel' athletes of a particular race into certain sports and activities?

Ethnographic barriers to participation

Clearly ethnicity, religion, and race combine to affect participation significantly, through the combination of cultural values and pressures. This may often also be

Harpal Singh

Harpal Singh is one of only a handful of Asian players in the football league. This is an extract from an interview from the Let's Kick Racism Out of Football website:

Q: How important is your identity and the fact that you're Asian?

A: I've always known it's going to be different with me being Asian but I'm proud to be Asian and don't see that as a problem. It makes me more determined to make it. I want to be the first Asian player to make it. The fans won't be used to seeing Asian players running around. I may get a bit of reaction. But they'll get used to it.

Q: What would you do if you don't make it in football?

A: I'd like to go into the leisure industry, maybe, to coach Asian kids and promote football.

Q: What would you say to any Asian youngsters trying to make it?

A: Be single minded about the way you approach the game. Don't think of yourself as an outcast, play your football and enjoy it and whatever happens, happens.

seen amongst youths in the form of street games they play in various ethnic neighbourhoods. Most will stay within their cultural zone and traditions. Sometimes this leads to communities who do not mix with other ethnic groups which can restrict the range of leisure activities.

activity

PESTLE

Thinking about race and gender and looking back over the topic, try to come up with as many factors you can that affect participation amongst different ethnic and gender groups. Organise the factors under PESTLE headings – Political, Economic, Social, Technological Legislative and Environmental.

Campaigns for leisure equality

In the 1970s, sport and leisure policies began to be aimed at providing blanket provision, trying to cover every need regardless of race, ethnicity age or ability. However, as inner-city social and economic problems emerged and public sector spending reduced in the 1980s, leisure and recreation provision also suffered.

Sport was seen as a low-cost option to help fill the need for constructive activities, so more specific sport campaigns were created for inner cities and deprived areas, introducing specific 'targeted' schemes for:

- Ethnic minorities
- The unemployed and low-income groups
- The elderly
- The disabled
- Women.

Are black athletes better suited to sprinting than other racial groups?

Sport and leisure schemes began to be targeted towards these groups to re-engage them in society through action. More recently, other agencies (the Commission for Racial Equality and the Professional Footballers Association) joined campaigns to help tackle racism on the football terraces. 'Kick Racism Out of Football' and 'Hit Racism for Six' (cricket) campaigns and began to shift the emphasis on to the perpetrators rather than the victims.

New Labour have overseen several policies including:

- A Sporting Future for All, 2000
- The Government Plan for Sport, 2001
- Game Plan, in 2004.

activity

BIG DIFFERENCES MADE AT A LOCAL LEVEL

All of these campaigns stress the need for tackling the issues on a local basis, rather than nationally. Why do you think this is?

Topic 4 Events, festivals and traditions

The Notting Hill Carnival

Issues in leisure relate to people, organisations or places. So far, you have looked at issues that relate mainly to people, but leisure events, festivals and traditions involve all three. From local fairs to regional gatherings and national and international festivals, you will have plenty to choose from for research in this area. Leisure events, no matter what size, have many aspects deserving of more in-depth study. In this topic you will explore:

- **The range of leisure activities**
- **The aims and purpose of leisure events**
- **Logistics – the complexity of successful event planning and management**
- **The value of events.**

Many of the ideas in this topic have been covered in part in earlier units. However, now you are thinking about them with a eye on your research proposal.

You can also draw on the practical experience gained from planning, organising and running an event from Unit 4 Leisure in Action.

You may choose to study a local event which provides easier access to the people involved and the possibility of carrying out primary research. You might alternatively choose a larger event to study at a distance and rely on secondary material for your data. With the Olympics coming to London in 2012 there will be plenty of material available for study in this field.

The range of leisure activities

Events in the leisure industry can be classified into common categories in order to help you choose an area that interests you. Try to think beyond this list as well – the possibilities are endless.

Type of event	*Example*
Sports	An athletics meeting
Festivals	The Edinburgh International Festival and the Fringe Festival
Music	The Glastonbury Festival
Drama	The National Student Drama Festival
Enthusiasts / Hobbies	The Hobbycrafts and Art Materials Live! Show at the NEC, Birmingham
Business	Book launch
Arts	The Walker Art Gallery, Liverpool
Shows	The Cheshire County Show
Educational	School reunion

Events can be classified by their locations, too. These are sometimes unique, making the event special. Examples of this are the Badminton Horse Trials, a cricket test match at Lords, or concerts in Hyde Park, London. Many of the oldest events ensure 'the place' is one of the unique selling points and in many spectators' or participants' eyes it would not be the same if run elsewhere. This was the case in 2005 when Royal Ascot was run at York Racecourse and when the FA Cup final was played at the Millennium Stadium, Cardiff between 2001 and 2005. Would the Oxford and Cambridge Boat Race be the same event if rowed on the River Ouse? So place, tradition and the occasion help to classify an event.

Events can also be classified according to which part of the calendar or season they fall in. For example, we associate:

- spring with Easter and gardening
- summer with outdoor music festivals and tennis
- autumn with bonfire night and Halloween
- winter with pantomimes and sledging.

Whether an event is run indoors or outdoors is another useful way of separating out the different types, as is whether they are oriented towards the spectator or the participant.

activity

PASSIVE OR ACTIVE?

Another way of classifying activities is to decide whether they are passive or active in nature. Make a list of events and classify them according to which term best describes them. Also consider what unique factors your examples include in terms of location, tradition and seasonality.

The aims and purpose of events

Aims are the visions behind the staging of an event and relates to both the organisers and the users. The London Marathon is primarily for participants to see if they can run the required distance, but other aims include simply running, finishing, raising money for charity, raising the profile of London and possibly even getting on television.

Most events will have set objectives to help guide organisers, staff and volunteers and these objectives will be focused on the aim or purpose. For example, if the aim of a music festival is to entertain various musical tastes, it may have some of the following as objectives:

- To attract 2,500 people to various venues to hear the bands.
- To attract five world-class musicians.
- To break even.

Additional objectives might be:

- Bringing income into an area.
- Providing jobs for local people.

You might wish to study how certain events meet their aims, objectives and purposes. Your analysis might focus on evaluating and rating success.

activity

AIMS AND OBJECTIVES

Set out aims, objectives and the underlying purpose for the following events:

1. **A coast-to-coast bike race.**
2. **An exhibition of paintings by a local artist.**
3. **A bonfire and fireworks party.**

In the following case study identify the aims, objectives and purpose:

Case study: New Nottingham event aims to encourage new talent

Development agency EM Media is to hold an event in Nottingham to discuss the future of young talent within the games industry, featuring speakers from Codemasters, Electronic Arts and De Montfort University. New Talent will look at issues such as the quality of university games development courses, the calibre of graduates and the question of overseas recruitment.

'The event is not the chance to try out a sales pitch or headhunt,' said EM Media, but 'a frank and open discussion of the art and science of games development.'

'Working with Universities and the companies here in the East Midlands there clearly is a gap to bridge when it comes to the life-blood of our industry Where do we find the next stars, how do we encourage people to move up in an organisation to a place where they want to be?' said Toby Barnes.

'With around 20 per cent of the UK's development occurring within the East Midlands and some of the biggest games icons born here, EM Media has recognised the need to support the games development sector in order to ensure it can grow and mature to produce the world's next top games, both in terms of sales and creativity and innovation.'

EM Media is a regional screen agency supported by the UK Film Council and Skillset as well as the East Midlands Development Agency and Culture East Midlands. Its aims are to develop a sustainable and accessible entertainment industry in the region.

The agency also offers a range of business development services for film, television, radio and digital media across the region. Public Domain is a series of events designed to support the East Midlands development community.

© 2002–2005 Eurogamer Network Ltd
Source: www.gamesindustry.biz

The target audience

Events are designed with a 'target audience' of spectators or participants in mind, and this aspect of planning needs careful research by the organisers.

Marketing theory suggests that a technique called 'segmentation' can be used first, to identify the segment of the population that the event should be aimed at and secondly, to identify what elements of an event they would find interesting. For example, in terms of age, young people are likely to be drawn to a fun fair, older people to a flower show. All event organisers need to carry out careful market research to get this right. Some events have a broad generational appeal and are attractive to all ages, such as football matches.

Segmentation techniques can also be applied geographically by targeting events at local communities, like regional games or county championships. The major world class events or hallmark events have global appeal and attract spectators and competitors from around the world. Equally so, events may be targeted on a gender basis.

You might choose to investigate how segmentation is used in some sectors of the event industry and what issues this involves for participants, organisers and the success of the event. Taking this theme a step further, you might choose to assess the promotional techniques (the four Ps) used for events by making comparisons.

Events may also target possible sponsors by trying to match up the audience to a particular brand.

activity

MATCH UP

Try the following exercise of matching up events at a seaside resort to target audiences and compare your ideas with others in your class.

Target audience	*Event*
Children under 14	Walking tour
Over 50s	Sandcastle competition
Males 24–35	Punch and Judy show
Females 18–35	Indoor go-karting competition
Families	Free performance by a band
Students	Fashion show

Logistics – the complexity of successful event planning and management

All events need planning and organising well in advance. Event managers and organisers are usually multi-skilled and knit many logistics together to make an event work. The process of how this is done may provide you with a valuable insight into event-management techniques.

Logistics are defined by the Council of Supply Chain Management Professionals: 'Logistics is that part of the supply chain process that plans, implements and controls the efficient, effective flow and storage of goods, services and related information from the point of origin to the point of consumption in order to meet the customer's requirements.'

What might these logistics be? Lighting, sound, special effects, catering, music and seating? You might be able to investigate the complexity of supplying or managing these at an event.

Consider the human side of logistics. It could involve volunteers, stewards, emergency services personnel, crowds, participants and suppliers.

The final set of logistics to cover are the financial ones – obtaining a sponsor, costing resources, estimating staff wages, budgeting for expenditure, pricing tickets, planning profit levels, dealing with cash, cheques and credit card payments, settling bills.

The opportunities for you to research a particular aspect are quite broad, such as:

- What technology is used to handle logistics?
- What are the most common problems and hitches?
- How do you plan the sequence in which logistics need to be tackled?
- How do organisers identify and arrange their logistical challenges?
- How are sponsors found and treated?

For some event organisers the challenge of managing their own logistics is too much and they bring in professional event companies to do the work for them.

The value of events

Events also carry a real value in several different ways, according to their nature and size. Events can have a value in different ways: Economically, socially, politically, culturally and environmentally.

Economic value

Large events bring jobs to an area for local people and they bring income to an area through purchases and supplies. If foreign visitors are attracted they bring currency into the country. The government gains money in tax and the locality enjoys inward investment, while the event company might (and usually, should) make a profit. The money that events directly and indirectly help to circulate is re-spent many times over. This is often called the economic multiplier effect.

zAt the beginning of the 1990s, when the International Convention Centre in Birmingham was built, it was estimated it would provide:

The International Convention Centre, Birmingham.

- Birmingham with a world-class image and venue
- annual investment of £40m in the area
- around 10,000 jobs
- related development of about £1.6 billion
- economic regeneration of the locality
- retail potential.

By the middle of the decade this was realised. You might be able to find a newly built venue for events and assess its effect on an area in economic terms. This is called an economic impact study. Alternatively you might carry out a benefit/cost analysis, because sometimes an event can push up local prices, making it more expensive for local people to live there.

Social value

- The opportunity to meet new people or people of similar interests
- The opportunity to experience or view new cultures
- Regeneration of an area
- Upgrading of an area's image or transport system
- New facilities for locals (after the event)
- Learning new skills
- Community pride is built up.

There can, of course, be social costs associated with an event coming to an area such as:

- Invasion of privacy
- Disturbance of local routines
- Congestion, pollution, noise, litter.

Political value

At first you might not think there would be many benefits, but consider the following:

- The 'feel good factor' the country might have after a famous victory at an event
- The image of government departments or officials, if responsible for or connected to, an event
- The skills base of the local people may be improved.

On the other side of the coin:

- The event may fail or gain a bad reputation
- Funds may be misspent
- The event may become a propaganda exercise.

Cultural value

Value is perceived through the exchange between people when attending an event, and the interaction with each other as spectators or players and participants. Hopefully this is a positive exchange and people get to know each other better. The Notting Hill Carnival is a good example of when cultures come together.

The cultural value of leisure events would lend itself well to further study, looking at both the positive and negative angles.

Environmental value

Many run-down areas have been regenerated through sport and leisure events. When it takes place in a city, it is called urban transformation and was a cornerstone of the UK's Olympic bid. However, there is often massive upheaval, pollution and disturbance during transformation, and the facilities' long-term use needs to be considered. Some Olympic sites have suffered from a lack of long-term activity as did the Millennium Dome. Clean up costs must never be forgotten after the event, either.

The development of the Eurostar encouraged urban transformation

activity

BENEFITS AND IMPACTS OF EVENTS

Create a chart grouping all the negative and positive effects that a large event of your choice can have. Group them under all of the above headings and try to research some examples of where these have actually occurred.

Topic 5 Government and policy in leisure

Jamie Oliver casts a critical eye over Government policy regarding school meals

Policy can be defined as a plan of action or an expression of purpose, adapted or pursued by an individual, government or organisation. Policy relating to leisure tends to be made at all levels of government – national, regional and local. The politicians and professionals making the policies hope that they will help to achieve a range of healthy social and economic benefits including maintaining and increasing participation. You have already learnt of different forms of policy in previous topics on issues, such as healthy living, providing equality, and race. In this topic you will explore more areas within the leisure industry that recent policy has focused on.

Policy is affected by the political climate, and as government and society changes so does policy.

Once a policy is stated it will be interpreted and possibly, although not always, implemented. There are many opportunities for misinterpretation or poor implementation which can send the original policy aims off track and cause conflict. Policy can also be influenced by lobbying and pressure from influential businesses.

The issues contained in this topic are:

- **Understanding policy**
- **Investigating leisure policy issues**
- **Leisure policy and crime**
- **Leisure policy and unemployment**
- **Leisure policy and regeneration**
- **Staging events**
- **Leisure in election campaigns.**

Understanding policy

Policies can be influenced by many forces. For example, Jamie Oliver's TV programme, *Jamie's School Dinners*, attacking the quality of food in schools, eventually persuaded the Minister for Education to rethink policies about the eating habits of children, as well as budgets. Equally so, very large organisations with a global presence influence policy makers all around the world over concerns such as oil, arms, the environment and human rights.

Leisure organisations who are quite powerful in influencing policy decisions are:

- Governing bodies of sport and activities, such as the Football Association (FA) and the British Olympic Association.
- Professional organisations, such as the Institute of Sport and Recreation Management (ISRM) and the Institute of Leisure and Amenity Management (ILAM).
- The media, such as newspapers, TV, radio and internet.
- Large businesses, such as sponsors.

They are influential because:

- they have a wide variety of resources at their disposal – expertise and communication channels
- they have large widespread organisational capabilities
- they often command considerable authority and respect.

Investigating leisure policy issues

When searching for a suitable area to research, some of the following might be of interest to you:

1. Why does Government devolve policy to many 'arm's length' organisations like Sport England and the Arts Council?
2. How much influence do local government officers have over politicians?
3. What difficulties are there implementing policy at school or club level for sports and other leisure activities?
4. How does Government calculate the needs of those in the leisure industry?

The main Government department which has a say in leisure policy is the Department for Culture, Media and Sport, (DCMS). Several other departments sometimes have an influence if the agenda covers tackling crime (Home Office), unemployment (Department for Work and Pensions), education (Department for Education and Skills), outdoor venues (Department for Environment, Food and Rural Affairs) or the promotion of healthier lifestyles (Department of Health).

The DCMS can serve as a case study using material from their website www.dcms.gov.uk.

The DCMS is responsible for Government policy on the arts, sport, the National Lottery, tourism, libraries, museums and galleries, broadcasting, film, the music industry, press freedom and regulation, licensing, gambling and the built heritage.

Their mission statement shows the intended direction of their policy. 'We aim to improve the quality of life for all through cultural and sporting activities, to support the pursuit of excellence and to champion the tourism, creative and leisure industries.' To try and achieve this they have developed four strategic priorities (policy directions):

- Children and Young People. Further enhance access to culture and sport for children and give them the opportunity to develop their talents to the full and enjoy the benefits of participation.
- Communities. Increase and broaden the impact of culture and sport, to enrich individual lives, strengthen communities and improve the places where people live, now and for future generations.
- Economy. Maximise the contribution that the tourism, creative and leisure industries can make to the economy.
- Delivery. Modernise delivery by ensuring our sponsored bodies are efficient and work with others to meet the cultural and sporting needs of individuals and communities.

At a more local level under the terms 'Competitive Performance Assessments' (formerly 'Best Value'), local councils or Metropolitan Boroughs have to produce a plan that includes leisure policies. You can probably visit your own local authority website or offices to gather details of what they have planned in terms of leisure. To give you a brief insight there is an extract from Scarborough Borough Council on the next page.

Case study: Scarborough Borough Council

The council aims to 'develop tourism and improve opportunities for leisure' under the wider objective 'to enhance the quality of life for those living in, working in, or visiting the Borough'.

The various objectives outlined by the council are very much in line with national strategies, whilst at a regional level, local authorities work together to share experiences and best practice.

The Council's corporate objectives are outlined in a downloadable pdf 'Corporate Plan 2003-8':

- Objective 1: To help ensure the provision of decent housing for all
- Objective 2: To reduce crime and disorder
- Objective 3: To keep the population of the Borough healthy
- Objective 4: To sustain and develop the local economy
- Objective 5: To develop tourism and improve opportunities for leisure
- Objective 6: To improve, protect and sustain the environment
- Objective 7: To help deliver an integrated transport system
- Objective 8: To promote the development of local democracy and accountability
- Objective 9: To provide leadership and vision to the local community

On top of this there are four key priorities:

- Protect and improve the wider coastal environment
- Address community disadvantage
- Facilitate better quality jobs and investment
- Deliver safer communities

The document goes on to show how each of these priorities will be achieved with targets in a clear effort to create synergies of thought and action.

Find out more at www.scarborough.gov.uk

Case study: Chichester District Council

Chichester District Council appointed a Crime Diversion Sports Officer to address social issues, potential criminality and substance misuse through positive and sustainable links through sports and leisure activities. The role seeks to create new and develop existing partnerships with many agencies to deliver exciting opportunities for young people and targeted communities within the Chichester District.

They have established partnerships with Sussex Police, the local authority's Youth Offending Team, the Drug and Alcohol Action Team, registered social landlords, residents associations, sports clubs, schools and young people. Recent projects have included:

Football in the Community

This crime diversionary project aims to:

- Tackle anti-social behaviour and create a diversion from youth crime
- Reduce boredom by the provision of activities

Leisure policy and crime

You may have noticed in the Scarborough case study that it mentioned reducing crime through more active involvement in leisure. In recent years it has become more apparent that constructive leisure activities can engage young people and help them break the habits of drugs, vandalism and disengagement.

When assessing this as a potential research topic, think about the following:

- What evidence can be found to show that involvement with sport or leisure activities reduces juvenile crime?
- From the evidence that is available, does this produce a permanent change?
- What particular schemes have been used and how do they evaluate their success or performance?

Some approaches can be illustrated through two case studies (below and right).

Some believe that, when compared to the costs of prosecution and detention, such programmes, even with a low success rate, are worthwhile, but there is disagreement. The major problem in identifying and measuring the effects of sport on crime is that the influence on crime is indirect. It is clearly not sufficient simply to measure outcomes and assume that these are 'sports-effects'. From a policy perspective, there is a clear need to understand the relationship between inputs and intermediate and final outcomes.

- Reflect young people in a positive way
- Promote essential life skills such as team work, respect and discipline
- Engagement and development the community
- Provide opportunities for education & training for young people and parents
- Reduce crime and anti-social behaviour in and around Housing Association properties.

Street Funk Dance

- Targets teenage girls and provides information on different issues surrounding health and well being
- Sessions are free for young people making them totally inclusive.
- Girls are also encouraged to choreograph their own dances as well as to learn material taught.
- Fun competitions are held to offer young people an opportunity to perform what they have learnt over the course.

The key to the projects' effectiveness lies in establishing what the young people want, by empowering them and consulting with youth club members and detached youth workers.

Find out more at www.chichester.gov.uk.

Case study: Positive Futures – Reading Borough Council

Positive Futures was launched in April 2000 in Reading. It is a national sports-based social inclusion programme funded and managed by the Home Office Drugs Strategy Directorate. The overall aim of Positive Futures is: 'To use sport to reduce anti-social behaviour, crime and substance misuse among 10–19 year olds.'

The project involves five weekly open house sports sessions for all local young people. Activities include generic sports such as football, basketball and cricket.

Where possible the sessions also give young people the opportunity to try new activities such as trampolining, skateboarding, ice-skating and paintballing. All the activities are aimed at giving young people a positive experience, confidence and self-esteem as well as developing skills such as self-discipline, problem solving, teamwork and communication.

You can find more at www.reading.gov.uk

Leisure policy and unemployment

Schemes and incentives to keep unemployed people or those on low income involved in leisure have been common for a few years. They are part of the Social Inclusion Strategy, in the belief that arts, sport and leisure activities have a role to play in countering social exclusion of the unemployed or low-income groups. They can help to increase:

- The self-esteem of individuals
- Community spirit
- Social interaction
- Health and fitness
- Employment.

The hope is that people who participate become more engaged with the community and are active in citizenship – one of the Government's policy objectives. This is part of the wider policy agenda to create a 'Giving Age' with more volunteering and the development of social capital in communities through contributions made to help less able or disadvantaged individuals and groups.

'Community development is the strengthening of the social resources and processes in the community, by developing contacts, relationships, networks, agreements and activities outside the household that residents themselves identify will make their locality a better place in which to live and work.'

Source: Thomas 'Community Development at Work: A Case of Obscurity in Accomplishment'

The Leisure Industries Research Centre in 1999 argued that 'one of the most valuable outcomes of a sports programme designed to reduce crime would be to enhance the participants' prospects for obtaining employment'.

activity

MAKING LIFE BETTER THROUGH LEISURE

In pairs, devise a six-week scheme of sports- and leisure-related activities for a mixed group of young people, which you think would help their social skills and confidence.

Leisure policy and regeneration

There are many examples of sport and leisure being used as focal points in regeneration schemes – for instance Don Valley in Sheffield, where new facilities include the Meadow Hall shopping precinct, the Hallam Arena, the Don Valley Stadium, the Ice Centre and the EIS centre. The same will be true for parts of London being rebuilt for the Olympics in 2012. However, many experts have concluded that 'although many claims are made for the contribution that this sector makes in terms of economic welfare, these are frequently based on assertion rather than concrete evidence. There is a need for a more systematic evaluation process to underpin strategies of support for sport both generally and in the region.

This comment indicates that there might be worthwhile study here to investigate the accuracy of claims. Here are two other examples which indicate what features of regeneration were measured:

1. It is estimated that the staging of the 1996 Masters Swimming Championships in Sheffield generated £3.9 million additional expenditure and 99 full-time equivalent jobs.
2. In 1997 the World Badminton Championships were held at Scotstoun Leisure Centre, in Glasgow. This created £668,000 additional expenditure in the Glasgow local economy, resulting in 58 full-time equivalent job years – of which 83 per cent were in the sectors of hotels, restaurants and catering.

Source: www.scotland.gov.uk

Working out the medium- to long-term effects of regeneration is difficult. In particular, there is a lack of available data on the regenerative impact of sport and leisure investments on local communities. Some experts refer to a certain scepticism about the extent to which community sport and leisure initiatives have a significant effect on local unemployed groups, because the type of jobs created are often temporary or seasonal and frequently part-time. Here too, there is potential scope for research into more recent schemes.

activity

DOES IT WORK?

Compare some of the opinions and points expressed above to those described in material and publications on the Sport England website – www.sportengland.org.uk. How successful do you think policy is in terms of regeneration, employment and crime-prevention?

Staging events

Staging events can have a beneficial effect on regeneration and employment. In terms of sports the UK have hosted the following international sporting events over past years:

The Homeless World Cup – Edinburgh 2005

The FIFA World Cup – England 1966

The Commonwealth Games – Wales 1958, Scotland 1970, 1986, England 2002

International Surfing Association World Championships – Newquay 1986

Olympic and Paralympic Games – London 2012

In certain sports the UK hosts events on an annual basis, such as the Open (Golf), Wimbledon (Tennis) and the World Snooker Championships, guaranteeing income to the area for the duration of the event.

activity

WORLD CUP TIDDLY-WINKS?

Given the huge range of leisure activities on offer round the world there is much that the UK could still stage, either on a one-off or regular basis. Can you think of any international events that would be practical and possible to consider pursuing, in terms of the policy aims of raising awareness and furthering social initiatives?

Leisure in election campaigns

As the provision of sports and leisure in England is non-statutory (it does not have to be provided), it does not usually feature highly in election manifestos. However, if it were to be compulsory what impact might that have on other election issues such as health, citizenship and education? Consider how often leisure issues are used to support these other policy areas. Indeed, leisure spending is often one of the easiest areas in which to make cuts for the very reason that it is non-compulsory.

activity

PARTY POLICY AND MANIFESTOS

Put yourself in the role of Members of Parliament for each of the three main parties. Do some research into where your party stands on leisure policy, either nationally or through your local party. Present your findings to the rest of the class and then decide:

1 whether any of the parties devote enough attention to leisure policy.

2 which party, in your opinion, presents the best policy. Your class could even hold a vote.

Topic 6 The media and commercial issues

It is often said that the relationship between the media and leisure (especially sport) is symbiotic – one can't live without the other. Consider how much of a newspaper is taken up by sport or how much leisure time is taken up watching TV or listening to the radio. The media acts as both a channel for the leisure industry and a leisure activity itself. It is important to think of the distinction when looking at each of the forms of media.

The relationship is rarely smooth, and many tensions exist between the media and players and leisure organisations. Some blame the media for employing sensationalism in order to sell more newspapers or attract higher audiences.

The influence of the mass media is very strong due to technological advances. The media has global presence and an increasing power to influence.

Such is the power and influence of the media that some sports and leisure events have been transformed to make them more suitable for viewing, such as changing kick-off times in football.

Discussion in this topic will cover the many types of media and the relationships that they have with sport, leisure organisations and activities. Possible research areas will be pointed out throughout the topic. For ease of study you can divide media into:

- Printed: newspapers, magazines, books
- Electronic: television, radio, the internet, film, mobile phones, music.

You will also look at some commercial issues such as sponsorship, advertising and celebrity in the media.

Printed media

Newspapers

Most of you will already be aware of the main national newspapers and the type of news they each cover. You may also be aware of your local newspaper and the role it plays in reporting and advertising leisure events. Newspapers have a number of sections targeted at leisure interests, including travel, sports and advertising. The business section and main home and international news pages will frequently report stories from the leisure industry.

Magazines

The magazine racks in most stores are bursting with choice – all interests are catered for. As such, very specific markets can be targeted. The range of magazines which relate to the leisure industry would be too many to mention, as they cover sport, fitness, hobbies, well-being, entertainment and travel. The popularity of leisure activities can be roughly worked out by the number of titles published on each subject. As important for the industry are the advertising opportunities of magazines through matching leisure consumers to providers.

activity

CONSIDER CONTENT

Carry out an analysis of two popular leisure magazines to assess the proportion of advertisements to actual articles. You could calculate it in terms of number of pages. Compare these with results found by your classmates.

Books

Books cover all tastes, but usually offer the reader more depth than a magazine. Reference and non-fiction books serve a large proportion of leisure users, such as a book on a particular interest or hobby Fiction is also important to consider because reading these books fills people's leisure time.

activity

READING HABITS

Some reading is for escape or relaxation; some is for learning and personal growth. Carry out a small survey amongst your classmates to assess reading habits.

What are motivations for reading?

What were the last three things you read (not including schoolbooks)?

How many prefer (or spend more time) reading magazines than books?

Electronic media

Rapid advances in technology have given us access to so many forms of electronic media that it is difficult to keep pace. You might focus on one of the following to create a research study area.

Television

TV is traditionally the major electronic medium that occupies our leisure time. It is affordable, global, accessible and in some households always on.

It's an important source of contact with sports, theatre, creative arts, history, and the news. Many of these subjects now have dedicated channels.

Watching TV is a common way of relaxing and being entertained, as an individual, in a group or with family. Increasingly homes have two or three TVs and people are able to watch what they want, when they want to, to fit around other activities. TV has the power to unite and bring people together – watching big sporting events or concerts, for example. The power and influence of television may make a useful research area.

Radio

Radio serves leisure audiences mainly through sports and music channels. Regional radio is a good place for information on local leisure events. Digitisation has enabled audiences to listen on demand and made it possible to listen to many specialist stations the world over.

The internet

Since the mid-1990s, this medium has revolutionised our listening and viewing habits. Virtually every leisure pursuit can be followed online in some way, from gambling to searching for local swimming pools. The leisure industry relies on the internet for making information available, and as a quick way of booking tickets, selling products and following discussion.

activity

WWW

Do you think that the internet has encouraged greater participation in leisure activities? Why?

Electronic games

There has been a lot of discussion about the validity of playing electronic games as a leisure pursuit. Although it has a huge market, there are concerns that it is addictive, contains too much violence, is anti-social and is very male-dominated. However, the educational advantages of electronic games cannot be overlooked. As new forms of electronic interaction are explored, a number of learning opportunities open up.

Films

Films nowadays, whether at the cinema, on DVD or through merchandising, have a huge market. The popularity of visiting the cinema may be under threat as home entertainment gets more sophisticated and affordable, but films continue to entertain and enthral. Think about the various leisure activities associated with films: Disneyland, Universal Studios, themed tours, exhibitions, themed parties and restaurants, open-air and drive-in cinemas, film festivals and visiting locations, reading the book of the film.

You might be able to do a study on a range of movie topics:

- Film-going figures and population profile.
- Film costs and revenues.
- New styles of multiplex cinema.
- The spread of home cinema systems.
- The impact of the internet and DVDs upon home viewing.
- The influence on buyer behaviour or fashions.

Mobile telephones

The role of the mobile phone has altered so quickly in recent years that it deserves a mention. Few people are without one, allowing them to connect with friends, family, the internet, take and send pictures and video, listen to music and play games.

Music

Music is another cultural medium that crosses the globe as a leisure interest, appealing to everyone in one form

A drive-in movie theatre.

or another. Music – whether live or recorded – generates many leisure activities in the form of concerts, festivals, discos, and dances, as well as accompanying an activity at sport events, bowling alleys and carnivals, for example. The diversity of musical genres ensures that a wide range of events is always on offer – a classical concert and a rock concert are obviously two very different experiences. Music can also influence lifestyles in terms of fashion and language (youth sub-culture).

activity

MUSIC

What was the last live music event you went to?

- Think carefully about how you learnt of it – through which form of media?
- Did the audience have anything in common?

What was the last bit of music you bought?

- How did you buy it and in what form (shop, internet download)?
- How and where do you listen to it (CD, ipod)?

Why do you think music is played

- in bars
- in gyms
- before football matches?

How important is music to the leisure industry?

Sport & the media feature

You will find quite a lot of discussion about how the media controls or interacts with sport through broadcasting rights. Often, if media broadcasters are paying a lot for rights they have some say in when events are staged and what content is included. Is this right? Cable channels who buy the rights to some events deny those with more basic terrestrial TV from watching. An increase in televised sports also contributes towards a decline in attendance in some sports. However, the breadth of coverage does mean that some sports are televised that weren't previously. The media can even influence what players and participants wear and which sponsors and advertisers gain the most exposure.

Many of these issues are there for you to explore if you wish to pursue a sports theme for your study.

activity

TV SPORT

Carry out some research in a weekly TV programme guide to assess:

- what the ratio of sports to other programmes is.
- the availability of channels that sports are on.
- how many sports feature women.
- whether a sport is staged for TV.

Commercial issues

With commercialisation found at every level of sport and in many aspects of leisure activities, there are a range of issues to be explored here. For example, in some sports there are fewer amateur players, but many more professional participants – sport is a profession with many rewards. Many national sport and leisure activity governing bodies are required to produce professional business and development plans as if they were commercial companies. Business-like practices and customer approaches are required when running a sports club or leisure activity. Why is this so? Why have the Olympics changed from being a loss-making exercise to being one of the most desirable events in the world? Commercial management techniques are required to manage public sector leisure centres and business performance targets are set.

Do these more commercial approaches detract from the simple running and enjoyment of a sport or activity? Or is the sport the winner in the end? Does it bring money, better organisation and development, improved technology and more participants and spectators?

Sponsorship

Sponsorship of sports, activities and events has enjoyed steady growth for several decades. Kettering Town became Britain's first sponsored football club in 1976. Sponsors generally seek to raise the awareness of their companies or test and launch new products. Siemens Mobile's deal with Real Madrid was worth £14m.

activity

HOW EFFECTIVE IS SPONSORSHIP?

Can you name which companies currently sponsor the following?

- **The England cricket, football and rugby teams. (There is a clue on the next page.)**
- **Liverpool Football Club.**
- **Andrew Murray (tennis).**
- **Tiger Woods (golf).**

Sponsorship can have its problems:

- Poor performances, corruption or disastrous results can tarnish the image of the sponsor.
- Sponsors may want to interfere with the running of an event or activity to suit their needs more.
- Sponsors may withdraw with little notice if their business performance is poor, or products do not sell well as a result of their sponsorship.
- Loss of business from rival fans. This is one of the reasons why Glasgow Celtic and Rangers football clubs share the same sponsor.

activity

WHEN SPONSORSHIP IS INEFFECTIVE

Carry out some research of your own to find cases where sponsorship did not work for a club, team or an event. You might look at old newspaper articles or online.

Advertising

Advertising is one of the most visible and important marketing tools available to leisure products and marketers. Although the mediums of advertising are changing quite regularly, the reason for it remains the same – it creates brand awareness and loyalty. For leisure products and services it also develops image and distinctiveness. But the bottom line for all adverts is that they must affect consumer buying behaviour.

Creating an advert for a leisure product or service follows tried and tested stages:

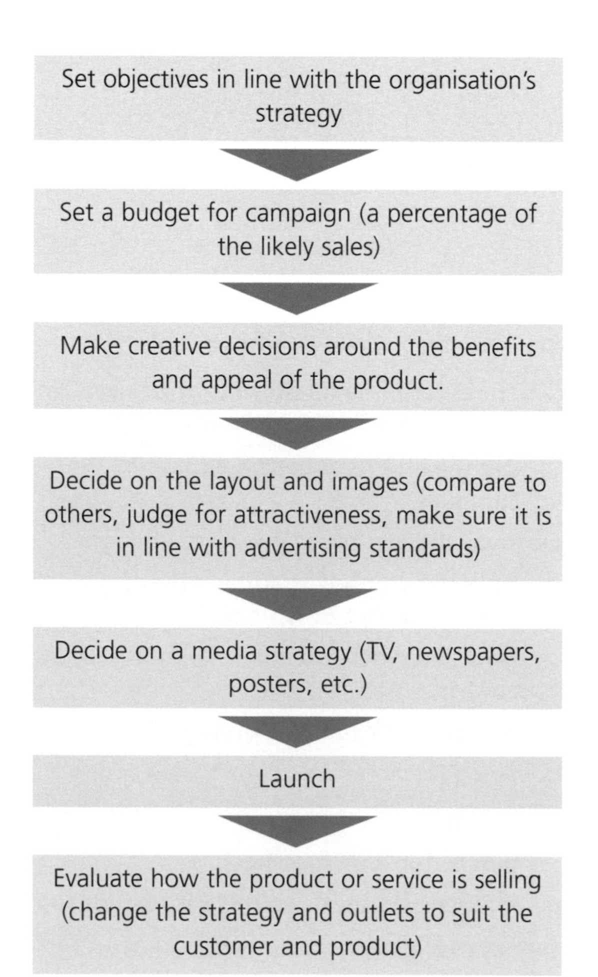

David Beckham faces the media

From a research point of view you might investigate a product range in the leisure industry, how it is advertised and how successful the ad campaign has been.

Celebrity and the media

Celebrity is difficult to define. The idea of a celebrity has evolved from royalty to include reality TV stars and many figures in the leisure industry including sportspersons. Heightened media frenzy around such figures has led to issues surrounding privacy. Some argue that celebrities' professions are in the public eye so they should expect some attention.

Celebrities can have a tremendous influence on young people, who often wish to emulate their heroes in terms of the clothes they wear, sports they play and products they buy. Having a celebrity endorse a product is a very valuable commodity.

Reputations are at stake, particularly in gossip magazines and tabloids, and careers have been irreparably damaged by sensationalist stories. In 2005 the British press praised George Best as a footballer – when he died. However, throughout his life he had been the subject of many newspaper scandals involving his behaviour and drinking.

activity

WHO?

Identify two celebrities who fit each of the descriptions given below.

Then debate what they actually offer the leisure industry.

Someone who:

- influences young people in terms of music and clothes
- uses their celebrity for good causes
- inspires you to play a sport
- endorses leisure products
- has been attacked in the media.

Topic 7 Selecting and planning a research project

In this topic ways in which to formulate your proposal will be explored. It is very important that you are clear about your aims and that they relate to what you produce in your project.

You need to decide what kind of data you will collect and which material you will consult. It is unlikely that you will undertake much experimental (primary) research for your research project; it will mostly be observational research and information from already published research (called desk research, consultation or secondary research).

Your research title can be decided upon and polished further on in your project. As long as you have a good proposal, set within a recognised subject area, you can use what is called a 'working title'. You might find that the title you were originally going to use needs altering as your findings develop.

Examples of research proposals will be provided to help guide you through.

This topic includes some important guidelines to get you on your way:

- Ensuring your topic is related to leisure (selecting from a range of topics)
- Assessing a research topic's feasibility (meeting learning and assessment outcomes)
- Setting parameters for the research
- Deciding what data to collect and how (methodology)
- Accessing and evaluating published material
- Phrasing the title of your project
- Timescale and budget.

There is a useful flowchart of the processes involved on page 155.

Ensuring your topic is related to leisure

In Unit 1 you covered a broad range of leisure activities. This is a good starting point for your selection process. To remind you of the scope look at this table.

Leisure activities by sector

Sector of the leisure industry	*Nature of this sector*	*Example organisations*
Active leisure	Playing sport or making visits	Sport England Next Generation A local authority leisure department
Passive leisure	Going shopping or to the cinema	Library Odeon cinemas
Home-based leisure	DIY, DVDs or cooking	Homebase Blockbuster videos

Leisure has many issues relating to academic areas of study, which might provide you with a focus.

Issues in leisure by area of study

Area of study	Example of research topic
Political	The Government's role in supporting leisure (refer to Topic 6).
Financial	Public expenditure in the leisure industry.
Social	Levels of participation.
Cultural	Cultural habits, trends, fashions and their impact on the industry. Demographics.
Technological	How advances in technology are shaping leisure activities.
Economic	The value of the leisure industry to the economy or the impact on the job market.
Legal	Laws on liability or negligence, and risk assessment at leisure events.
Geographical	The geographic spread of leisure provision.
Environmental	The effect of environmental issues on leisure activities.
Psychological	Understanding what motivates people to pursue certain leisure activities
Commercial	Reaching leisure consumers through marketing. Customer relations in the leisure industry.
Historical	The development of a particular leisure pursuit over the years

As well as a subject area, you might want to consider a research topic in terms of a specific place.

Issues in leisure by place

Places	Example of research topic
Country parks	What are the environmental impacts of leisure events on country parks?
Theme parks	What incentives are theme parks providing to boost numbers?
Urban sports centres	Do urban sports centres solve the problems they set out to address?
Private clubs	Do exclusivity and membership fees help the leisure economy grow?
Cities	How have Athens, Sydney, Atlanta and Barcelona benefited from hosting the Olympic Games?
The home	Is technological change altering the way we approach leisure activities around the home?

In addition, here are a few more ideas based around a variety of issues.

Further issues in leisure

Area of research	Example of research topic
The arts	An audit of provision for the arts.
Sport	How is the provision of sport influenced by religion in the UK?
Hospitality	What training will be needed for the 2012 Olympics?
Adventure tourism	How significant is risk to the future of adventure tourism?
Shopping	How are certain leisure retailers dominating the high street?
Theatre	Are regional theatres viable without subsidies?
Bingo	Why is Bingo viewed as a leisure activity mainly for women?
Pay and conditions for young employees in leisure	Does the current wage structure in the leisure industry increasingly de-motivate staff?
Technology	Has the increase in home entertainment killed the art of conversation?
Hunting	Is hunting a justifiable leisure activity? Should all forms of hunting be banned?
The elderly	Is the over-50s market underserved for leisure?
Fishing	Why is fishing one of the most popular male leisure activities?

Which issues could be studied with regards to a theme park like Pleasure Island?

activity

MATCH UP

Match the following topic areas to the research questions (more than one might apply):

Topic areas

- Inclusion
- Blood sports
- Healthy living
- Government policy

Research questions

- Examine the political, economic and social effect of the fox-hunting ban on a rural community.
- Why do school children spend fewer hours-per-week doing P.E. than several years ago? What is being done to reverse this?
- How have adventure holiday companies ensured that opportunities exist for all types of customers?
- Account for the annual rise in gym membership in the months of January and February.

It should be clear that there are many variations available, many more than shown here or described in any of the six units that make up this course. It is best if you can find something which interests you, something that you would like to discover more about. You might already have a topic area in mind, but at this stage you still have plenty of opportunities to open up to new ideas – you may change your mind and find something more workable.

Assessing a research topic's feasibility

A number of criteria can be applied when you are trying to assess whether to proceed with any topics. Some important questions can be asked to help you test feasibility:

1 Is the topic of sufficient interest to you? There might not be one topic of research that will motivate and stimulate you consistently over a period of time. You need to be aware that some aspects will require concentration, time and effort. Not everything will go smoothly – it would be a small miracle if it did. The ups and downs of your research process will inevitably affect your motivation, so if you choose something you feel strongly about or have a lot of interest in, it should help sustain your dedication to the project.

2 Is it possible to obtain data appropriate to the subject? This will be your first major concern. You will not be able to 'massage' data into the required format, so it is better to adjust the focus of your question or proposal to suit what you can find.

3 Are research techniques available to you? Take time to ensure you can carry out the appropriate testing or research technique (see Topic 8) and that the resources are available.

4 Is time going to be a problem? Overall feasibility is usually linked to time and cost. Deadlines will inevitably apply. You are not a full-time researcher and you may have to juggle a number of other studies with this project.

5 Have you got adequate knowledge of the chosen subject area? If you choose a study based at a tennis club you need to make sure you have enough knowledge (technical and theoretical) about the sport to gather, analyse and present data. It might be that you can learn as the study progresses, so don't let this question dissuade you from researching something you are genuinely interested in.

6 How well does the subject fit into current avenues of research? This requires an in-depth knowledge of the subject and you are unlikely to know this at the outset. It is not essential, but a research proposal that clearly furthers previous studies will be proof of insight and relevance.

7 Is the study of enough contemporary significance? It might help if the issues you are looking at are in the news, or have been in recent years.

8 Is the study going to help you meet the assessment criteria?

Setting parameters for the research

One of the best ways to set the parameters (boundaries) for the research is to identify areas such as those listed in the tables earlier in this topic.

The issue under investigation must be properly defined so that it is not too broad or unmanageable. Attempting to do too much is the most frequent problem encountered by new researchers.

Explanatory research might be undertaken to show the relationship between two variables in a leisure context, such as leisure spend and disposable income.

Your reading might then provide you with accepted theories, which relate to your study. Through both of these processes you are beginning to set the scope of your study.

A more challenging approach might be to tackle an evaluative study – assessing the *performance* of something, such as a policy or programme.

One other strategy might be to increase the intensity of study in a limited area to give more depth.

Honestly report the limitations and drawbacks known to you at the outset, such as bias in reporting or incomplete data. This opportunity should not be used to make excuses for poor research techniques or inadequate preparation.

Setting the parameters of the study should involve:

- setting a limit on the variables to be considered
- describing the key features of the study
- clarifying the data to be collected
- explaining what will be done with the subjects and variables
- clarifying the title (see under heading Phrasing the title of your project).

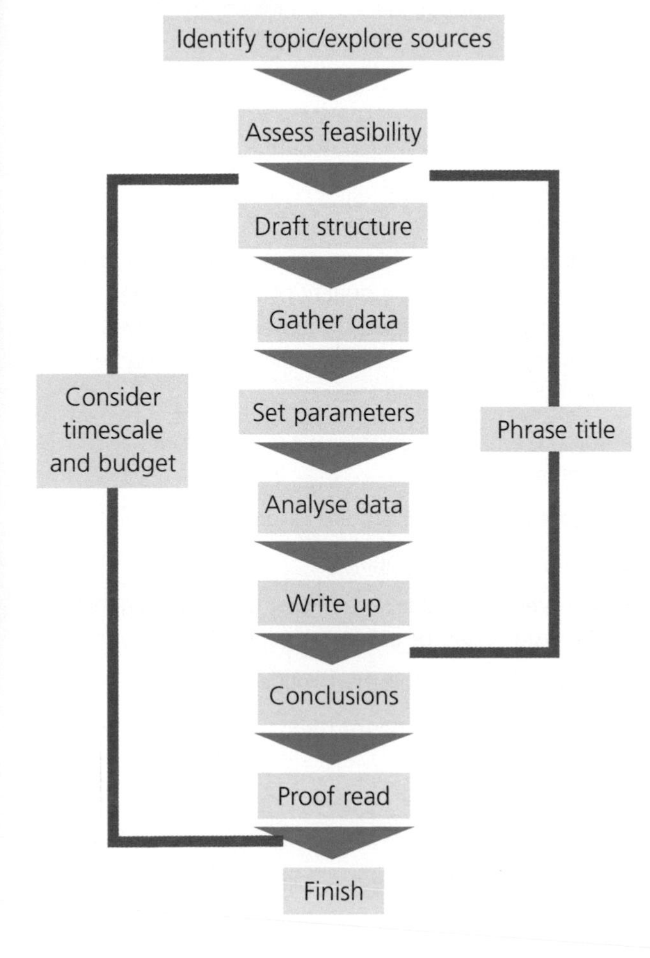

Deciding what data to collect and how (methodology)

Definition of methodology

The means by which a topic is researched, ways of collecting data appropriate to the topic being studied.

You looked at various types of data collection in Unit 4 during your leisure event. Now you get to apply them to your research project. Deciding what information needs to be collected to answer your research question is an important part of your work.

Two aspects are crucial at this stage when deciding what data to collect – validity and reliability.

- Validity is defined as 'the extent to which the measure truly reflects the phenomenon being considered'.

Leisure research is notoriously difficult in terms of validity because research is largely concerned with people's leisure habits and attitudes, there is no definitive data, and the sample taken might not be a true snapshot. Quantitative data might be highly opinionated or even false, without any way of knowing.

- Reliability is 'the extent to which research findings would be the same if the research were repeated again or with a different sample'.

Rarely in leisure research can the exact 'laboratory' conditions be replicated. Findings are really only appropriate to that time, for the sample group, in those conditions.

The most common methods used in leisure research are:

- Consultation – analysing existing papers and published material
- Observation
- Surveys based on questionnaires, interviews or focus groups.

The task at this stage is to match your research question with possible means of data collection. For example, if you are analysing the attendance levels at swimming pools you might consult existing material from swimming governing bodies and/or your local pool, observe practices at your local pool, survey users at your local pool, or refer to existing surveys.

activity

WHAT DO I COLLECT?

What type of data might you collect and assess to answer this research proposal: 'Compare some of the twenty Premiership football clubs and how they provide for grass-roots football and community schemes in their region'?

In some instances you may realise that the data you need to sample or collect is too complex, so you might need to adjust your planning or simplify your question to reduce the workload and complexity. You may not find out until after all the hard work is done that the information does not answer the question (or hypothesis) that you first posed. Some data might simply not be available. At this point you might need to return to the scope and scale of your research and adjust accordingly.

Accessing and evaluating published material

Knowledge of literature in your chosen field of study can be as crucial as your methodology, particularly as secondary material is likely to form the larger share of your research.

Part of your research will be to look at what has already been published on a topic by others and develop an understanding of how the topic has been researched before. As you read, you might identify gaps or weakness in material on the subject, or it might persuade you to alter the focus of your project. You might find that your project has been done many times before.

Consultation material that you might use could be:

- text books
- research papers
- reports
- magazine articles.

Sources for material are:

- libraries
- internet
- periodicals (includes newspapers, journals and magazines).

You have to put in the reading time around your chosen subject to build up your knowledge. In the end it will enhance the quality of your work and the depth of your study (and the grade you achieve). However, too much reading could waste valuable time. Try to find a balance.

If comprehensive enough, your reading could produce the following:

- Evidence of similar studies or data.
- Valuable ideas or theories.
- An overall broader and deeper understanding of the study area, or at least a general background.
- Evidence of where others made mistakes.
- Ideas of how you might make your work different.

activity

DOES YOUR LIBRARY PROVIDE?

Check out your college's library and your local library to see what is available. Make a list of what you think you might need, what is available and what isn't, so that you identify gaps in your sources. Discuss with your tutor how you might fill these gaps.

Phrasing the title of your project

By the time you are in a position to formulate your proposal you should have

- a field of study in leisure to research
- a suitable approach to your research
- plans for data collection
- an idea of the existing material and how to get hold of them.

The next step is to work out how the wording of your title will shape your project.

Your title can be arranged as one of the following:

- Proposal – It sets out what you propose to look into: *A study into the efforts of Macclesfield Council to improve leisure facilities in the Borough.*
- Hypothesis – An unproved theory or suggested explanation as a basis for further work: *There are fewer participants in the game of badminton today than 20 years ago. Account for the extent of this decline.*
- Question – Posed in order to draw out a response: *Have host cities at the Olympic Games benefitted economically and socially from the experience?*

The way you phrase your title can really help you to clarify the parameters of your study. Don't make it too general or vague, such as *A study into home-based leisure pursuits.* Instead, add elements to narrow it down, such as *A study into the rise of electronic home-based leisure pursuits amongst 18–35-year-olds.*

If your title takes the form of a question, the way you phrase it can determine the way you answer it.

- Those beginning with *To what extent…, How far…, How significant…* ask for two sides of an argument with factors under both 'yes' and 'no' headings.
- Those beginning with *Account for…, Why…* ask for a more straightforward explanation.

Remember that a working title means it can be altered at a later point to fit in with your findings or new ideas.

activity

EXPAND AND REDUCE

1 Using the title provided below, decide how else you could widen the study.

How do annual wages amongst 16–21-year-old female seasonal workers in the Italian Alps compare to other sectors of the leisure industry?

2 Using the title provided below, decide how you could limit the study.

Is Wembley Stadium good?

Timescale and budget

At this stage you also need to make some sort of timescale plan which takes account of the stages described above. It is probably best to plan backwards from your date of submission. Allow time for (working backwards) printing, typing up, analysis, data collection, further planning, reading. And allow some time for things going wrong.

Not to be overlooked are the costs and resources. Costs may be incurred through postage, phone calls, paper and printing.

activity

YOUR PROPOSAL

Formulate a broad research proposal now to show what is to be done, as well as how it is to be done, and when it will be done.

In Topic 8 more discussion, illustration and depth of understanding of each of the research areas and methods introduced in this planning topic are given. This will help you structure your work and make more informed decisions about how to carry out the project, assess your outcomes and present the final report.

Topic 8 Final planning and writing of your research proposal

In Topic 7 you looked at ways to formulate your proposal and considered what sort of data to collect, and how. You should now have a good idea about the research topic you want to cover, having looked at suggested issues from the previous topics. Most importantly, you should have identified a research proposal that reveals that the chosen leisure issue has the range and potential for the intended methods of research.

This topic will provide guidance about how to complete the planning process so that you can go ahead, acting as a reminder of what needs to be done:

- **Finalising your proposal**
- **Finalising the research methods**
- **Project format**
- **References and bibliography**
- **Applying ethical standards.**

Finalising your proposal

A research proposal's aims need to give a clear overview and state a general purpose. They must not be vague, but be clear and simple. The objectives provide more depth and give the study an element of measurability – they are the targets or specific goals of the proposal. One common way of remembering the role of aims and objectives is the acronym SMART:

Specific
Measurable
Achievable
Realistic
Timed

If you apply this to your proposal to date it should prompt you to evaluate each objective. Use these questions to test your preparation and proposal to date:

1. Are your objectives specific enough? Specific objectives involve setting quantifiable categories appropriate to your study. This means focusing on those objectives which apply to the core of your study and possibly rejecting some wider objectives. Try to have no more than three objectives.
2. Can you explain how the project aims will encourage meaningful research?

   If you can do this in your introduction, it will help you to gain a higher mark.
3. Are any of your objectives truly measurable? Do they use percentages, volumes, numbers, proportions, scores or ratings, and do you have the necessary skills and tools (maths, IT and graphics) to present the data?
4. Is your proposal feasible? This needs to be judged in terms of time available and volume of work. Have you set out a timescale for each stage of the project?

Finalising the research methods

Secondary

Leisure studies is a relatively new subject area academically and topics will be wide-ranging and multi-disciplinary. Narrowing down research methods will be a demanding task, but one you must not avoid.

The first consideration is working out where you need to look to read around the subject and find appropriate sources of information:

- Bibliographies – lists of textbooks, reports, studies, surveys, articles in magazines and journals, articles on the internet.
- Library catalogues – key word, author title and topic searches all might bear fruit. Your local library may also have an inter-library loan service or access to the British Library. All libraries will have online capabilities and may have access to e-journals or digital learning resources.
- Indexes are published by leisure-related organisations such as the World Leisure and Recreation Association, the Leisure Industry Research Centre, the Leisure Studies Association, Sport England, the Institute of Leisure and Amenity Management, the Institute of Sport and Recreation Management, and the Central Council for Physical Recreation.
- Related subject areas, such as sociology, economics, culture and media, may publish similarly useful sources.

Try to ensure that you use a substantial amount of information from a variety of sources, but not so much that it overwhelms you.

Care should be taken to adopt the Harvard referencing system so that you can present your references correctly in your bibliography and while quoting in your report. At assessment your sources will be checked via these references. See below for more details.

The second consideration is analysing data. If you know where to look, it can save a lot of time avoiding large-scale primary research. Sources of leisure data are:

- The General Household Survey – Uses national sampling data and although general, it is reliable and valid. It captures data such as age ranges, activities, time periods, social characteristics and participation.
- The Family Expenditure Survey – A voluntary survey of a random sample of private households in the United Kingdom carried out by the Office for National Statistics.
- The Census from the Office for National Statistics – The most comprehensive survey of the UK population. This offers a good range of material on population profiles (demographics), gender balance, age range, occupational groups, family type and sizes, etc. The most recent was conducted in 2001 and the survey is taken every 10 years.

All are available from www.statistics.gov.uk

Specialist studies are carried out by consultancy groups and market researchers. You won't be able to afford the full reports as these are expensive, but you may find summaries published on associated websites. These studies might cover specific sports, membership of gyms, accident rates and group leisure travel.

It helps if you are able to understand the relevance of what has been written previously. If you can identify a pattern of thought, gaps, mistakes or opportunities for further study in previously published material you will gain a higher mark. Throughout your project you can report such findings, highlighting opportunities for further study in your conclusions.

activity

LIST OF SOURCES

Using the information given above and sources you may have already, compile a comprehensive list of sources that you are likely to use or consult. This should be split into textbooks, magazines, journals, websites, newspaper articles, official reports and surveys.

Primary

If you do choose to undertake some fieldwork, the following is worth bearing in mind. Decide whether qualitative data (see box below) or quantitative data (observation techniques, interviews, ethnography) is more appropriate to your area of study. What results do you expect to get?

Five useful types of qualitative data:

1. Descriptive – covering a single group
2. Comparative – covering two or more groups
3. Relationships – correlations between various traits
4. Inferential – observed data from a sample are used to make generalisations
5. Predictive – the unknown is predicted from the known and measurable.

You don't want to waste too much time by carrying out a lot of primary research, the results of which you cannot use, so choose your methods carefully and explain the reasons for using them in your project.

The most important thing to remember is to **explain**. Explain your:

- aims
- objectives
- methodology
- analysis
- conclusions.

Project format

Your introduction will contain the aims and objectives. You will then need to write about the methodology used and its relevance to the subject. You can then present your findings and provide analysis. Your conclusions will bring together your main findings, including any outstanding questions that you might consider for further research. The structure is completed by a list of references and a bibliography.

References and bibliography

All statements, opinions, conclusions, etc. taken from another writer's work should be cited, whether the work is directly quoted, paraphrased or summarised. One of the more popular systems of referencing is the Harvard system (see box overleaf).

The Harvard referencing system

In your main text – where you have quoted someone's work – you just put, in brackets, the author's surname and the year of publication.

Example: (Hamilton, 1995).

In the Bibliography, you must put all the details needed by the reader to find the source, if they want to. All the entries are arranged alphabetically, in one list. This means that the reader, who won't know from the main text whether a reference is to a book, an article or a website, can always find the details. These details are laid out in a standard way, which varies for books, articles and internet sites:

Books

- Author's surname, followed by their initials
- Year of publication in brackets
- Title of publication – in italics
- Place of publication
- Publisher

Example: Hamilton, F. (1995) *Tourism and Crime*, London: Collinson.

Articles in journals, magazines or newspapers

- Author's surname, followed by their initials
- Year of publication in brackets
- Title of article – in quotation marks
- Name of the journal, magazine or newspaper – in italics
- Day and month of publication
- Page number (abbreviated to p.)

Example: Selvey, S. (1999) 'Caught in a pitch and toss', *Guardian*, 13 June, Travel p.10.

Internet sites

- Author's surname, followed by their initials (If no name is given, use the name of the organisation.)
- Year in brackets (If no publication date is given, put 'no date'.)
- Title in italics, followed by 'online' in brackets
- 'Available from:' website address (the URL – Universal Resource Locator – or at least the website homepage address)
- The date when you accessed it – in brackets.

Example: Rough Guides (no date), *Australia* (on-line). Available from: http:// www.hotwired.com/rough/australia (accessed 10 April 2000).

For more information on this method of referencing you may visit your local library or see the website www.libweb.apu.ac.uk.

Applying ethical standards

Ethical issues arise in a number of ways related to research. There are issues surrounding:

Privacy – research should never invade an individual's or organisation's privacy. Permission may be granted for some information.

Confidentiality – Sensitive information should not be used, e.g. financial data, personal information, unless permission is granted.

Data protection – Information may not be passed on to third parties unless permission is given.

research**focus**

Graham Saffery, teacher

Blackpool Sixth Form College

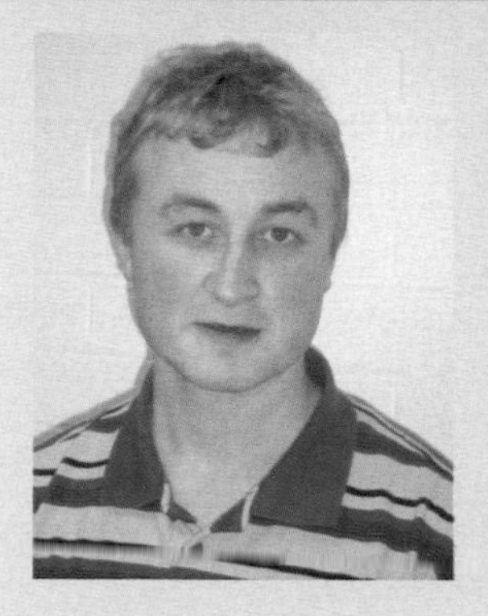

Graham Saffery teaches A level PE, BTEC Sport and BTEC Sports Science at Blackpool Sixth Form College. He has also taught research and scientific methods at various levels for the past seven years and supported HND students with their dissertations.

He is used to giving advice about research projects, so you should find his practical advice very useful, especially if you still have any outstanding questions about how exactly to proceed.

Q When your students are starting some research what advice do you give them, with regard to:

planning their work?

- READ, READ, and READ prior to deciding on your title; once you have a good feel for the topic you should be able to choose an appropriate title.
- Never rush into a piece of work.
- Consider using a pilot study.
- Choose a topic that you are interested in – you will be spending a lot of time working on the topic.
- Speak to your tutor before deciding on a topic. They will be able to discuss potential pitfalls with you and advise you about what to concentrate on.
- Produce a schedule setting out clear dates, for example, deadlines for each of your drafts.

finding out what has been done previously?

- It is important to consider any research, in the form of articles, reports or studies, which have been done previously on your chosen topic. This will help you know your project better and understand what areas have either not been covered, or have been exhausted by previous research.
- Even if an article is not directly related to your project, you might find that something in it may be useful as a discussion point.
- See below for details on accessing useful sources of information.

carrying out their research?

- Work in an organised manner using files, labeling systems, diaries, databases and schedules.
- Never throw anything away; you may need the information at a later date. Make sure you keep your raw data such as tables or completed questionnaires.
- Keep your work together, whether it is paper-based or electronic. It can be time-consuming if you lose parts of the project.

presenting their work?

- Use an appropriate style and format (the font, for example, should be either Times Roman or Arial, size 12).
- Use one and a half or double line spacing. This is so your tutor can make appropriate comments between the lines – it will help them provide feedback.
- Have a contents page and number pages.
- Reference all quotes, figures, diagrams, tables and pictures that are other people's work (be aware of plagiarism).
- Have clear bold headings and subheadings (this will allow you to check your progress).
- Have a clear gap between paragraphs.
- Use the Harvard system for referencing.
- Get someone to proofread your work. NEVER rely on a spell checker, it doesn't find *everything*.
- If you have appendices, make sure they are relevant and clearly labeled. An appendix is not a dumping ground for paper, it is an active part of the project.

accessing useful sources of information?

- A good starting point – often over-looked – is using the referencing within the textbooks you use. Usually there will be a list of further reading, which will give you a clearer idea of the previous research.

Throughout this book you can find links to a large variety of organisations (see list on pages 8–9) and websites (see list on pages 164–5) from all over the leisure industry. Some contain reports and studies written by professionals.

- Ask your tutor who may be able to guide you with some key articles or researchers names in your field of study.
- Ask your Learning Resource Centre staff for help – they often have useful information which you may not be aware of.
- Even if your Learning Resource Centre does not have a wide range of books, the staff will be able to order the book you want through the British Library system.
- Remember that you have a wide variety of resources at your disposal, such as the internet, books, audiotapes, video, DVD, newspapers, radio and TV.

Q What would you say are the most common mistakes that students make while conducting their studies?

- Failing to keep references up-to-date. This means that near the end of compiling the project, students are searching for references to pieces they have used and cannot find.
- Not spending enough time researching and reading. This helps set parameters early on and can actually save time by avoiding further research at the writing up stage.
- Losing sight of the original aims and objectives. These should always be at the forefront of the mind.
- Failing to expand on discussion points. Throughout the topic ask yourself the question: 'what does this mean, or what are the implications?'
- Failure to get your work proofread. Fresh eyes always spot the basic errors that the writer will miss. Small mistakes can make a project look unprofessional.

Q What advice would you give students considering researching a leisure topic in areas such as health and lifestyle, gender and race, and equality and diversity.

Within these areas there a multitude of research topics you may choose. It is therefore important that you start off with one fairly narrow, simple idea or study topic, for example, the influence of computer games on physical activity in children aged 13–15. Do not aim to cover a wide area. Remember you are doing a research project, not a PHD.

Q Finally, what would you advise if a student's motivation is dwindling?

- Speak to your tutor at the earliest opportunity. The later the problem is left, the more exaggerated it will become.
- Perhaps reconsider your topic area if it does not hold enough interest for you. However, this can only be done during the earlier stages. There comes a point when starting over would simply be unmanageable.
- Carry out the project in digestible chunks. This helps you appreciate the progress you make.
- If needs be, rearrange your schedule from your original plan, so that completing the project is still realistic and achievable. Do not set impossible deadlines and give appropriate amounts of time to tasks.
- Speak to the college support services, as they will offer a lot of practical advice and will be familiar with this issue.
- Take breaks. I have never worked on a Saturday afternoon because that is my time for watching football. Use these reward times for whatever interests you have. These times will seem even more special if you have worked hard during the week.

How Unit 6 is assessed

Unit 6 is assessed through coursework, in this case a research project, which you have to complete on your own, on a topic of your own choice from the leisure industry.

Your work must include evidence of:

- a research plan that identifies the topic together with the project aims and methodology
- research that includes references related to the research topic
- presentation of the completed research project
- an evaluation of the research project.

How you present the final version may well depend on a number of factors and the nature of the study. Indeed no two research projects in your class should, or are likely to, be the same. However, the key content and guidance is given below:

- Give a clear description of the subject to be examined and its relevance to leisure studies.
- Give a detailed plan of action, describing your objectives – not an outline.
- Assess the feasibility of the whole project before undertaking detailed work.
- Demonstrate where you have taken your knowledge and ideas for research from.
- Clearly lay out how you will carry out your research (methodology) for both primary and secondary data collection, describing any weaknesses or opportunities in the material that you notice.
- A section on your findings clearly presented.
- An evaluation section covering conclusions, analysis and any recommendations.

It would be wise to keep your tutor fully informed of progress to ensure the suitability of your proposal and work pattern.

Improving your grades

In general, you will get better grades by giving more comprehensive explanations, including good examples and showing a deeper understanding of the subject of your project. Your school or college should be able to help you in more detail, or you could visit the Edexcel website: **edexcel.org.uk** for more guidance.

General guidelines on presentation of assignments

Whilst the way in which you present your assessment evidence will not directly affect your grade, it is important that you strive to present it in a professional and well-structured way. The following are a few tips on achieving good presentation.

1. All assignments should be word processed, using a suitable font, such as Ariel. Try to avoid 'casual' fonts, such as Comic Sans.
2. You can use a different font for titles if you wish, but do not use more than two fonts in your work.
3. Be consistent in your font size. Generally, 14 or 16 is suitable for titles, and 12 for the main text.
4. Only use bold for titles – not the whole report.
5. Use italics and 'quotation marks' to show when you have copied text from another source, and indicate the source in brackets after the quote.
6. If you choose to use more than one colour in your work, limit this to two, for example, blue for titles and black for the main text.
7. Avoid using 'Wordart' for titles.
8. Use 1.5 line spacing throughout your work.
9. Do not cut and paste cartoon-style clipart into your work.
10. If you use photographs in your work, label each image underneath.
11. Insert page numbers into your finished work.

Useful websites

Public sector

Advisory Conciliation and Arbitration Services	acas.co.uk
Arts Council	artscouncil.org.uk
BBC	bbc.co.uk
Bristol City Council	bristol-city.gov.uk
Carmarthen Council	carmarthenshire.gov.uk
Census 2001	statistics.gov.uk
Charter Mark	cabinetoffice.gov.uk/chartermark
Chichester District Council	chichester.gov.uk
Commission for Racial Equality	cre.gov.uk
Connexions	connexions.gov.uk
Countryside Agency	countryside.gov.uk
Depart of Trade and Industry (DTI)	dti.gov.uk
Department for Culture, Media and Sport	culture.gov.uk
Department for Education and Skills (DfES)	dfes.gov.uk
Department for Environment, Food and Rural Affairs	defra.gov.uk
Department for Work and Pensions	dwp.gov.uk
Department of Health	dh.gov.uk
English Heritage	english-heritage.org.uk
Environment Agency	environment.gov.uk
Equal Opportunities Commission	eoc.gov.uk
Family Expenditure Survey	statistics.gov.uk
General Household Survey	statistics.gov.uk
Health and Safety Executive	hse.gov.uk
Highland Council	highland.gov.uk
Hounslow Borough Council	hounslow.gov.uk
Manchester City Council	manchester.gov.uk
Reading Borough Council	reading.gov.uk
Scarborough Borough Council	scarborough.gov.uk
Social Exclusion Unit	socialexclusionunit.gov.uk
Sporting Equals	cre.gov.uk
UK Sport	uksport.gov.uk
Westminster Council	westminster.gov.uk

Private sector

Accolade Corporate Events UK	accolade-corporate-events.com
Acorn Adventure	november.acumedia.co.uk
Alton Towers	alton-towers.co.uk
Anywork Anywhere	anyworkanywhere.com
Boat Race	theboatrace.org
Bourne Leisure	bourneleisure.co.uk
Camp Beaumont	campbeaumont.com
Center Parcs	centerparcs.com
Concerto Group	concertogroup.co.uk
David Lloyd Leisure	davidlloydleisure.co.uk
Disney	disneyinternational.com
DTB International – Hospitality and Events Management	dtbsportsandevents.com
Fitness First	fitnessfirst.com
Flamingo Land	flamingoland.co.uk
Haven Holidays	havenholidays.com
Henley Royal Regatta	hrr.co.uk
HF Walking Holidays	hfholidays.co.uk
International Convention Centre, Birmingham	theicc.co.uk
LA Fitness	lafitness.co.uk
Leisure Opportunities magazine	leisureopportunities.co.uk
Leisurejobs	leisurejobs.co.uk
Maximillion Events Ltd	maximillion.co.uk
McDonalds	mcdonalds.co.uk
Odeon Cinemas	odeon.co.uk
PGL	pgl.co.uk
Royal Ascot	royalascot.co.uk
Scarborough Spa	scarboroughspa.com
Silverstone (home of British Grand Prix)	silverstone-circuit.co.uk
Weight Watchers	weightwatchers.co.uk
Welcome Host	welcometoexcellence.co.uk
Wimbledon (All England Lawn Tennis Club)	wimbledon.org
Youth Hostels Association	yha.org.uk

Charities

Childline	childline.org.uk
Greenwich Leisure Limited	gll.org
Mencap	mencap.org.uk
National Society for the Prevention of Cruelty to Children	nspcc.org.uk
National Trust	nationaltrust.org.uk
Raleigh International	raleighinternational.org
Ramblers Association	ramblers.org.uk
Royal National Institute for the Blind	rnib.org
Sense (UK deafblind charity)	sense.org.uk
Sportsaid	sportsaid.org.uk
TimeBank	timebank.org.uk

Professional bodies

Association of Exhibition Organisers	exhibitions.work.co.uk
British Association of Leisure Parks	balppa.org
Chartered Institute for Personnel Development	cipd.co.uk
Institute of Leisure and Amenity Management (ILAM)	ilam.co.uk
Institute of Occupational Safety and Health	iosh.co.uk
Institute of Sport and Recreation Management (ISRM)	isrm.co.uk
Recreation Managers Association	rma-ofgb.org
Skills Active	skillsactive.com
Trade Unions Council (TUC)	tuc.org.uk

Sporting bodies

British Olympic Association	olympics.org.uk
British Paralympics Association	paralympcs.org.uk
Capital Sport	capital-sport.co.uk
FIFA (Fédération Internationale de Football Association)	fifa.com
Fitness Industry Association	fia.org.uk
Football Association	thefa.com
International Association of Athletics Federations (IAAF)	iaaf.org
International Olympic Committee (IOC)	olympic.org
Lawn Tennis Association	lta.org.uk
National Coaching Foundation	sportscoachuk.org
Rugby Football Union	rfu.com
Sport England	sportengland.org.uk
Women's Sports Foundation	wsf.org.uk

Other

Advertising Standards Authority	asa.org.uk
Business in Sport and Leisure	bisl.org
Central Council of Physical Recreation	ccpr.co.uk
Disability Rights Commission	drc-gb.org
Drugs in Sport	drugsinsport.net
EM Media	em-media.org.uk
English Federation of Disability Sport	efds.net
European Leisure & Recreation Association	elra.net
Flora London Marathon	london-marathon.co.uk
International Organisation of Standardization (ISO)	iso.org
Investors in People	investorsinpeople.co.uk
Let's Kick Racism Out of Football	kickitout.org
London 2012 official site	london2012.org
Long Way Round (EwanMcGregor and Charlie Boorman)	longwayround.com
National Railway Museum	nrm.org.uk
Quest	quest-uk.org
Team Ellen (Ellen MacArthur)	teamellen.com
VisitBritain	visitbritain.com
World Anti-Doping Agency	wada-ama.org

Glossary

absenteeism persistent absence

accessible easy to reach or get into

Act of Parliament a part of the law passed by Parliament

action plan a strategy for achieving results

active being physically energetic

administration the management of affairs of an organisation

AIDA awareness, interest, desire, action

aims overviews of what you want to achieve

amenity a useful facility or service

anorexia a disorder characterized by fear of becoming fat and refusal of food, leading to weakness and even death

appraisal the process of considering and evaluating the performance of an employee with the objective of improving job performance

apprenticeship a form of training which involves workers committing themselves to one employer for a period of time during which they acquire the skills of the trade

brainstorming a technique for generating ideas in which members of a group express ideas as they think of them

break-even the short-run rate of sales at which a supplier generates just enough revenue to cover his fixed and variable costs

budget an organisation's predetermined financial plan for a given future period

chauvinistic having a smug, irrational belief in thesuperiority of one's own sex or race

clerical administrative activities such as typing and filing

commercial having profit as the main aim

community the people living in one locality or the locality in which they live. A group of people having cultural, religious, ethnic, or other characteristics in common. The public in general

commute a regular journey between one's home and place of work

consultation a process where people seek the views of others before finally deciding what course of action to take

contingency plans plans which would be adopted in the event of an organisation's original plans being thwarted to avoid disruption

contract a legally enforceable agreement between two or more parties (contract of employment)

corporate culture the distinctive culture of an organisation that influences the level of formality, loyalty and general behaviour of its employees

corporate identity the ethos, aims and values of an organisation, presenting a sense of its individuality which helps differentiate it from its competitors

critical path analysis a method of planning, scheduling and controlling projects involving interrelated but distinct activities

culture ideas, beliefs, traditions and practices, or the way of life of a particular group of people

customer (external) a private customer or a customer from another organisation

customer someone who receives a service

customer (internal) a customer from another part of the same organisation

customer charter a statement detailing what an organisation will do for the customer. A customer charter is a statement of intent and is generally not part of the contract that a service deliverer makes with its customer

customer service/customer care the marketing and technical functions which deal direct with customers to ensure a healthy relationship

CV curriculum vitae, personal data for a job application

data items of information

deadline a time limit for an activity

demographics data resulting from the study of the growth, size, distribution, movement and composition of human populations

desk research see primary research

direct mail/mailshot a form of marketing aimed at obtaining and retaining customers where the supplier contacts customers directly by mail

disciplinary procedure a set of rules governing the way managers should conduct investigations into infringements of company rules or unsatisfactory performance by employees

discrimination unjust treatment of people of which the main forms are: sex discrimination; race discrimination; disability discrimination

disengagement not being involved in an activity

dismissal the termination of an employee's employment with an organisation, or firing

equality of opportunity approaches to equality that promote equal access and by providing a fair and equal chance to gain access to resources or opportunities

ethnicity a social profile used to classify people according to their social and cultural heritage and identification

evaluation judgement on the quality of something

expenditure that which is spent

facilities a space or building providing supporting capability

feasibility study a study designed to determine the practicability of a system or plan

feedback information in response to an inquiry

finance the system of money

flyers leaflets used as a promotional tool

focus group a group of people brought together to give their opinions on a particular issue or product

gender the social and cultural attributes and expectations that society attaches to men and women through notions of appropriate masculinity and femininity

hallmark event distinguished event

hazard something can be dangerous

health and safety the regulation of organisation's working methods so as to discourage dangerous practices

homophobia hatred or fear of homosexuality

hospitality receptiveness and kindness towards customers

HRM human resource management

implement to carry something out or put into action

incentives a motivating influence or additional payment made to employees as a means of increasing production

inclusion being part of, or included, in something

induction the initial training an employee may receive at the start of employment to familiarise themselves with the organisation

investigating enquire or examine thoroughly and systematically

labour the human input to work activity

leave permission to be absent or the duration of such absence, officially excused from work

legislation written, or statute laws that have been passed by parliament

lifestyle a combination of attitudes , habits or behaviours that have a significant influence on the way a person lives and experiences their daily life

lobbying an attempt to influence in the formation of policy

local authority an administrative body, such as a county council, city council or metropolitan borough council

logistics the functions involved in moving materials

market research the collection and analysis of information about a particular market

marketing the managerial process of identifying customer requirements and satisfying them by providing customers with appropriate products in order to achieve the organisation's objectives

marketing mix see Ps (the four)

maternity leave a period of paid absence from work to which a woman is legally entitled to during the months immediately before and after childbirth

motivation the force or process which drives people to behave in the way that they do

national insurance state insurance based on weekly contributions from employees and employers and providing payments to the unemployed, the sick, the retired and medical services

NOS National Occupational Standards

not-for-profit sector the collective term used to describe organisations who provide services on a basis where profit making is not required

notice period the time between an advanced notification of intention to end a contract (leave a job) and the act of doing so

nutrition the process of taking in and absorbing nutrients, the process of being nourished

NVQs national vocational qualifications

obesity a very overweight state, usually defined by a body mass index of 30 or more

objectives the goals which an organisation sets for itself, which in turn determine the strategic and operational policies it adopts

orientation a course, programme or lecture introducing somebody to a new situation or environment

parameters constant or limiting factors

participants someone who is actively involved in something

partnership event an event where organisations from a mixture of the public, private or voluntary sector are involved

passive not active or not participating noticeably in an activity, like a spectator

paternity leave a period of paid absence from work which a father is legally entitled to

peer group/peers a group of approximately the same age who see themselves, and are seen by others, as associated, or belonging together in some way

peer review the process of screening and evaluating the work of peers

piece rates rates of pay for completion of a job

PEST(LE) analysis a framework used by strategists to identify those factors which affect an organisation's activities: political, economic, social, technological (legislative, environmental)

policy a plan of action or an expression of purpose, adopted or pursued by an individual, government or organisation

population all people living in a defined area or place

prejudice an unreasonable or unfair dislike or preference. Prejudices are typically reflected in negative attitudes towards particular groups of people

premises buildings, particularly as in a place of business

price-skimming a pricing technique designed to allow a business to charge each potential customer the most that he or she would be willing pay for a given product or service. The product or service is first offered at the highest price that customers will pay, and the price is incrementally dropped until it reaches a level designed to be viable for the long term

primary research when data is collected specifically for the study at hand. It can be obtained either by the investigator observing the subject being studied, or communicating directly or indirectly with the subject

prioritising arranging items to be attended to (in order of their importance)

private sector the collective term used to describe leisure businesses and the self-employed who provide services on a commercial, profit-making basis

product lifecycle the typical sales pattern of a product over time from its introduction

profit the difference that arises when sales revenue is greater than total costs

promotional techniques the means which an organisation can use to inform prospective customers of the nature and attributes of its products. Made up of advertising, sales promotion, personal selling, direct marketing, internet marketing and public relations

P's (the four), the marketing mix product, place, price, promotion

public relations (PR) a general means of promoting an organisation's company image

publicity the technique or process of attracting public attention to people, public interest resulting from information supplied by such a technique

public sector the part of an economy that consists of state-owned institutions, including services provided by local authorities, such as leisure centres

race a group of people of common ancestry, distinguished from others by physical characteristics

racism a hostile attitude or discriminatory behaviour, based on racial prejudice, towards members of other races, usually on the grounds that they are somehow inferior

recruitment and selection the process of filling job vacancies in an organisation by hiring new employees, often recurring

redeployment assigning to a new position (job)

redundancy the termination of an individual's employment when the employer ceases trading or the job ceases to be required because of rationalisation, change of product, etc

regeneration physical renewal or revitalisation of an area

remuneration the pay or reward to workers and managers for their labour services, in the form of wages, salaries and bonuses

resources an input (e.g. raw material, people, machinery) which is combined with other inputs to supply a good service

risk assessment the process of identifying and evaluating the possible impact of risks or hazards that exist

seasonal occurring at a certain season or part of the year

secondary research when a project requires a summary or collection of existing data

short list a list of suitable applicants for a job, a list of preferred items

SMART specific, measurable, achievable, realistic, timed

spectator a person viewing anything, such as a sport

sponsor a provider of funds, resources or services to an individual, event or organisation, which in return receives some rights and association which may be used for commercial advantage

staff a group of people employed by a company

staffing audit an inspection, correction and verification of staff

statute another term for an Act of Parliament or legislation

stereotype to characterise and label all members of a social group in some way, regardless of the differences between such people. A simplistic generalisation

strategy overall plan

suppliers a producer or distributor of a good or service

SWOT analysis a framework for identifying the internal strengths and weaknesses of something, the external opportunities open to it and threats it faces which an be used in formulating a strategy

timescale the span of time within which certain events occur, or are scheduled to occur, considered in relation to any broader period of time

USPs unique selling points

VDU visual display unit

venue any place where an organised gathering, such as a concert, is held

voluntary sector the collective term used to describe organisations who provide services on a voluntary basis

volunteers a person who serves or acts in a specified function without promise of payment

working time regulations laws that address what hours are acceptable to work to during a week

working title a provisional or temporary title of a report

Many of the defintions used in this glossary can be found in the *Collins internet-linked dictionary of Business* (ISBN: 000720583X).

Ideal for more in-depth explanations to all the key areas of business theory and practice:

- marketing
- production
- finance
- human resources
- business policy
- international business

All of these areas are covered in the *Leisure Studies AS and A2 for Edexcel* books and and the *Collins internet-linked dictionary of Business* provides a practical companion to this book.

Index

absence from work 93
absenteeism 94
accident report sheet 43
action plans 37, 54, 55
administration 21
  administrative systems 42–3
  evaluation 60
  non-routine work 42–3
  routine work 42
adoption leave 95
advertising 19, 26, 34, 150–1
  recruitment 70, 71, 82–3
Advisory, Conciliation and Arbitration Service (ACAS) 82, 87, 96
AIDA 34
aims 13, 16, 19, 25, 30, 60, 137
  see also objectives
Alton Towers 13
annual leave 92–3
anorexia nervosa 124
ante-natal care, time off for 95
Anywork Anywhere 77–8
application forms 84, 85
  see also job applications
appraisals 97, 100
apprenticeships 78
assessment
  Unit 4 61, 64–5
  Unit 5 66, 116–17
  Unit 6 163
Athens Olympics 2004 43

bar charts 43
Beckham, David 151
Best, George 151
bonuses 103
books 147
Boorman, Charley 56
Bourne Leisure 100
brainstorming 14, 36, 154
break-even 19, 33
Brentford Fountain 114–15
Bristol City Council 90, 92
British Olympic Committee (BOC) 41
brochures 26
budgets 21, 39
bulimia 124

Carmarthen Council 129
case studies
  Billy Jones 73
  Bourne Leisure 100
  David Lloyd Great Mile Runs 23
  disability discrimination 107
  girl saved from drowning 112
  Greenwich Leisure Limited 76
  HF Walking Holidays 17
  People 1st 73
  The Adventure Motorcycling handbook 56
cash flow 21
casual staff 76, 109
Charter Mark 28, 100
Chartered Institute for Personnel Development (CIPD) 82, 87
checklists 37, 54, 55, 57, 62
Chichester District Council 142–3
children
  employment of 110–11
  protection of 113
Commission for Racial Equality 107
communication 50–1, 56
  checklist 57
  with customers 28
  external 51, 56
  peer review 59
  team communication 50, 56
competitive pricing 33
complaints procedure 28
confidentiality 160
Connexions 78
contact database 55
contingency fund 39
contingency plans 47, 60, 62
contracts of employment 74, 78–9, 109
corporate culture 102
covering letter 85
curriculum vitae (CV) 73, 84, 85
customer care 30, 56
customer charter 27
customer communications 28
customer needs 26
  assessing 19
  external customers 26–7, 55
  identifying 30
  internal customers 27, 55
  meeting 27
customer relations 27–8
customer satisfaction 28–9
customer service 27–9

data protection 160
database of contacts 55
David Lloyd Great Mile Runs 23
deadlines 56, 57, 60
Department for Culture, Media and Sport (DCMS) 141
diary 10, 16, 17, 42, 44, 47, 54, 55
diet 123
direct mail 34
direct marketing 26
disability discrimination 106–7
Disability Rights Commission 107
Disability Sport 125
disciplinary procedures 95–6
discount pricing 33
discrimination 105–7
  see also equality
dismissal 97
Disneyland 102, 112
diversity 127–8
drug dependency 122–3

eating disorders 124
election campaigns 145
electronic games 148
EM Media 137

employment contracts 74, 78–9, 109
Equal Opportunities Commission 107
equal pay 105–6
equality 126–7
campaigns for leisure equality 133, 134–5
gender issues 130–2
homosexuality 132–3
race and ethnicity 133–4
see also discrimination
evaluation 22, 47
areas to evaluate 58
customer care 56
effectiveness of planning 60, 62
feedback 58–9, 62
marketing 30, 35, 60
meeting deadlines 60
peer review 59
personal evaluation 59
success of event 60
team effectiveness 61
triangle diagram 61
events
administration 21
aims and purposes 137–8
choosing 14–15
complexity, assessing 13–14, 16, 60
cultural value 139
economic value 138–9
environmental value 139
feasibility 18–19, 20, 23
legal aspects 14, 22, 45–6, 60
marketing *see* marketing
parameters 15, 16
physical resource needs 20, 62
political value 139
reviewing 22, 47
seasonal 13, 136–7
social value 139
sources of information 63
staffing 21, 62
staging 145
success 60–1
value 138–9

feasibility 18–19, 36, 60
assessing 23
financial 21
of research topic 154
testing 18–19
feedback 19, 29
giving and receiving 58–9
informal 29
peer review 47, 59
personal evaluation 59
sources 58–9
films 148
finance 31, 38, 60
budgets 21, 39
cash box 39
cash flow 21
contingency fund 39
financial feasibility 21
objectives 33
payment methods 39
records 39
reporting after the event 39
resource costs 39
start-up costs 21, 39
firework display 13
flexible working 90
focus groups 29, 35
Football Association (FA) 141
free events 19, 33
full-time work 69–70

gender issues 130–2
see also equality; sexual discrimination
Greenwich Leisure Limited 76
Grey-Thompson, Tanni 107
grievance procedures 95–6

health and safety 14, 45, 111–13
healthy living campaigns 125
heart disease 122
Herzberg's motivators and satisfiers diagram 49
HF Walking Holidays 17
Highland Region local authority 129
homosexuality 132–3
hours of work 89–90
flexible working 90
part-time jobs 71–2, 109
scheduled breaks 90–2
Working Time Regulations 89, 91–2, 108–10
Human Resource Management (HRM) 40, 80, 101
see also staffing

incentives 102–3
inclusion schemes 128–9
induction 88–9
industry focus 62, 114–15, 161–2
Institute for Employment Studies 90
Institute of Leisure and Amenity Management (ILAM) 126, 141
Institute of Sport and Recreation Management (ISRM) 126, 141
insurance 21, 45, 46
International Olympic Committee (IOC) 10
International Organisation of Standards (ISO) 28, 100
internet 148
interviewing 86–7
Investors in People (IIP) 28, 90, 100

job adverts 70, 71, 82–3
job analysis 81–2
job applications
application forms 84, 85
curriculum vitae (CV) 73, 84, 85
letter of application 84, 85
see also recruitment; selection
job descriptions 82, 84
job interviews 86–7
job share 75

KISS principle 13, 14

leadership 49–50
choosing a leader 50
style 49
Tannenbaum and Schmidt Continuum 49
Learning Skills Council 78
legal aspects 14, 22, 45–6, 60
health and safety 45
risk assessment 45–6
security procedures 46
Leisure Industries Research Centre 144
letter of application 84, 85
log book 10, 16, 17, 21, 42, 44, 50, 55
logistics 62, 138
London Olympics bid 38, 43

MacArthur, Ellen 52
McGregor, Ewan 56
magazines 125, 146
Manchester City Council 127, 133
market research 34–5
marketing 13, 19, 30–5
evaluation 30, 35, 60
four Ps 19, 30, 32–4
market research 34–5
marketing mix 32–4
marketing plan 30–2
PEST analysis 30, 31
place 19, 32

price 19, 33
product 19, 32
promotion 19, 34
segmentation 137–8
SWOT analysis 30, 31
Master Tournament
Royal Albert Hall 13
Masters Swimming Championships 1996 144
maternity leave 94
Mayo, Elton 99
media 146–51
sport and 149
methodology 155
mobile telephones 148
motivation 49, 56, 98–9, 162
Herzberg's motivators and satisfiers diagram 49
management methods 99
motivational flowchart 98
motivational theory 98–9
remuneration and incentives 102–3
staff development and training 100–1
working environment 101–2
music 148–9

National Railway Museum 129
National Vocational Qualifications (NVQs) 78
newspapers 146
notice periods 95
Nova International 23

obesity 120–1
objectives 12, 13, 16, 19, 25–6, 30, 137
discussing 26
evaluation 60
financial 33
flowchart 25
meeting 60
SMART 25, 39, 60, 99, 158
see also aims
Oliver, Jamie 140, 141
Olympic Games 10
organisational culture 102
orientation 88

parental leave 95
part-time jobs 71–2, 109
term time only 72
twilight shifts 72
zero hours 72
participant needs 18
see also customer needs
partnership events 10
paternity leave 95
pay 102–3
equal pay 105–6
payment methods 39
peer review 47, 59
peer evaluation 59
peer evaluation chart 40
People 1st 73
performance measurement 40
swingometer chart 16
performance-related pay 103
person specifications 82, 84
personal evaluation 59
chart 41
personal selling 26, 34
personnel see staffing
PEST analysis 30, 31
PESTLE 01, 131
piece rates 103
portfolio 10, 55, 61, 64
Positive Futures 143
price 19, 33
price-skimming 33
privacy 160
problem solving 51
flowchart 52
problems
reacting to 57
product positioning 26
professionals 40, 41
profit-related pay 103
project overview 24
promotion 19, 34
AIDA 34
techniques 13, 19, 26, 34
see also marketing
public relations 26, 34

Quest 28, 100

race and ethnicity
equality 133–4
race relations 106
racial discrimination 106
Racial Equality Charter for Sport 133
radio 147
Reading Borough Council 143
recruitment 80–3
advertising 70, 71, 82–3
job analysis 81–2
job description 82, 84
person specifications 82, 84
see also selection; staffing
redeployment 96–7
redundancy 95, 96, 97
regeneration 144
remuneration 102–3
research project
assessing feasibility 154
data protection 160
ethical standards 160
evaluation 60
final planning 158–60
finalising proposal 158
methodology 155, 158–9
project format 159, 161
published material 156
references and bibliography 159–61
research methods 155, 158–9
selecting and planning 152–7
setting parameters 154
time scale and budget 157
title 157
resources 36–8
access to 53
action plan 37
checklists 37
effective use 38
finding 37–8
human resources *see* staffing
identifying needs 36–7
management 13
physical resources 20
premises and facilities 37
quality 37
resource costs 39
rest breaks 90–2
risk assessment 45–6
Royal Albert Hall 13

salaries 103
sales promotion 26
sampling 19, 35
Scarborough Borough Council 142
scheduled breaks 90–2
seasonal events 13, 136–7
seasonal work 72–3
security 14, 45, 46, 118
segmentation 137–8
selection
appointment 87
forms of application 84–5
interviewing 86–7
processes 84–7
short-listing 85–6
see also recruitment
self-employment 70–1, 109
sexual discrimination 105
see also equality; gender issues
short-listing

events 14
job applicants 85–6
sickness absence 93
Singh, Harpal 134
SkillsActive 78
SMART objectives 25, 39, 60, 99, 158
Social Exclusion Unit 128
social inclusion 128–9, 144
social trends 31
Spa Complex, Scarborough 62
special populations 124–5
spider diagram 16
sponsorship
of events 19, 26, 27, 34, 138
of sports 150
Sport England 77, 144
Sporting Equals 133
staff development 100–1
staffing 21, 40–1, 62
assessing performance 40
Human Resource Management 40, 80
identifying needs 81
peer evaluation chart 40
personal evaluation chart 41
planning needs 80–1
professionals 40, 41
suppliers 40, 41
volunteers 40, 41
see also recruitment; selection; team
staffing plan 82, 90
start-up costs 21, 39
stereotyping 131
stress 124
suppliers 40, 41
surveys 19, 29, 35
swimming coaches 113
swingometer chart of performance 16
SWOT analysis 30, 31, 40

Tannenbaum and Schmidt Continuum 49
targets 22
meeting 60
personal targets 44
setting 44
team targets 44
team
allocating roles 16, 41, 50
communication 50–1
dealing with team-mates 55–6
effectiveness 61
evaluation 60, 61
formal structures 49
informal structures 49
leadership 49–50
motivation 49, 56
number of people 15
overall purpose 48–9
recommendations 61
recording involvement 16–17
resources, access to 53
roles and responsibilities 15, 16, 40, 41, 50
selection 15
skills and abilities 15
structure 15, 41, 49
supporting other members 56
swingometer chart of performance 16
SWOT analysis 40
team-building and interaction 52–3
working environment 53
see also staffing
teamwork 51, 62
flowchart 51
problem solving 51
Tuckman's forming to performing model flowchart 51
technology 32

television 147
sport on 149
temporary workers 75–6, 109
term-time only employment 72
time management 54
planner 55
TimeBank 77
timescales 14, 22, 43–4
bar charts 43
calendar style timetable 43
critical path analysis 43
deadlines 43
flowcharts 44
individual 44
personal planner 44
training 78, 100–1
treasure hunt 13
Tuckman's forming to performing model flowchart 51
twilight shifts 72

unemployment 144

variable pricing 33
victimisation 105
voluntary work 73, 77–8
volunteers 40, 41, 56

wages 103
Westminster Council 129
work/life balance 70
Working Time Regulations 89, 91–2, 108–10
World Badminton Championships 1997 144

zero hours employment 72
Zijlaard-van Moorsel, Leontien 124